0 kilometres   20

0 miles   20

Apostolos
Andreas ●

Dipkarpaz
(Rizokarpaso) ●

Aigialousa
(Yenierenkoy) ●

● Trikomo (Iskele)

NORTH CYPRUS

Famagusta
(Gazimağusa/
Ammochostos) ●

Agia Napa ●

Larnaka ●

South Nicosia
Pages 116–127

Southern Cyprus
Pages 64–87

North Cyprus
Pages 128–157

EYEWITNESS TRAVEL

CYPRUS

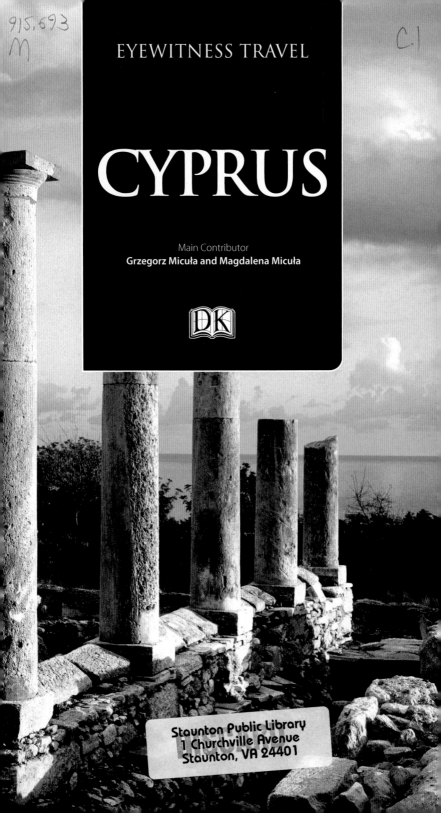

EYEWITNESS TRAVEL

CYPRUS

Main Contributor
Grzegorz Micuła and Magdalena Micuła

DK

LONDON, NEW YORK,
MELBOURNE, MUNICH AND DELHI
www.dk.com

Produced by Hachette Livre Polska sp. z o.o., Warsaw, Poland

Senior Graphic Designer
Paweł Pasternak

Editors
Agnieszka Majle, Robert G. Pasieczny

Main Contributors
Elżbieta Makowiecka, Grzegorz Micuła, Magdalena Micuła

Cartographers
Magdalena Polak, Michał Zielkiewicz

Photographer
Dorota and Mariusz Jarymowicz, Krzysztof Kur

Illustrators
Michał Burkiewicz, Paweł Marczak, Bohdan Wróblewski

Typesetting and Layout
Elżbieta Dudzińska, Paweł Kamiński, Grzegorz Wilk

Printed and bound in China by L. Rex Printing Co., Ltd.

First American Edition, 2006
Published in the United States by DK Publishing,
345 Hudson Street, New York, New York 10014

14 15 16 17 10 9 8 7 6 5 4 3 2 1

Reprinted with revisions 2008, 2010, 2012, 2014

Copyright © 2006, 2014 Dorling Kindersley Limited, London
A Penguin Random House Company

Published in Great Britain by Dorling Kindersley Limited.
A catalog record of this book is available from the Library of Congress

ISSN 1542 1554
ISBN: 978-1-46541-192-1

Floors are referred to throughout in accordance with American usage;
ie the "first floor" is at ground floor level

MIX
Paper from
responsible sources
FSC
www.fsc.org   FSC™ C018179

**The information in this
DK Eyewitness Travel Guide is checked regularly.**
Every effort has been made to ensure that this book is as up-to-date as
possible at the time of going to press. Some details, however, such as
telephone numbers, opening hours, prices, gallery hanging arrangements
and travel information are liable to change. The publishers cannot accept
responsibility for any consequences arising from the use of this book, nor for
any material on third party websites, and cannot guarantee that any website
address in this book will be a suitable source of travel information. We value
the views and suggestions of our readers very highly. Please write to:
Publisher, DK Eyewitness Travel Guides, Dorling Kindersley, 80 Strand, London
WC2R 0RL, Great Britain, or email: travelguides@dk.com.

Front cover main image: Paphos Fort, Kato Pafos harbour

◀ Sanctuary of Apollo Ylatis, near Kourion

Contents

Introducing Cyprus

Cypriot saint, Agios Mamas, the Byzantine
Museum in Pafos

Beach in the bustling resort of Agia Napa in
southeast Cyprus

Ruins of the Sanctuary of Apollo Ylatis, near Kourion

Picturesque Kyrenia harbour, one of the most beautiful in Cyprus

Baklává, a typically Cypriot dessert

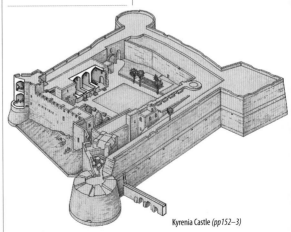
Kyrenia Castle *(pp152–3)*

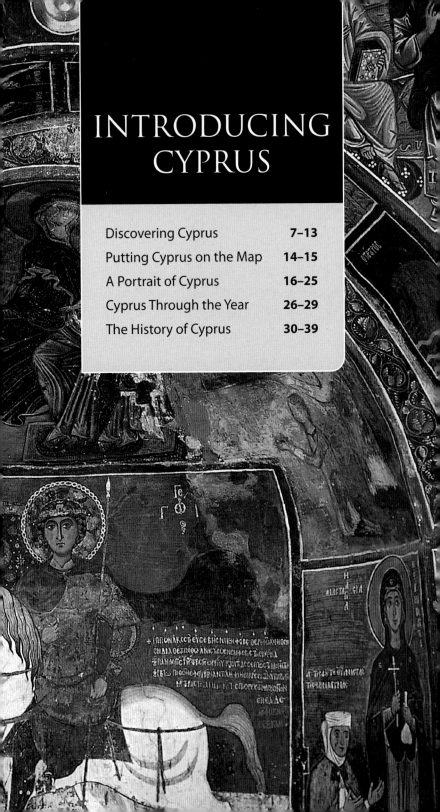

INTRODUCING CYPRUS

DISCOVERING CYPRUS

The following itineraries cover the highlights of Cyprus, and are of varying lengths: mix and match these to create your ideal Cypriot holiday. First are a couple of two-day tours of the island's most walkable towns, Nicosia and Pafos. Next, a 3-day driving tour of the UNESCO World Heritage-listed frescoed churches of the Troodos mountains. Of the week-long itineraries, one covers western Cyprus – essentially the hinterland of Pafos – with its hill villages, pristine beaches, country monasteries and chapels, and natural beauty spots. The other is end-to-end North Cyprus, taking in its many monuments, towns and beaches.

Agios Neofytos monastery
Founded by the hermit monk Neofytos in the 12th century, the *encleistra* (hermitage) was carved out the mountain by Neofytos himself; the monastery contains fine Byzantine frescoes dating from the 12th to 15th centuries.

A Week in Western Cyprus

- Squeeze through the frescoed, cut-from-living-rock *encleistra* of Agios Neofytos monastery.

- Contemplate the sensual, water-sculpted sides of the unspoilt Avakas Gorge.

- Learn about sea-turtle nesting at the Lara Bay hatchery station.

- Discover the elegant stone-built villages of the Akamas peninsula.

- Sample Cyprus' cleanest sea, the supposed bathing spot of the goddess Aphrodite, at Chrysochou Bay.

- Marvel at intricately painted archaic amphorae in the Marion–Arsinoe Archaeological Museum.

- Pick up a bottle of the monks' own wine at the Chrysorrogiatissa monastery.

- View the cedar groves of Cedar Valley.

- Purchase fine lacework and woven wall-hangings in Fyti.

Avakas Gorge
This deep ravine of towering limestone cliffs, with the river Avgas runing through it, is popular with both rock climbers and hikers.

◀ Detail of the interior of Asinou Church in the Troodos mountains

Kyrenia Castle
Built on the site of a Roman fort by the Byzantines, the castle affords magnificent views of the harbour below.

Apostolos Andreas

Nangomi (Golden) Beach

Dipkarpaz

Agios Thyrsos

Sipahi

Kantara Castle

yrenia (irne)

Kyrenia (Girne) beaches

Mediterranean Sea

Bellapais

Antifonitis Monastery

Trikomo (İskele)

Buffavento Castle

NORTH CYPRUS

Nicosia (Lefkoşa)

St Barnabas Monastery

Salamis

Royal Tombs

Famagusta

LARNAKA

Larnaka Bay

llias

Tremithos

Bellapais Abbey
These romantic ruins date back to the 13th century, when the Gothic abbey housed Augustinian monks fleeing Jerusalem.

0 kilometres | 25
0 miles | 25

Key

—— A Week in Western Cyprus

—— A Week in Northern Cyprus

A Week in Northern Cyprus

- From Kyrenia's imposing castle, gaze over the picturesque port.

- Savour Lusignan Gothic style at Bellapais abbey.

- Visit the royal apartments of St Hilarion Castle.

- Study the north's best-preserved Byzantine frescoes in situ at the Church of Panagia Theotokos, Trikomo.

- Walk on geometric mosaic flooring at Agia Trias basilica in Sipahi.

- Stretch out on Golden Beach (Nangomi), the island's longest and wildest, on the Karpasia peninsula.

- Explore the colonnades, Roman theatre, mosaics and baths of ancient Salamis.

- Peruse the Gothic architecture of old Famagusta, especially Lala Mustafa Pasha Mosque.

Two days in Pafos (Paphos)

Pafos (pp52–7) offers ancient sites, worthwhile museums, a well-loved shore promenade and a lively bazaar.

- **Arriving** Pafos (PFO) airport lies 15 km (9 miles) to the southeast; take a bus, taxi or hire car to/from town.

Day 1
Morning Your first stop is the Roman mosaics in **Kato (Lower) Pafos** *(pp56–7)*, then stroll along the harbourfront to the old fort for views from its roof, or head north to the restored Roman odeon, then east across Apostolou Pavlou to the **Agia Solomoni catacombs** *(pp54–5)*, with their sacred pool. From there, thread through the Kato Pafos backstreets to medieval **Agia Kyriaki church** *(p54)*, before stopping for lunch.

Afternoon Take a swim at one of the pocket **beaches** *(p55)* along the municipal promenade leading east from the old port. Then change direction to follow the shoreline walkway north for an hour to the subterranean **Tombs of the Kings** *(p54)*, off the road to Coral Bay.

Day 2
Morning Explore **Agora** *(p52)*, the covered bazaar, and the lanes between Agora and Kanari streets in Ktima, best on Saturday when there's a street

The stone church of Agia Kyriaki, built in the 12th century and still in use today

produce market. Downhill at the base of the escarpment is the **Mehmet Bey Ebubekir** *(p52)*, with panels detailing the old public baths of Cyprus. Lunch at a traditional bazaar taverna on Votsi Street.

Afternoon Continue into Moutallos, with its time-warped 1960s houses and **Gothic Selimiye Camii** mosque *(p52)*. Return to the centre of town to visit the **Byzantine and Ethnographic museums** *(both p53)*. From the nearby municipal gardens, it's a short bus ride southeast to the **Archaeological Museum** *(p55)*. Finish the day with a traditional meze.

Two days in Nicosia (Lefkoşa)

Old, walled Nicosia has experienced a revival, with numerous restaurants and boutiques lining its pedestrianized streets.

- **Arriving** Larnaca airport is 45km southeast of Nicosia, with bus services to the edge of the city, and ample hire-car facilities.

Day 1
Morning Allow 2 to 3 hours for the **Cyprus Museum** *(pp126–7)*, one of the Mediterranean's great collections of ancient art, with special distinction in Bronze Age, Geometric and archaic artefacts. Follow this with lunch at one of the city's growing number of quality new restaurants just southeast.

Afternoon Enter the old walled town via Plateia Solomou and head east across Ledra Ave for the excellent **Leventis Museum** *(p125)*. From here, stroll north past the ornate **churches of Trypiotis and Fanermeni** *(p126)* and the **Araplar Mosque** *(p126)*, before turning east towards the **Municipal Arts Centre** *(p122)*, aka "the Powerhouse", as it used to be an old Electricity Authority building. Admire the exhibits, then head south for a peak inside the **Omar**

The Gothic façade of Selimiye Camii mosque (Aya Sofya Cathedral)

Mosque *(p123)* before dining at one of the old quarter's traditional tavernas.

Day 2
Morning Enter old Greek Cypriot Nicosia from its far eastern corner, into Chrysaliniotissa, with its tottering Ottoman-era houses. Explore the **Chrysaliniotissa church** *(p124)* from c.1450, then meander southwest to reach the **Municipal Cultural Centre** *(p124)*, home to superb Byzantine art rescued from desecrated churches in North Cyprus. If time permits, peek inside the nearby **Hadjigeorgakis Kornesios House** *(p123)* with its ethnographic displays. Then go to the **Ledra Street checkpoint** *(p125)* between the two sectors of Nicosia – don't forget your passport. Have lunch at one of the restaurants around **Selima Mosque** *(pp132–3)*, after admiring this Gothic place of worship inside and out.

Afternoon West of the mosque, the craft shops of the well-restored Ottoman **Büyük Han** *(p132)* beckon. Nearby, the **Mevlevi Tekke** *(p134)* museum unveils the former monastery of the Whirling Dervishes. From here, stroll southwest to the central mosque of **Arabahmet district** *(p135)*, North Nicosia's answer to Chrysaliniotissa. Finally, head back to the Ledra–Lokmacı crossing for a night on the town in livelier south Nicosia.

Painted Churches of the Troodos

This itinerary explores the frescoes and murals of churches in and around the Troodos mountains, most of which are on the UNESCO World Cultural Heritage list. Stay overnight in Kakopetria, Agros and Kalopanagiotis to minimize driving.

- **Duration** This is a 3-day tour.
- **Transport** A car is necessary for this itinerary.

Day 1
Morning Take the E110 road up from the A6 motorway at Limassol to Kalo Chorio, bearing right for the small **Chapel of St Mamas** *(p115)* in Louvaras village. Continue uphill on the E110 to Potamitissa village for Pelendri village and its grander 14th-century church of **Timios Stavros** *(p102)*. Retrace your route to Potamitissa, continuing east to **Agros** *(p115)* for lunch.

Afternoon Head north via Chandria to Lagoudera and the **Panagia tou Araka** *(pp104–5)*, with its superb late-12th-century frescoes. If time and daylight permit, head one valley

The interior of Panagia Forviotissa (tis Asinou)

east, via Platanistassa village where the key-keeper lives, to visit remote **Stavros tou Agiasmati** *(p105)* church and more vivid frescoes. Return to Agros for the night.

Day 2
Morning Return to the ridge road at Chandria, then head west via Karvounas junction, Troodos resort and Prodromos, descending to Pedoulas and the late 15th-century **Church of the Archangel Michael** *(p93)*. Continue to Moutoullas village and the oldest painted church in these mountains, **Panagia tou Moutoulla** *(p93)*. Arrive down valley at the scenic **Kalopanagiotis** *(p93)* village in time for a spot of lunch.

Afternoon Cross the river to take in the rambling **Agios Ioannis Lambadistis monastery** *(pp92–3)*, the frescoes in its triple church recently restored by students from London's Courtauld Institute, and the excellent icon museum adjacent. Retrace your tyre treads to Pedoulas and the useful link road east to **Kakopetria** *(p103)*, a good place to spend the night.

Day 3
Morning Start the day with a pilgrimage to **Agios Nikolaos tis Stegis** *(pp102–3)* on Kakopetria's outskirts. Next, head to the nearby village of Galata, where you'll be shepherded around three churches, including **Panagia tis Podithou** *(p103)*, with frescoes by master Simeon Axenti. Stop here for some lunch.

Afternoon Drive north towards Nicosia on the fast B9 road, turning off at Koutrafas for access to **Panagia Forviotissa (tis Asinou)** *(p104)*, perhaps the finest of the UNESCO-listed churches, with frescoes of similar date to Agios Nikolaos tis Stegis. Proceed from here to Nicosia, pausing en route at Vyzakia to admire the Venetian-style frescoes in its **Archangel Michael Church** *(p104)*.

The UNESCO ancient church of Panagia Podithou

A Week in North Cyprus

- **Arrival/departure** Ercan airport, northeast of Lefkoşa (North Nicosia), or Larnaka airport in the south for a greater selection of flights.

- **Transport** This tour is best undertaken with a hire car.

Day 1: Kyrenia and Bellapais
Kyrenia (Girne) (pp150–53) has long been the crown jewel of Cypriot tourism. The huge castle with its two museums, and the medieval Venetian port, are in-town highlights; after lunch, head up to **Bellapais village** (p149), graced by an exquisite Lusignan-era abbey. Bellapais and adjacent villages have a variety of restaurants for dinner. Spend the night in Bellapais or Kyrenia proper.

Day 2: Vouni and Soloi
Still using Kyrenia or Bellapais as a base, head west, then southwest via Morphou, to the ancient sites of **Soloi** (pp156–7), with its mosaic-floored basilica, and the enigmatic hilltop citadel of **Vouni** (p157). Have a swim and some lunch at one of the tavernas nearby at Yedidalga or Yeşilirmak before returning to Kyrenia or Bellapais.

Day 3: Castles and Kyrenia Beaches
Climb up from the Kyrenia area to the fairy-tale Byzantine-Lusignan **St Hilarion Castle** (p149), best viewed in the early morning. Return to sea level and drive east for a swim or – if nesting season – a spot of turtle-watching at **Algadi beach**. Contact the Society for Protection of Turtles (www.cyprusturtles.org) for more information. Afterwards, drive up the good road to Beşparmak pass and take the track west from there to **Buffavento Castle** (p148) in time to take in the dramatic sunset views.

Day 4: Into the Karpasia (Karpas) Peninsula
Head east from the Kyrenia area, leaving the coast road briefly to take in the damaged but still worthwhile 12th-century frescoed monastery of **Antifonitis** (p148). Continue east to Kaplıca and the sharp climb up to **Kantara Castle** (p144), the gateway of Karpasia. Once on the peninsula trunk road, pause at **Sipahi village** (p145), where vast mosaics cover the Agias Trias basilica floor. After a restorative lunch near **Agios Thyrsos** (p145), there's time for a swim nearby before reaching abundant accommodation just outside **Dipkarpaz** (p145), your base for the next couple of nights.

Day 5: Exploring the Karpasia Peninsula
After taking in the half-ruined Levantine-fantasy church of **Agios Philon** (p145), with its flanking palm trees, pack a picnic and take the peninsula trunk road beyond Dipkarpaz to the northeastern-most cape of Cyprus, the cave-riddled **Kastros** (p145). On the return journey, stop to pay your respects at the rambling **Apostolos Andreas monastery** (p145), and spread your towel and picnic lunch at **Nangomi (Golden) Beach** (p145), the island's longest and another haven for nesting sea turtles. Meander back to Dipkarpaz, dining at one of the excellent fish tavernas outside the village.

Day 6: Salamis and Around
With an early start, a southwesterly drive out of

Salamis, the largest archaeological site on Cyprus

Dipkarpaz brings you to Trikomo (İskele) and its **Panagia Thetokos church** (p144), sheltering the only intact Byzantine frescoes in North Cyprus. Further along the main coastal road, the sprawling site of ancient **Salamis** (pp138–9), and the beach fringing it, demands a few hours of your time until lunch. Nearby, the Bronze Age **Royal Tombs** (p136), and the **St Barnabas monastery** (p137) with its catacomb and museum, will fill the afternoon. Overnight at a beachfront hotel.

Day 7: Famagusta
Spend the day in the walled city of **Famagusta** (pp140–43), admiring the **Citadel** (p142), the façade of the **Lala Mustafa Pasha** (p140) mosque (originally a Lusignan Gothic cathedral) and the **chapels of the Knights Templar and Hospitaller** (p141), before a late lunch in the *medrese* next to the mosque. Drive back to Ercan airport, or for crossing into Southern Cyprus for Larnaka airport.

The formidable ruins of Bellapais abbey

For practical information on travelling around Cyprus, see pp200–3

A Week in West Cyprus

- **Arrival/departure** Pafos (PFO) Airport.
- **Transport** A car is needed for this itinerary.

Day 1–2: Pafos
See the Two Days in Pafos itinerary on p10.

Day 3: Around Pafos
Pause in Empa for its imposing **Panagia Chryseleoussa** *(p51)*, sporting expressive, if damaged, 15th-century frescoes. Next, continue inland to **Agios Neofytos monastery** *(p51)*, where the eponymous saint dwelt in the intriguing, rock-cut *encleistra*. After lunch, stop in **Geroskipou** *(p50)* village to admire the six-domed, vividly frescoed **Agia Paraskevi** *(p50)* church. Its frescoes – of similar date to those at Empa – were recently consolidated. Continue along the B6 highway to the ancient site and museum **Palaipafos (Old Pafos)** *(pp48–9)*, a powerful city-state in ancient times. Undergoing continuing excavations here is the **Sanctuary of Aphrodite** *(p49)*. Finally, continue southeast to **Petra tou Romiou** *(p48)* for a late swim, and admire the sunset over this noted beauty spot. Then, return to modern Kouklia village next to Palaipafos for supper at one of its many tavernas; overnight in Pafos.

Day 4: Safari to the Akamas Peninsula
Take the initially paved coast road beyond Coral Bay to the mouth of the **Avakas Gorge** *(p58)*, whose spectacular narrows take just over 2 hours return to hike from the parking area. Have lunch at one of the nearby snack bars before forging north on a much rougher track to **Lara** *(p58)* and its two flanking beaches – the northerly one is idyllic and has a sea-turtle research and protection station. After a swim, backtrack slightly to the narrow but paved track up to **Ineia** *(p58)* and other Akamas

The arched Venetian bridge of Roudia

peninsula villages, spending the night in **Drouseia** or **Kathikas** *(both p58)* after tastings at one (or more) of the local wineries.

Day 5: Chrysochou Bay
From Drouseia or Kathikas, descend the fast ridge road to the **Polis** *(p62)* area and enjoy a swim at one of the best beaches in West Cyprus. A 15-minute walk from town – is one of the peninsula's marked nature trails from the **Baths of Aphrodite** *(p59)*, with fine views of Chrysochou Bay and Cape Arnaoutis. Spend the night on the resort strip here between Polis and the Baths of Aphrodite.

Day 6: Polis and Beyond
Stroll the tiny old town of Polis, stopping at diminutive **Agios**

Agios Neofytos monastery lies in what once was a secluded valley

Andronikos *(p62)* church to view its fine frescoes, then take in the excellent **Marion-Arsinoe Archaeological Museum** *(p62)*. (Keys to Agios Andronikos are available here if the church is unattended.) Afterwards, your course lies northwest along a rugged, wild coast to **Pomos** *(p47)* with its fish tavernas and pocket beaches, detouring halfway at **Gialia** *(p47)* to explore a 12th-century Georgian monastery excavated in 2005–07. Spend the night at **Lysos** *(p47)*, in the foothills above Polis.

Day 7: The Pafos Forest
From Lysos, head east into the wild, forested **Tilliria** *(p92)* region, via **Stavros tis Psokas** *(p92)* forestry station and the famous cedar groves of **Cedar Valley** *(p92)*, before veering southwest to **Panagia** *(p63)*, birthplace of Archbishop-President Makarios III. Just 2 km south, the **Chrysorrogiatissa monastery** *(pp62–3)* has exceptional woodwork and offers quaffable products from its very own Monte Royia winery; there are more wineries in the area, such as Vouni Panagia. After a late lunch here, search out the historic medieval **bridge of Roudia** *(p63)*, built by the Venetians, before heading north to **Fyti** *(p47)*, famous for its lacework and woven wall-hangings. From here it's a scenic drive back to Lysos.

Putting Cyprus on the Map

Situated in the eastern Mediterranean Sea, Cyprus is its third largest island
(after Sicily and Sardinia), covering an area of 9,250 sq km (3,571 sq miles)
with a 720 km- (447 mile-) long coastline. Divided since 1974 into the Greek
Cypriot-governed Republic of Cyprus in the south and the Turkish-sponsored
Turkish Republic of North Cyprus in the north, both regions share Nicosia as
a capital. The rocky Pentadaktylos mountain range runs along the north,
while its central part is dominated by the mighty massif of the Troodos
mountains. The wildest and least accessible areas are the Akamas and
Karpasia (Karpas) peninsulas.

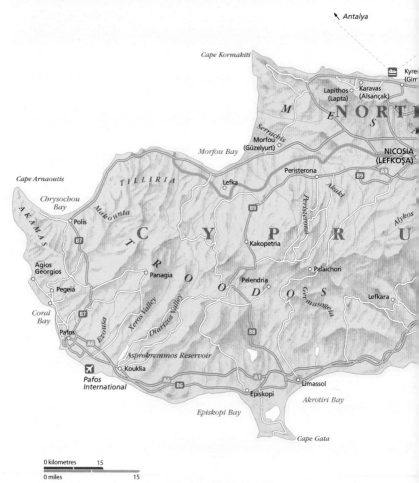

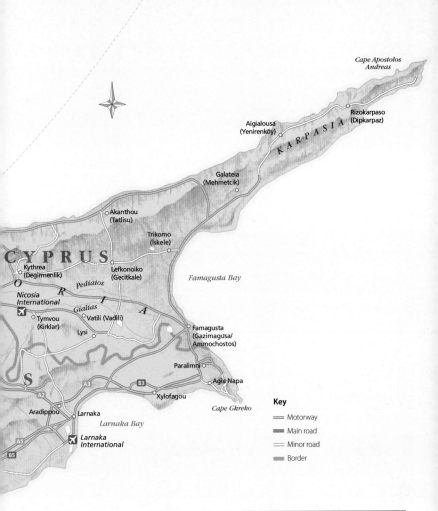

Taşucu

Cape Apostolos
Andreas

Rizokarpaso
(Dipkarpaz)

Aigialousa
(Yenirenköy)

K A R P A S I A

Galateia
(Mehmetcik)

Akanthou
(Tatlisu)

Trikomo
(İskele)

C Y P R U S

Kythrea
(Değirmenlik)

Lefkonoiko
(Gecitkale)

Famagusta Bay

O R I A

Nicosia
International

Pediaios

Gialias

Tymvou
(Kirklar)

Vatili (Vadili)

Lysi

Famagusta
(Gazimagusa/
Ammochostos)

Paralimni

Agia Napa

S

A2

A3

B3

Xylofagou

Cape Gkreko

Aradippou

Larnaka

A5

Larnaka Bay

Larnaka
International

B5

Key

══ Motorway

▬▬ Main road

── Minor road

▓▓ Border

Europe

North
Sea

SWEDEN

ESTONIA

LATVIA

RUSSIAN
FEDERATION

DENMARK

LITHUANIA

REP. OF
IRELAND

UNITED
KINGDOM

BELARUS

POLAND

NETH.

GERMANY

BELGIUM

CZECH
REPUBLIC

SLOVAKIA

UKRAINE

Atlantic
Ocean

FRANCE

SWITZ.

AUSTRIA

SLOV.

HUNGARY

MOLD

CROATIA

ROMANIA

ITALY

BOSNIA
HERZ.

SERBIA

MONTEN.

KOS.

BULGARIA

Black Sea

SPAIN

MAC.

ALBANIA

GREECE

TURKEY

PORTUGAL

MOROCCO

ALGERIA

TUNISIA

Mediterranean
Sea

CYPRUS

SYRIA

LEBANON

ISRAEL

For map symbols see back flap

A PORTRAIT OF CYPRUS

The legendary birthplace of Aphrodite, Cyprus enjoys a hot, Mediterranean climate moderated by sea breezes. Visitors bask in the sun on its many beaches, but within an hour's drive can find themselves in the mountains, enjoying the shade of cool herb- and resin-scented cedar woods, villages set amid orchards and peaceful vineyards, as though time stands still here.

Cyprus is an idyllic destination for romantics, with so many old castles, ancient ruins and secluded mountain monasteries to explore. The exploration of these historic sights is enhanced by plentiful sunshine – over 300 days of it per year. Cyprus also has a great number of scenic beaches, and the warm waters encourage bathing and relaxation.

Tucked away in the shady valleys are monasteries with ancient icons of the Virgin, at least one of which was supposedly painted by St Luke. The tiny churches, listed as UNESCO World Heritage Sites, hide unique frescoes – some of the most magnificent masterpieces of Byzantine art.

In the Pafos district, valleys overgrown with pine and cedar forests provide a home to the moufflon – a shy mountain sheep. Its image can be seen on Roman mosaics in Pafos.

Cypriot meadows are at their loveliest in springtime, when covered with motley carpets of colourful flowers: anemones, cyclamens, hyacinths, irises, peonies, poppies and tulips, among others. Orchid lovers will find over 50 species of these beautiful flowers growing in the sparsely populated regions of the island – in the Akamas peninsula, in the Troodos mountains and on the Pentadaktylos mountain range. The island lies on a route for bird migration. Thousands of birds, including

A symbol of Cyprus – an olive tree against the backdrop of a sapphire-blue sea

◀ Anchored catamaran along the coastline

View over the northern part of Nicosia, with the Turkish Cypriot flag carved into the hillside

flamingos, cormorants and swans, can be seen wintering on the salt lakes at Larnaka and Akrotiri.

Historic Divisions

The winds of history have repeatedly ravaged this beautiful island. Cyprus has been ruled in turns by Egyptians, Phoenicians, Persians, Romans, Byzantines, Crusaders, Franks, Venetians, Turks and the British. Each of these cultures has left its mark on the architecture, style, cuisine, language and the mentality of the island's inhabitants.

Above all, the island has been shaped by the conflict between the Greeks and the Turks. The Greeks first arrived over 3,000 years ago. The Turks began to settle here following the conquest of the island by Sultan Selim II in 1571.

People and Society

Cypriot society has been composed of two completely separate cultures since the division of the island in 1974 into the Turkish-occupied North and the Greek-speaking Republic of Cyprus in the south. Greek Cypriot society has

always been highly traditional, particularly among country people. This is partly due to the power of the Orthodox Church. Life proceeds at a slow pace in the villages, where it centres around cafés where men spend hours playing backgammon and discussing politics. Village women

An Orthodox priest out shopping

excel in sewing and embroidery. There has been gradual change, however, with many villages becoming deserted as their residents move to towns, where life is generally easier and the standard of living higher, but this decline is gradually being reversed; old houses are frequently bought by artists, often foreigners, in search of tranquillity. In Fikardou, two abandoned houses have been turned into a museum of village life, and awarded the Europa Nostra medal for the preservation of architectural heritage. Overall, the Republic of Cyprus is highly urbanized. Women play a great role in the modern economy – running businesses, hotels and restaurants. Life in the cities of Larnaka, Nicosia and Limassol proceeds at a speedy pace.

In the Turkish North, life proceeds at a far gentler pace, partly due to the international boycott that has afflicted tourism and hampered development since 1974. The North is quite separate from southern Cyprus in both atmosphere and landscape, as well as politics. It is far less affluent and more sparsely populated, and Islam is the main religion.

The Cape Gkreko area – one of the most beautiful areas in Cyprus

A lace-maker at work

Following the Turkish invasion of Cyprus and the displacement of tens of thousands of its people, it seemed that the island would never recover. Over thirty years on, the southern part of the island has seen great prosperity.. After the 1974 invasion, hundreds of thousands of refugees from the North found new homes and began new lives. Since then, national income has increased several fold. The economy is flourishing, based on tourism, maritime trade and financial services, despite the island being hit hard in the Eurozone crisis of 2013. The same cannot be said of the northern part of the island, where the standard of living is much lower, caused by the isolation of North Cyprus.

Modern-day Cyprus

The Republic of Cyprus lives off tourism. Its towns are bustling and – like the beaches – full of tourists. Tourist zones have been established in Limassol, Larnaka and Pafos, and around Agia Napa.

This small island provides everything for the holiday-maker, from beautiful scenery to delicious food, excellent hotels, gracious hosts and historic sights.

Relaxing at an outdoor café on a summer afternoon

Landscape and Wildlife

The Cypriot landscape is surprisingly varied. Besides high mountains covered with pine and cedar forests, and the rugged crags of Kyrenia, the central part of the island is occupied by the fertile plain of Mesaoria. The crowded beaches of Limassol, Pafos and Agia Napa contrast with the less developed coastal regions of the Karpasia (Karpas) and Akamas peninsulas. In spring, the hills and meadows are covered with colourful flowers. The forests are the habitat of the moufflon – mountain sheep – while the Karpasia peninsula is home to wild donkeys.

A flock of goats grazing freely – a typical sight in the Cypriot landscape

The Coast

Besides beautiful sandy and pebble beaches, the coastline features oddly shaped rocks jutting out of the sea and rugged cliffs, which descend steeply into the water. The northern part of Famagusta Bay and the Karpasia and Akamas peninsulas feature virtually empty sandy beaches where loggerheads and green turtles come to lay their eggs. The exposed Jurassic rocks near Coral Bay, northwest of Pafos, are being destroyed by erosion.

Lizards, particularly the ubiquitous sand lizard, can be seen almost everywhere. The largest Cypriot lizard, Agama (Agama stelio cypriaca) can reach up to 30 cm (12 in) in length.

Rocky coastlines are created wherever mountain ranges reach the sea. The rocky coast near Petra tou Romiou (Rock of Aphrodite) is being worn away over time by erosion.

Sandy coastlines are found at Agia Napa, Famagusta Bay and the Karpasia peninsula, but the loveliest beaches are on the Akamas peninsula.

Rock Formations

The Troodos mountains, in the central part of Cyprus, are formed of magma rock containing rich deposits of copper and asbestos. The Kyrenia mountains (the Pentadaktylos range), running to the Karpasia peninsula in the northeast part of the island, are made of hard, dense limestone. The lime soils in the southern part of the island, near Limassol, are ideally suited for the growing of vines.

Salt lakes – near Larnaka and on the Akrotiri peninsula – are a haven for pink flamingos, wild ducks and the Cyprus warbler (Sylvia melanthorax).

Copper mine at Skouriotissa

Mountains

The island features two mountain ranges, separated by the fertile Mesaoria plain. The volcanic Troodos massif in central Cyprus, dominated by Mount Olympus at 1,951 m (6,258 ft) above sea level, is covered with pine and cedar forests. The constant mountain streams in the Troodos mountains even have waterfalls. Spring and autumn bring hikers to the cool forests and rugged valleys, while winter brings out skiers. The Kyrenia mountains (the Pentadaktylos or "Five-Finger" range) in North Cyprus rise a short distance inland from the coast. The highest peak is Mount Kyparissovouno, at 1,024 m (3,360 ft).

The Troodos mountains are largely forested but vines are grown on the southern slopes and apple and cherry orchards abound in the valleys.

In springtime wild flowers carpet the hillsides and meadows of the island with a colourful, fragrant display.

The Cypriot moufflon is a spry mountain sheep, living wild in the forests of Pafos, in the western part of the island.

Mountain streams flow year-round, bringing cooling water to lower ground.

Other Regions

The island's interior is occupied by the vast, fertile Mesaoria plain, given mainly to grain cultivation. The northern area around Morfou (Güzelyurt) is full of citrus groves, and to the south, in the region of Larnaka, runs a range of white semi-desert mountains stretching for kilometres. The sun-drenched region of Limassol, with its limestone soil, is a patchwork of vineyards, which yield grapes for the production of the sweet Commandaria wine.

The Akamas peninsula is a remote region in the west of Cyprus. It features the island's most beautiful wild, sandy beaches (see pp59–61).

Donkeys can be seen in the Karpasia peninsula. These ageing domesticated animals have been turned loose by their owners.

Pelicans with wing-spans up to 2.5 m (8 ft) visit the island's salt lakes. Some stop for a few days, others remain longer. These huge birds can also be seen at the harbours of Pafos, Limassol and Agia Napa, where they are a tourist attraction.

The Karpasia peninsula is a long, narrow strip of land jutting into the sea. Its main attractions are its wild environment and historical sights (see pp144–5).

Cypriot Architecture

The long and rich history of Cyprus is reflected in its architecture, and some true gems can be glimpsed amid the ocean of nondescript modern development. The island has a number of Neolithic settlements as well as Bronze Age burial chambers, ruins of ancient buildings (including vast Byzantine basilicas), medieval castles, churches and monasteries. From the Ottoman era, relics include mosques and caravanserais. The British left behind colonial buildings. In villages, particularly in the mountains, people today still live in old stone houses.

The Roman II Hotel in Pafos, built to a design based on ancient Roman architecture

Ancient Architecture

The Greeks, Phoenicians, Romans and Byzantines who once ruled over Cyprus left behind numerous ancient buildings. Archaeologists have uncovered the ruins of ancient Kourion, Amathous, Kition, Soloi, Salamis and Pafos with temples, theatres, basilicas, bath-houses and palaces. These ancient ruins include fragments of the old defence walls, sports stadiums, gymnasiums, and necropolises. Some Roman theatres are still in use today for shows and festivals.

The palaestra in Salamis (see pp138–9) is surrounded by colonnades and statues. It was devoted to the training of athletes and to staging sporting competitions.

Kourion, a beautiful, prosperous city, was destroyed by an earthquake in the 4th century AD (see pp70–71).

Medieval Architecture

During the 300 years when Cyprus was ruled by the Crusaders and the Lusignans, many churches were built, including the opulent cathedrals in Famagusta and Nicosia. Added to these were charming village churches and chapels, Gothic monasteries and castles. The Venetians, who ruled the island for over 80 years, created the magnificent ring of defence walls around Nicosia and Famagusta, whose mighty fortifications held back the Ottoman army for almost a year.

Angeloktisi Church in Kiti is one of a number of small stone churches on the island whose modest exteriors often hide magnificent Byzantine mosaics or splendid frescoes (see p80).

This beautifully carved capital crowns the surviving column of a medieval palace in South Nicosia.

Bellapais, with its ruins of a Gothic abbey, enchants visitors with its imposing architecture (see p149). Every spring international music festivals are held here (see p26 and p29).

Islamic Architecture

Following the conquest of Cyprus by the army of Selim II, new structures appeared, including Turkish mosques (minarets were often added to Gothic cathedrals), bathhouses, caravanserais and covered bazaars. In many villages you can still see small mosques with distinctive pointed minarets.

Büyük Han in North Nicosia is a magnificent example of an Ottoman caravanserai, with a *mescit* (prayer hall) in the courtyard *(see p132)*.

The Hala Sultan Tekke *(see p81)* is Cyprus's most sacred Muslim site. It comprises a mosque and a mausoleum with the tomb of Umm Haram, aunt of the Prophet Mohammed.

The Colonial Period

British rule on the island from the 18th to 19th centuries marked the beginning of colonial-style architecture, including churches, government offices, courts of law, army barracks, civil servants' villas, bridges and other public buildings. The British administration also admired the Greek Classical style, and commissioned, designed and built a great number of Neo-Classical buildings.

The Faneromeni School in South Nicosia *(see p126)* is an example of a Neo-Classical public building. When it was founded in 1852, it was seen as a connection to the students' Greek roots.

The Pierides Museum in Larnaka is a typical example of colonial architecture with shaded balconies resting on slender supports *(see p82)*. Its flat roof and wooden shutters complement the image of a colonial residence.

Modern Architecture

Following independence in 1960, the architectural style of Cypriot buildings, particularly of public buildings such as town halls, offices, banks and hotels became more modern and functional. Most of these buildings were erected in Nicosia and in Limassol, which has since become the international business capital of Cyprus. The majority of modern buildings lack architectural merit.

Limassol's modern architecture is largely limited to functional office buildings constructed of glass, concrete and steel, located in the eastern business district of town.

Traditional Homes

For centuries, Cypriot village houses, particularly in the mountains, were built of stone, offering the benefit of staying cool in summer and warm in winter. While some new homes imitate the traditional style, most are built of breeze-block and reinforced cement.

A modern stone building reminiscent of a traditional village home

Christianity and the Greek Orthodox Church

Christianity gained an early foothold in Cyprus, when saints Barnabas and Paul introduced the religion to the island in the first century AD. For 500 years the Church remained relatively unified. However, subsequent divisions led to the emergence of many parallel Christian creeds. The Great Schism of 1054 marked the split between East and West, resulting in the emergence of the Orthodox and Roman Catholic Churches. One of the groups of the Eastern Orthodox Church is the Greek Orthodox Church, and the majority of Greek Cypriots are devoutly Orthodox. Most of the churches in the south are still consecrated and can be visited; in the North, most have been converted into mosques or museums.

Byzantine frescoes, some of the most splendid in existence, decorate the walls of small churches in the Troodos mountains. Ten of them feature on UNESCO's World Heritage List.

The late Father Kallinikos from St Barbara's Monastery *(Agia Varvara)* was regarded as one of the greatest icon painters of recent times. His sought-after icons are sold at the monastery *(see p80)*.

Neo-Byzantine churches are topped by a grooved cupola with a prominent cross. They have distinctive arched windows and portals.

Saint Nicholas

Saint Barnabas and Saint Paul

Two saints are associated with Cyprus – Barnabas (a citizen of Salamis, and patron saint of the island), and Paul. Together, they spread Christianity to Cyprus in 45 AD. Paul was captured and tied to a pillar to be flogged. It is said that the saint caused his torturer to go blind. Witnessing this miracle, the Roman governor of Cyprus, Sergius Paulus, was converted to Christianity. Barnabas was stoned to death in 61 AD.

St Paul's Pillar in Kato Pafos

Saints' days are celebrated by placing an icon of the saint on a small, ornamental table covered with a lace cloth.

Icons with images of Christ or the saints, depicted in traditional Byzantine style, play a major role in the Orthodox Church. They are painted on wood, according to strictly defined rules.

The Royal Doors are found in the central part of an iconostasis. They symbolize the passage from the earthly to the spiritual world. The priest passes through them during the service.

The Iconostasis is a "wall of icons" that separates the faithful from the sanctuary.

Royal Doors

Monasticism

Cypriot monasteries, some of them hundreds of years old, are scattered among the mountains. These religious communities of bearded monks live in accordance with a strict regime. Built on inaccessible crags or in shadowy green valleys, they were established in the mountains to be closer to God and further from the temptations of this world. The monasteries hide an extraordinary wealth of frescoes, intricate decorations and magnificent iconostases. The best known of the Cypriot monasteries is Kykkos – the Royal Monastery (see pp94–5) which is a place of pilgrimage for the island's inhabitants.

Two monks in the courtyard of Kykkos Monastery

Divine Liturgy

This is a liturgy celebrated in commemoration of the Last Supper. In the Greek Orthodox Church the service lasts longer than in the Catholic Church and there is no organ, only a choir. The service consists of two parts: the "catechumen liturgy", during which psalms and the Gospel are read; and the "liturgy of the faithful" – the main Eucharist when all worshippers (even children) receive holy communion in the form of bread and wine.

Icons on both sides of the Royal Doors depict Mary and Jesus. The second from the right usually depicts the patron saint of the church.

CYPRUS THROUGH THE YEAR

Cypriots hold strongly to their traditions, which are manifested in the celebration of numerous religious festivals. The Orthodox Church, to which most Greek Cypriots belong, has a great influence on their lives. Besides local village fairs and public holidays, the festivities include athletic events and beauty contests. Added to this, every village has its own *panagyri* – the patron saint's day celebration –

the equivalent of church fairs. The villagers celebrate them with copious food, drink, dancing and song.

In North Cyprus, Muslim feasts are more common. The main ones include Şeker Bayrami, which ends the 40 days of Ramadan; Kurban Bayrami, which is held to commemorate Abraham's sacrifice (rams are slaughtered and roasted on a bonfire); and Mevlud, the birthday of Mohammed.

Olive trees flowering in the spring

Spring

This is the most beautiful season on the island. The slopes of the hills begin to turn green and the meadows are carpeted with a profusion of colourful flowers, though in places it is still possible to ski. The main religious festival held in spring is Easter.

March
International Skiing Competition *(mid-Mar)*, Troodos. Since 1969, competitive ski races have been held on the slopes of Mount Olympus *(see p96)*.
Evangelismós, Feast of the Annunciation *(25 Mar)*. Traditional folk fairs held in the villages of Kalavasos *(see p78)* and Klirou, as well as in Nicosia *(see pp116–27)*.
Easter *(varies – Mar to May)*. A week before Easter,

the icon of St Lazarus is paraded through Larnaka. In all towns on Maundy Thursday, icons are covered with veils, and on Good Friday

Winners of the May Cyprus International Rally in Limassol

the image of Christ adorned with flowers is carried through the streets. On Easter Saturday, icons are unveiled and in the evening an effigy of Judas is burned. Easter Day is celebrated with parties. Orthodox Easter is based on the Julian calendar, and may occur up to five weeks after Easter in the West.

April
Wild Flower Festival *(Mar & Apr)*. This celebration of nature's blooms is held every Saturday and Sunday in many towns throughout southern Cyprus.
International Spring Concerts *(Apr & May)*, Bellapais. Performances by musical ensembles, singers and choirs are held in the Gothic abbey *(see p149)*.

May
Anthistiria Flower Festival *(mid-May)*, Pafos, Limassol. The return of spring is celebrated with joyful processions and shows based on Greek mythology.
Orange Festival *(mid-May)*, Güzelyurt (Morfou) *(see p156)*. Held since 1977 to celebrate the orange harvest, with two weeks of parades, folk concerts and art exhibitions.
Cyprus International Rally *(May)*. Three-day car rally starting and ending in Limassol *(see pp72–75)*.
Chamber Music Festival *(May–Jun)*, Nicosia *(see pp116–27)* and Pafos *(pp52–5)*. Top international orchestras and ensembles travel far and wide to perform here.

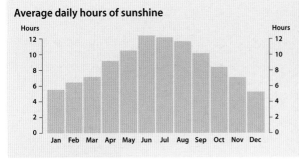

Average daily hours of sunshine

Hours

12 –
10 –
8 –
6 –
4 –
2 –
0 –

Jan Feb Mar Apr May Jun Jul Aug Sep Oct Nov Dec

Hours

12
10
8
6
4
2
0

Average Hours of Sunshine
In June and July, the amount of sunshine reaches nearly 13 hours per day. These months mark the peak holiday season. December, January and February have the fewest hours of sunshine, but the winter sun is pleasant and warm.

Children at the Wild Flowers Festival in Larnaka

Summer

Summer is rich in cultural events, especially art festivals, fairs and music concerts. Tourist resorts, hotels and attractions vie with one another to organize attractive cultural events for their guests. There are numerous folk

The popular Limanaki Beach in Agia Napa, Southern Cyprus

fairs held in the mountain villages, particularly in August. This is also the hottest and sunniest time of the year.

June

St Leontios' Day *(mid-Jun)*, Pervolia village. Traditional religious fair.

Pancyprian Choirs Festival *(late Jun)*, Kato Pafos *(see pp56–7)*. During this festival, choirs perform in the ancient Roman Odeon.

Pentecost-Kataklysmos Fair (Festival of the Flood) *(7 weeks after Easter)*. Coinciding with Pentecost, this is celebrated over several days with processions and sprinkling each other with water, to symbolize cleansing.

Shakespeare at Kourion *(late Jun) (see pp70–71)*. This charity performance of a Shakespeare play takes place at the ancient amphitheatre.

July

International Music Festival *(Jun–Jul)*, Famagusta *(see pp140–43)*.

Moonlight Concerts *(Jul, during full moon)*, Pafos *(see pp52–5)*, Limassol *(pp72–5)*, Agia Napa *(p86)*. These concerts are organized by the Cyprus Tourism Organization.

Larnaka International Summer Festival *(Jul)*, Larnaka *(see pp82–5)*. Performances are staged by theatre, music and dance groups. Acts range from local groups and those from Greece, the UK and other European cities.

August

Ancient Greek Drama Festival *(Aug)*, Pafos ancient Odeon *(see pp56–7)*. Theatre festival with Greek dramas.

Assumption of the Virgin Mary *(15 Aug)*. Traditional fairs in Kykko *(see pp94–5)* and Chrysorrogiastissa monasteries and in the Chrysospiliotissa church *(see p110)* in Deftera.

Commandaria Festival *(late Aug)*. Food, wine, music and theatre at Kalo Chorio in the Limassol district to mark the beginning of the grape harvest.

Dionysia *(late Aug)*, Stroumbi near Pafos. Cypriot and Greek dances and music. An all night party with local wine and food.

Pomegranate from the environs of Larnaka

Public Holidays in South Cyprus

New Year's Day (1 Jan)

Fóta Epiphany (6 Jan)

Green Monday (varies)

Greek Independence Day (25 Mar)

Good Friday (varies)

Easter Monday (varies)

Pentecost-Kataklysmos (varies)

Greek Cypriot National Day (1 Apr)

Labour Day (1 May)

Assumption (15 Aug)

Cyprus Independence Day (1 Oct)

Ochi Day (28 Oct)

Christmas Eve (24 Dec)

Christmas Day (25 Dec)

Boxing Day (26 Dec)

Average monthly rainfall

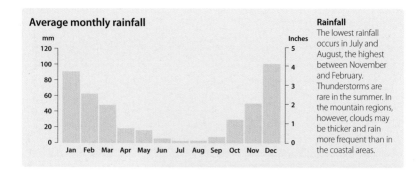

Rainfall
The lowest rainfall occurs in July and August, the highest between November and February. Thunderstorms are rare in the summer. In the mountain regions, however, clouds may be thicker and rain more frequent than in the coastal areas.

Autumn

After the summer heat, autumn brings cooler weather. With the end of the peak holiday season many resorts slow down. The Cypriots celebrate successful harvests, with particular prominence given to the grape-gathering festivals. Many towns and villages hold local fairs. The Wine Festival in Limassol attracts hordes of visitors.

Troodos mountains in their autumn colours

September
Wine Festival *(early Sep)*, Limassol *(see pp72–5)*. Wine tasting and dancing in the Municipal Gardens.
Aphrodite Opera Festival *(Sep)*, Pafos *(see pp52–5)*. One of the main cultural festivals, with a cast that includes major international singers. Some years the festival starts at the end of August.
Agia Napa International Festival *(mid-Sep)*, Agia Napa *(see p86)*. This seaside resort becomes a gathering place for

Autumn harvest of grapes in the wine-growing village of Vasa

folk musicians and dancers, theatre groups, opera ensembles, traditional and modern singers, and magicians.
Elevation of the Holy Cross *(14 Sep)*. One of the oldest religious feasts in the Greek Orthodox Church calendar. Traditionally, men tucked basil leaves behind their ears on this day.
International North Cyprus Music Festival *(Sep–Oct)*, Bellapais *(see p149)*, and **Kypria International Festival** *(Sep-Oct)*, Larnaka *(see pp78–81)*. Both of these classical music festivals feature performances by all manner of musical virtuosos: soloists, ensembles, orchestras, piano recitals and vocal groups.

October
Afamia Grape and Wine Festival *(early Oct)*, held in Koilani village *(see p98)* in the Limassol region.
Agios Ioannis Lampadistis *(early Oct)*, Kalopanagiotis *(see p93)*. Traditional folk festival combined with a fair.

Participant in the Elevation of the Holy Cross

International Dog Show *(mid-Oct)*, Pafos *(see pp52–5)* with the Kennel Club.
Agios Loukas *(mid-Oct)*. Traditional village fairs in Korakou, Koilani *(see p98)* and Aradippou.
Turkish National Day *(29 Oct)*.

November
Feast of Archangels Gabriel and Michael *(mid-Nov)*. Festival and fair in the St Michael monastery southwest of Nicosia *(see p110)*, in the village of Analiontas.
Cultural Winter *(Nov– Mar)*, Agia Napa *(see p86)*. A cycle of concerts, shows and exhibitions organized by the Agia Napa Municipality and Cyprus Tourism Organization.
Cultural Festival *(Nov)*, Limassol *(see pp72–5)*. Music, dancing, films, theatre and opera performances held in the Rialto theatre.
TRNC Foundation Day *(15 Nov)*. Celebrating the foundation, in 1983, of the Turkish Republic of Northern Cyprus, which is recognized only by Turkey.

Average monthly temperature

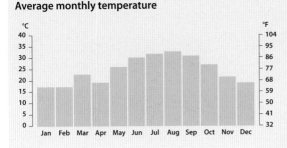

Temperature
In the summer, temperatures may reach up to 40° C (104° F). Many people enjoy visiting the island out of the high season. Only the higher sections of the Troodos mountains, which are covered with snow in winter, record temperatures below freezing.

Winter

The winters in Cyprus are mild, and the days are usually sunny. At times winter brings rain, but snow is limited to the upper reaches of the Troodos mountains. Many cultural events are organized by local authorities at this time. Christmas is traditionally celebrated within the family circle.

December

Winter Solstice *(22 Dec)*. The Solstice is observed at ancient Amathous *(see p78)*, the Sanctuary of Apollo and also at the Sanctuary of Aphrodite and Agios Tychonas in Limassol *(see pp72–5)*.
Christmas *(25 Dec)*. All over Cyprus family celebrations are held after attending church.
Carols Evening *(25 Dec)*. This occurs in the central square in Agia Napa *(see p86)*. Events include carol singing, rides in Santa's sleigh and food markets with traditional Cypriot dishes.

Welcoming the New Year *(31 Dec)*, in all towns. In Agia Napa *(see p86)*, free wine is served in the town's main square.

January

New Year (Agios Vassilios) *(1 Jan)*, formally celebrated with the exchange of presents.
Fóta – the Epiphany *(6 Jan)*. Greek Orthodox churches hold processions and bless water. In coastal towns and villages, young men compete with each other to retrieve a crucifix hurled into the water.
St Neofytos' Day *(late Jan)*. A traditional fair held in the Agios Neofytos monastery *(see p51)* near Pafos.
Şeker Bayrami (Sugar Festival) *(varies)*, North Cyprus. A religious feast and a family occasion marking the end of Ramadan, the annual Muslim fast.

February

Carnival, Limassol *(see pp72–5)*. Ten days of wild revelry preceding Lent end with Green Monday, which in Limassol features parades and fancy-dress balls.

Salt excavation from the salt lake near Larnaka

Presentation of Jesus to the Temple *(mid-Feb)*. Traditional fair in the Chrysorrogiatissa monastery *(see p62)*, in the Pafos district.
Kite-flying Competition *(late Feb)*, Deryneia *(see p87)*.

Public Holidays in North Cyprus

New Year's Day (1 Jan)
Children's Day (23 Apr)
Labour Day (1 May)
Youth and Sports Day (19 May)
Peace and Freedom Day (20 Jul)
Social Resistance Day (1 Aug)
Victory Day (30 Aug)
Turkish National Day (29 Oct)
Independence Day (15 Nov)
Şeker Bayrami (varies)
Kurban Bayram (varies)
Birth of the Prophet Mohammed (varies)

Winter sports on the slopes of the Troodos mountains

THE HISTORY OF CYPRUS

Lying at the crossroads of the eastern Mediterranean, Cyprus has long been a prize coveted by surrounding lands: Egypt and Aegia, Persia and Greece, Rome and Byzantium, and finally Venice and Turkey. Its rich copper deposits ensured the island's continuing worth to the prehistoric world. Even the name Cyprus probably derives from the late Greek word for copper – *Kypros*.

The location of Cyprus, at the point where the Eastern and Western civilizations met, determined its history to a large extent. Many rulers tried to conquer the island that occupied such a strategic position. Cyprus has been ruled in turn by the Egyptians, Mycenaeans, Phoenicians, Assyrians, Persians, Ptolemies, Romans, Byzantines, Crusaders, Franks, Venetians, Turks and British.

Stone Age

Not much is known about the earliest inhabitants, who lived in coastal caves and did not leave much trace of their habitation. Recent evidence from archaeological discoveries at Aetokremmos (Eagle Cliff), however, indicates that Cyprus has been inhabited since at least 8,000 BC. The settlements of Petra tou Limnitis and Tenta existed here in the Neolithic era (late Stone Age), around 7,000-6,000 BC.

The first permanent settlements appeared in the 6th millennium BC. These early settlers are thought to have come from Asia Minor. They built round or oval huts of broken stone, covered with branches and clay. A settlement of this type was discovered in the area of Choirokotia. The inhabitants engaged in primitive farming, livestock rearing (one species of sheep was domesticated at that time) and fishing. The scarce flint stones and obsidian were used to make tools, and vessels were gouged out of limestone. Burial practices included weighing down the bodies with stones, in the belief that this would stop the dead disturbing the living.

From this period until around 4,500 BC there is a gap of information on the activities on the island. Archaeologists have discovered traces of settlements in the vicinity of Çatalköy (Agios Epikitotos), in the North, and Sotira in the South, where they found early "combed pottery" – the oldest ceramics in Cyprus. This pottery was produced by dragging a comb-like tool over the wet vessel to create straight or wavy lines.

After 4,000 BC the Chalcolithic era ushered in the first small-scale use of metal – copper, in addition to the widespread use of stone.

8000 BC	5000 BC	4000 BC	3500 BC	3000 BC

c.6000 BC Choirokotia is Cyprus' earliest known settlement

5250 BC Existence of monochromatic and linear-pattern painted ceramics

After 4000 BC Chalcolithic settlements emerging in the western part of the island

c.8000 BC evidence of Neolithic era (Stone Age) human habitation

Howling Man *from Pierides Museum in Larnaka (5500–5000 BC)*

3400–2300 BC The earliest copper mines are established; copper vessels and steatite (soapstone) images of female idols are produced

◄ Richard the Lionheart, who conquered Cyprus in 1191

Neolithic settlement of Tenta

The Copper and Bronze Ages

The transitional period between the Stone and Bronze ages was known as the Chalcolithic era (after the Greek words for copper and stone: *chalkos* and *lithos*); it saw the small-scale use of copper for tools and implements. Most Chalcolithic villages were discovered in the previously unsettled western part of Cyprus. Figurines of limestone fertility goddesses from Lempa and cruciform figurines in picrolite (blue-green stone) from Yala indicate the growing cult of fertility.

The Troodos mountains contained large deposits of copper, and thanks to this the power of Cyprus began to increase in the third millennium BC. Cyprus became the largest producer and exporter of copper in the Mediterranean basin. The technology of bronze-smelting had by then spread throughout the entire Mediterranean basin. Copper, the main component of bronze, became the source of the island's wealth.

Trade with Egypt and the Middle East developed during this period. Along with vessels of fanciful, often zoomorphic shapes, human figurines and statuettes of bulls associated with the cult of fertility

were produced. By the start of the second millennium BC, there were towns trading in copper. The most important of these was the eastern harbour town of Alasia (modern-day Egkomi). At that time, cultural influences brought by settling Egyptian and Phoenician merchants intensified.

Flourishing trade necessitated the development of writing. The oldest text found in Cyprus is a Minoan incised clay tablet from the ruins of Alasia (16th century BC), a form of writing which came about through links with the Minoan civilization of Crete.

During the 16th and 15th centuries BC, the most important towns were Kition (modern-day Larnaka) and Egkomi-Alasia. Mycenaean culture left a permanent imprint on the future development of Cypriot culture. Despite diverse influences (from

Choirokotia, one of the earliest settlements

c.2500 BC Early Bronze Age, with the earliest bronze smelting occuring in Mesaoria		**2000–58 BC** The island ruled by Mycenaeans, Egyptians, Phoenicians, Assyrians and Persians		*Statuette of an idol, 1900 BC*	
2500 BC	**2350 BC**	**2200 BC**	**2050 BC**	**1900 BC**	**1750 BC**
c.2500 BC Red polished ceramics spread across the island; growth of the cult of fertility (its symbol a bull)	 *Ceramic pot from Vounous, 2500–1900 BC*			**1900–1650 BC** Middle Bronze Age; settlements appear on the south and east of the island, as a result of overseas trade	

Egypt, Mesopotamia, Phoenicia and Persia), it was Greek culture that would dominate.

Around the 12th century BC, marauders known as the "sea peoples" invaded Cyprus, destroying Kition and Alasia. They settled in Maa (Paleokastro) in the west of the island, among other places. But with the mass arrival of Mycenaeans in the 11th century BC, balance was restored. The Greek language, customs and culture were widely adopted, and a flourishing cult of Aphrodite also developed. The Temple of Aphrodite in Palaipafos rose in status and soon became the main shrine of the goddess in the ancient Greek world.

Ruins of Phoenician-populated Kition

Female figurine from the Temple of Aphrodite

Around 1,050 BC, an earthquake devastated Cyprus, heralding the island's Dark Ages. Kition and Alasia were reduced to rubble, and their inhabitants relocated to Salamis.

Iron Age

The first millennium BC ushered in the Iron Age throughout the entire Mediterranean area, although it in no way diminished the demand for copper from Cyprus. During this time, Cyprus was divided into kingdoms, ruled by local kings. The most important were Salamis, Marion, Lapithos, Soli, Pafos, Tamassos and Kourion. By the 9th century BC the wealth of Cyprus lured Phoenicians from nearby Tyre, who established a colony at Kition. The joint influences from the Phoenicians, Mycenaeans and the Cypriots fuelled this era of outstanding cultural achievement, with the building of new towns and the development of metallurgy.

In about the 8th century BC Amathous (east of modern-day Limassol) began to develop, and Kition (modern-day Larnaka) became a major trading hub and the centre of the cult of the Phoenician goddess, Astarte.

Archaic Era

In about 700 BC, Cyprus fell into the hands of the Assyrian kings, who did not wish to rule but merely demanded payment of tributes. This period saw the creation of Ionian-influenced limestone statues, pottery decorated with images of people and animals, and votive terracotta figurines.

Amathous, one of the oldest Cypriot towns

c.1400 BC Mycenaean merchants and craftsmen begin to settle on the island

12th century BC Invasion by the "sea peoples"

1050–750 BC Geometric era

Gold jewellery 1650–1150 BC

| 1600 BC | 1450 BC | 1300 BC | 1150 BC | 1000 BC | 850 BC |

16th century BC The earliest Cypro-Minoan writing on a tablet found in the ruins of Alasia

c.1050 BC A violent earthquake destroys Cypriot towns, including Alasia and Kition

c.1000 BC Phoenicians arrive from Tyre and settle on the southern plains

Sarcophagus from Pierides Museum in Larnaka

Classical Period

In the early 6th century BC, Cyprus was ruled by Egyptians, but their influence on local art was negligible. The most distinctive architectural features of the period are the subterranean burial chambers, resembling houses, unearthed in Tamassos. In 545 BC, Egypt was conquered by the Persians, under whose control Cyprus fell. The small Cypriot kingdoms were forced to pay tributes to the Persians and to supply battleships in the event of war.

Although the kingdoms were not at first involved in the Persian Wars (490–480 BC), strife akin to civil war erupted. Some kingdoms declared themselves on the side of the Greeks, while others supported the Persians (especially the Phoenician inhabitants of Kition and Amathous, as well as Marion, Kourion and Salamis). In the decisive battle at Salamis, insurgents were defeated and the leader, Onesilos, was killed. The Persians went on to conquer other kingdoms. The last to fall were Palaipafos and Soloi (in 498 BC). Having quashed the revolt, the pro-Persian king of Marion built a palace to watch over Soloi.

By the start of the 5th century BC, Cyprus had ten kingdoms, the existing ones having been joined by Kyrenia, Idalion, Amathous and Kition, while Soloi submitted to the rule of the king of Marion. Cyprus became a battleground for the Greek-Persian Wars. The Athenian general, Kimon, who was sent to the island failed to conquer Cyprus, despite a few minor victories, and was killed during the siege of Kition.

Despite the difficult political situation, the influence of Greek culture on Cyprus grew considerably. This was especially noticeable in sculpture; hitherto the portrayal of gods and men had been stiff, endowed with an obligatory "archaic smile", and now it became more naturalistic.

Hellenistic Era

When Alexander the Great attacked the Persian Empire in 325 BC, the Cypriot kingdoms welcomed him as a liberator, providing him with a fleet of battleships for his victorious siege of Tyre. The weakening of Phoenicia resulted in greater revenues from the copper trade for Cyprus. But the favourable situation did not last. After Alexander's death in 323 BC, Cyprus became a battleground for his successors – the victor was the Greek-Egyptian Ptolemy I Solter. Kition, Kyrenia, Lapithos and Marion were destroyed and Nicocreon,

Marble statue of Apollo from Lyra, 2nd century AD

---

800 BC Phoenicians settle in Kition		570 BC Egyptians assume control of Cyprus		294 BC Island falls under the control of theEgyptian Ptolemys
		546 BC Start of Persian rule		
			Jug (5th century BC)	

700 BC	**600 BC**	**500 BC**	**400 BC**	**300 BC**

| 8th century BC Assyrians leave control of the island to Cypriot kings, demanding only an annual tribute | c.500 BC Ionian cities revolt against the Persians | 381 BC Evagoras, King of Salamis, leads revolt against the Persians | 333 BC Alexander the Great occupies Cyprus |

Lion from a tomb stele (5th century BC)

Ruins of Kambanopetra basilica in Salamis

the King of Salamis who refused to surrender, committed suicide. Cyprus became part of the Kingdom of Egypt, and its viceroy resided in the new capital – Nea Pafos. Cultural life was influenced by Hellenism, with the Egyptian gods joining the pantheon of deities.

Roman Rule and Christianity

In 58 BC, Cyprus was conquered by the legions of Rome. The island was given the status of a province ruled by a governor, who resided in a magnificent palace in Nea Pafos. The largest town, port and main trading centre was still Salamis, which at that time numbered over 200,000 inhabitants. The imposing ruins of Salamis bear testimony to its prosperity, while the Roman floor mosaics in Pafos are among the most interesting in the Middle East. The flourishing city of Kourion was the site of the temple and oracle of Apollo – which continued to be of religious significance. Roman rule lasted in Cyprus until the end of the 4th century AD.

Mosaic from the house of Theseus in Kato Pafos

Christianity came to Cyprus with the arrival from Palestine of the apostle Paul in AD 45. He was joined by Barnabas, who was to become the first Cypriot saint. In the same year they converted the Roman governor of Cyprus, Sergius Paulus. The new religion spread slowly, until it was adopted as the state religion by Emperor Constantine. His edict of 312 granted Christianity equal status with other religions of his Empire. St Helena, the mother of Constantine the Great, stopped in Cyprus on her way back from Jerusalem, where she found fragments of the True Cross. She founded Stavrovouni monastery, which is said to house a fragment of the cross.

Saranda Kolones in Kato Pafos

58 BC Rome annexes Cyprus

1st century BC Cyprus hit by violent earthquakes

Eros and Psyche (1st century AD)

200 BC | 100 BC | AD 1 | AD 100 | AD 200 | AD 300

AD 45 The apostles Paul and Barnabas arrive as missionaries to spread Christianity to Cyprus

313 Edict of Milan grants freedom of worship to Christians throughout the Roman Empire, including Cyprus

115–116 Jewish rebellion put down by Emperor Hadrian. Salamis destroyed

In 332 and 342, two cataclysmic earthquakes destroyed most of the Cypriot towns, including Salamis and Palaipafos, marking the end of the era.

View from St Hilarion Castle

Byzantine Period

The official division of the Roman realm into an Eastern and Western Empire in 395 naturally left Cyprus on the eastern side of the divide, under the Byzantine sphere of influence.

The 5th and 6th centuries were flourishing times. The centres of pagan culture linked to the cults of Aphrodite and Apollo (Pafos and Kourion) lost importance, while the role of Salamis increased. Renamed Constantia, it became the island's capital. New towns also arose, such as Famagusta and Nicosia, and vast basilicas were built.

Beginning around 647, the first of a series of pillaging raids by Arabs took place. In the course of the raids, which continued over three centuries, Constantia was sacked and many magnificent buildings were destroyed.

In 965, the fleet of the Byzantine emperor Nicephorus II Phocas rid the island of Arab pirates and Cyprus again became safe. But not for long. From the 11th century, the entire Middle East became the

Christ Pantocrator from the church of Panagiatou tou Araka

scene of new warfare. Anatolia, Syria and, above all, the Holy Land were captured by the Seljuk Turks. Byzantium was incapable of resisting the onslaught, and Crusades were organized in Europe to recover the Holy Land and other lost territories.

Crusades and Lusignan Period

Successive crusades took place throughout most of the 12th and 13th centuries to recover the Holy Land from the Muslims. After considerable effort, the first succeeded in capturing Jerusalem (1099). European knights set up the Kingdom of Jerusalem, but surrounded as it was by Turkish emirates, it was unable to survive. Further crusades were launched but mainly suffered defeats. The Sultan Saladin conquered nearly the entire Kingdom of Jerusalem in 1187. The next crusade was organized in 1190. One of its leaders was

Pendant from the early Byzantine period

488 Following the discovery of the tomb of St Barnabas, Emperor Zenon confirms the independence of the Cypriot Church

688 Emperor Justinian II and Caliph Abd al-Malik sign a treaty dividing control of the island

| 300 | 450 | 600 | 750 | 9 |

395 Partition of the Roman Empire; Cyprus becomes part of the Eastern Roman Empire

7th century Arab raids

David in the Lion's Den, *a 7th-century AD relief*

Richard I (the Lionheart), King of England, whose ships were forced onto Cyprus by a storm. The local prince, Isaac Komnenos, who had proclaimed himself King of Cyprus, plundered the ships and tried to imprison the sister and the fiancée of Richard. In reprisal, Richard smashed the Komnenos artillery on the Mesaoria plain and chased his enemy, capturing him in Kantara Castle.

As spoils of war, Cyprus passed from hand to hand. Richard turned it over to the Knights Templar, and they in turn sold the island to the knight Guy de Lusignan, who started the Cyprian Lusignan Dynasty and introduced the feudal system to Cyprus. A period of prosperity for the nobility ensued, partly due to trade with Genoa and Venice, although local Cypriots experienced terrible poverty. Magnificent cathedrals and churches were built, and small churches in the Troodos mountains were decorated with splendid frescoes. The state was weakened by a devastating raid by the increasingly powerful Genoese in 1372, who captured Famagusta. Finally, the widow of James, the last Lusignan king, ceded Cyprus to the Venetians in 1489.

A costume from Venetian times

Venetian Rule

Venetian rule over Cyprus lasted less than a century. The island was a frontier fortress, intended to defend the Venetian domains in the eastern Mediterranean from the Ottoman Empire. The most formidable fortifications around the ports and towns date from this period (including Kyrenia and Famagusta). Still, these were no match for the overwhelming power of the Ottoman Empire. When the Turkish army of Sultan Selim II landed on Cyprus in 1570, one town after another fell to the invaders. Nicosia was able to defend itself for just a few weeks; when it fell, the Turks slaughtered 20,000 people. The defence of Famagusta lasted longer – 10 months – and was one of the greatest battles of its time. The Venetian defenders did not survive to see the arrival of the relief army, and were forced to capitulate. The Turkish commander, Lala Mustafa Pasha, reneged on his promises of clemency and ordered the garrison to be slaughtered, and its leader Bragadino to be skinned alive.

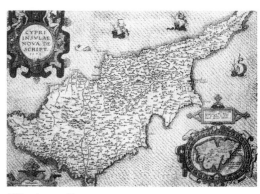

A 16th-century map of Cyprus

The Ottoman Era

This was the start of 300 years of Turkish rule. The conquerors destroyed most of the monasteries and churches, turning others into mosques. They abolished the hated feudal system, and divided land among the peasants. The Orthodox clergy were allowed to adopt some Catholic churches and monasteries, and later the archbishop was recognized as the Greek community's representative.

The Turks brought their compatriots to settle on the island, and squashed the regular rebellions. In 1821, after the beginning of the Greek War of Independence, the Turkish governor ordered the execution of the popular Archbishop Kyprianos and many other members of the Orthodox clergy.

In the mid-19th century, Great Britain came to play an increasingly important role in the Middle East. In exchange for military

Selima Mosque in North Nicosia

aid in the war with Russia, Turkey handed over occupation and administrative rights of Cyprus to Britain in perpetuity in 1878, though the island would continue to be a Turkish possession.

British Rule

Cyprus's strategic location was vital in defending the sea routes to India and in safeguarding British interests in the Middle East. During their rule, the British introduced the English justice system, reduced crime and built roads and waterworks. Following the outbreak of World War I, when Turkey declared itself on the side of Germany, Britain annexed Cyprus.

After World War II, Greek Cypriots pressed for *enosis* (unification with Greece), which was strongly opposed by the Turkish minority. Rising

Hadjigeorgakis Kornesios mansion

Hoisting of the British flag in Cyprus

1570 Cyprus invaded by Ottoman Turks

1754 The sultan confirms the Orthodox archbishop as a spokesman for the Greek Cypriots

The hanging of Archbishop Kyprianos

1600	1650	1700	1750	1800

1571–1878 Ottoman era

1660 Ottoman authorities recognize the legitimacy of the Archbishop's office with the Greeks

Büyük Han in North Nicosia

1779 Establishment of the dragoman (intercessor between the Turks and the Greeks)

1821 Bloody suppression of the Greek national uprising by the Turks

tensions led to the establishment of the organization EOKA (National Organization of Cypriot Fighters) in 1954 by Archbishop Makarios and Greek General George Grivas. Its aim was to free Cyprus from British control. EOKA embarked on a terrorist campaign, first aimed at property and later, at people. In 1958, Turkish Cypriots founded the Turkish Resistance Organisation (TNT), which provided a counterbalance to EOKA.

Archbishop Makarios, first president of the Republic of Cyprus

The terror and growing costs of maintaining order led the British to grant independence to Cyprus. A constitution was drafted that, among other things, excluded *enosis* and *taksim* (partition of Cyprus between Turkey and Greece favoured by Turkish Cypriots). Britain, Greece and Turkey signed a treaty that obliged them to ensure Cyprus's independence. Archbishop Makarios, who had been interned by the British, returned to Cyprus in triumph and was elected President of the Republic of Cyprus. Independence was officially declared on 16 August 1960.

Independent Cyprus

In December 1963, animosity between Greek and Turkish Cypriots erupted into warfare. The Greek army intervened and the Turkish air force bombarded the environs of Polis. In 1964, United Nations troops arrived to restore peace between the warring parties within three months. The mission failed and troops remain to this day.

On 15 July 1974 a coup d'état, encouraged by Athens and staged by rebel units of the Cypriot National Guard (led by Greek army officers), ousted Makarios. The conspirators killed several hundred Greeks and Turks, which provided the Turkish government in Ankara with a pretext to send troops to Cyprus. After a short battle, the invading army controlled the north, and the resettlement of the population began. The "Green Line" buffer zone still divides the Turkish-occupied North from the South, and continues to be patrolled by UN troops.

In November 1983 the Turks declared the Turkish Republic of Northern Cyprus (TRNC), which is recognized only in Turkey. In April 2004 a referendum preceding Cyprus's entry into the European Union failed to unify the island. The leaders, President of the Republic of Cyprus Nico Anastasiades and President of the TRNC Dervis Eroglu, make repeated attempts at reunification by participating in frequent rounds of talks.

Referendum on the reunification of Cyprus (2004)

878 Great Britain takes over the administration of Cyprus

1925 Cyprus becomes a British colony

1950 Makarios is elected Archbishop

1960 (16 August) Proclamation of independence. Archbishop Makarios III becomes President of the Republic of Cyprus

General George Grivas

1850	1900	1950	2000	2050

1914 Outbreak of World War I; Great Britain annexes Cyprus

1963–4 Fighting erupts between Greek and Turkish Cypriots; UN troops arrive

1974 Coup d'état against President Makarios. Turkish invasion of North Cyprus

1983 TRNC is declared

2013 Eurozone crisis

2010 Festivals mark 50 years of independence

2008 Southern Cyprus adopts the euro

2004 Referendum on reunification

CYPRUS REGION BY REGION

Cyprus at a Glance

Cyprus has a wide variety of historic sites. Visitors can find everything from Neolithic settlements and ancient towns to medieval cathedrals and small mountain churches decorated with exquisite frescoes, castles built by the Crusaders and Venetian fortresses, and modern buildings and museums. The island abounds in picturesque towns and villages, beautiful coastal areas, and scenic mountains, with diverse wildlife and friendly people.

Nicosia is the world's only divided capital city. A highlight of its southern part is the Byzantine-style Archbishop Makarios Cultural Centre, housing an impressive collection of icons (see p122).

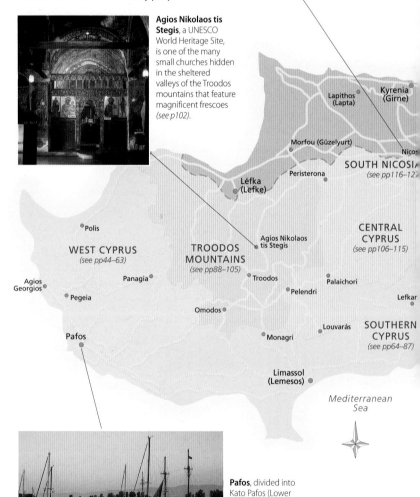

Agios Nikolaos tis Stegis, a UNESCO World Heritage Site, is one of the many small churches hidden in the sheltered valleys of the Troodos mountains that feature magnificent frescoes (see p102).

Lapithos (Lapta)

Kyrenia (Girne)

Morfou (Güzelyurt)

Nico

Peristerona

SOUTH NICOSIA (see pp116–12

Léfka (Lefke)

Polis

WEST CYPRUS (see pp44–63)

Agios Nikolaos tis Stegis

CENTRAL CYPRUS (see pp106–115)

Panagia

TROODOS MOUNTAINS (see pp88–105)

Agios Georgios

Pegeia

Troodos

Palaichori

Lefkar

Pelendri

Pafos

Omodos

Louvarás

SOUTHERN CYPRUS (see pp64–87)

Monagri

Limassol (Lemesos)

Mediterranean Sea

Pafos, divided into Kato Pafos (Lower Pafos) and Ktima, is full of history. With its picturesque harbour, it is also one of the most beautiful towns in the Mediterranean (see pp52–7).

◄ Aerial view of rooftops in the mountain villages of Cyprus

Buffavento Castle in the Kyrenia mountains was one of three castles, along with Kantara and St Hilarion, that defended Cyprus against attacks along the north coast *(see p148)*.

Aigialousa
(Yenierenkoy)

0 kilometres   15

0 miles   15

Bogazi
(Boğaz)

Trikomo (Iskele)

favento
tle

Kythrea

NORTH CYPRUS
(see pp128–157)

Salamis

Famagusta
(Gazimağusa/
Ammochostos)

Lysi

Idalion

Kellia

Agia Napa

Larnaka

Pyrga

Kiti

Salamis was the island's most important port and trading town for almost one thousand years, and also its capital. Now it is one of the largest archaeological sites *(see pp138–9)*.

In Larnaka the remains of the 18th-century Kamares Aqueduct stand beside the Larnaka–Limassol highway. Known as the Kingdom of Kition in ancient times, today Larnaka is a large port town with a thriving tourist zone *(see pp82–5)*.

Famagusta, a city surrounded by Venetian defence walls, contains Gothic churches that have been transformed into mosques with minarets *(see pp140–51)*.

WEST CYPRUS

West Cyprus is a varied region, made up of mountains, historical sights and a lovely coastline. It was once the most neglected part of the island, remote from the main cities and harbours. Now it is becoming a popular attraction due to its wild natural environment. Lovers of antiquities are sure to be enchanted by the Roman mosaics in Pafos, while mythology buffs can see the place where the goddess Aphrodite emerged from the sea at Petra tou Romiou.

Pafos's Hellenistic, Roman and Byzantine relics are among the most interesting in the island, especially the Roman mosaics.

The modern town is divided into a bustling tourist zone on the coast, with dozens of luxury hotels, taverns, pubs and restaurants, and Ktima – the old town of Pafos – which is only a short drive inland but a world away from the tourist zone.

This region has a slightly milder climate than the rest of the island, as witnessed by the banana plantations north of Pafos. And though there is practically no industry, it has the most extensive forest areas in Cyprus, including the famous Cedar Valley inhabited by wild moufflon.

The Akamas peninsula, with its rugged hills overgrown with forests, is home to many species of wild animals, and the beautiful beaches provide nesting grounds for sea turtles. This is a paradise for nature lovers and is one of the best places to hike in Cyprus. Movement around the peninsula is hindered by the lack of roads, but there are trails for use by walkers.

This is the land of Aphrodite, goddess of love, who is said to have been born in the south of the island by the rocks jutting out of the sea, which are named after her. North Akamas, on the bay of Chrysochou, is the goddess's bath, which she used after her amorous frolics with Adonis.

Boats and yachts moored at Paphos harbour on a sunny day

◄ Sunset over Petra Tou Romiou beach

Exploring West Cyprus

The best place to begin exploring West Cyprus is Pafos, which has the largest concentration of hotels and the most developed tourist infrastructure. Here you will also find a wealth of historic relics that have made Pafos a UNESCO World Heritage Site.
They range from Bronze Age dwellings (Maa Paleokastro at Coral Bay), royal tombs dating from the Hellenic era and Roman floor mosaics to Byzantine castles and churches. Pafos forest is home to wild moufflon. Cape Lara, to the northwest of Pafos, has beautiful beaches, and further on is the Akamas peninsula.

Lempa is a favourite place with watersports enthusiasts

Getting There

The easiest way to arrive is by air to the international airport east of Pafos, where a motorway links the town with Limassol, offering easy access to the west coast. It is also possible to get here via a parallel road running along the coast and over the southern slopes of the Troodos mountains. However, the mountain roads are not of the best quality, and driving around the Akamas peninsula is best done in a four-wheel-drive vehicle.

Sights at a Glance

1. Petra tou Romiou
2. Palaipafos
3. Geroskipou
4. Pafos *pp52–7*
5. Lempa
6. Agios Neofytos
7. Coral Bay
8. Pegeia
9. Agios Georgios
10. Lara
11. Baths of Aphrodite
12. Akamas Peninsula
13. Polis
14. Marion
15. Panagia Chrysorrogiatissa
16. Xeros Valley
17. Diarizos Valley

Walking in the Akamas Peninsula pp60–61

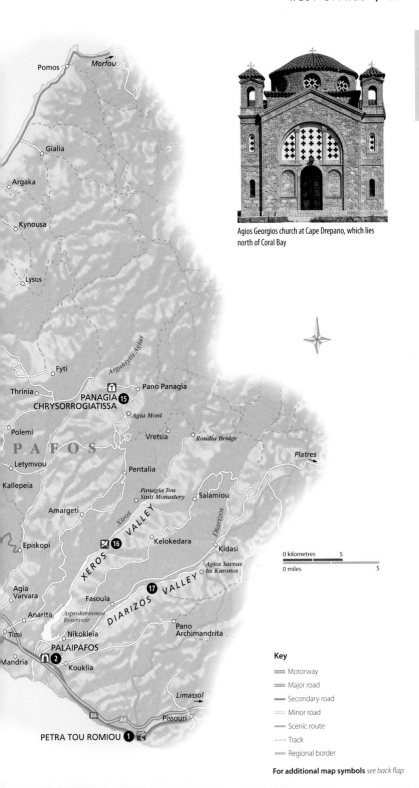

Agios Georgios church at Cape Drepano, which lies
north of Coral Bay

Pomos

Morfou

Gialia

Argaka

Kynousa

Lysos

Fyti

Argakiytis Agias

Thrinia

**PANAGIA
CHRYSORROGIATISSA** **15**

Pano Panagia

Agia Moni

Polemi

Vretsia

Roudia Bridge

P A F O S

Letymvou

Pentalia

Platres

Kallepeia

*Panagia Tou
Sinti Monastery*

Salamiou

Amargeti

Xiros VALLEY

Diarizos

Episkopi

16

Kelokedara

Kidasi

XEROS

*Agios Savvas
tis Karonos*

17

DIARIZOS VALLEY

Agia
Varvara

Fasoula

Anarita

*Asprokremmos
Reservoir*

Pano
Archimandrita

Timi

Nikokleia

PALAIPAFOS **2**

Mandria

Kouklia

Limassol

Pissouri

B6   A6

PETRA TOU ROMIOU **1**

0 kilometres   5

0 miles   5

Key

━━━ Motorway

▦▦▦ Major road

━━━ Secondary road

╌╌╌ Minor road

━━━ Scenic route

--- Track

▦▦▦ Regional border

For additional map symbols *see back flap*

Petra tou Romiou, the legendary birthplace of Aphrodite

❶ Petra tou Romiou

Road Map B4. 25 km (16 miles) east of Pafos.

The area between Pafos and Limassol includes what is probably the most beautiful stretch of the Cyprus coast, dominated by limestone crags rising from the blue sea. At Petra tou Romiou there are three huge, white limestone rocks known collectively as the **Rock of Aphrodite**. In Greek mythology it was here that Aphrodite, goddess of love, beauty and fertility, emerged from the sea foam. She sailed to the shore on a shell towed by dolphins and rested in nearby Palaipafos, where a temple was built to her.

The location of these picturesque rocks is beautiful, with clear blue water beckoning swimmers. The large beach near the rocks is covered with fine pebbles and stones polished smooth by the action of the waves. A word of caution,

however: the road between the car park and the beach is dangerous, and you are advised to use the underground passage.

Nearby you can see trees on which infertile women tie handkerchiefs or scraps of fabric to appeal for help from Aphrodite. They are joined by others who are lonely and unlucky in love, beseeching the goddess of love to help them. A local legend says that swimming around the jutting rock at full moon will make you a year younger with each lap. Other legends lead us to believe that the amorous goddess, after a night spent in the arms of her lover, returned to this spot to regain her virginity by bathing in the sea.

On the slope of the hill above the Rock of Aphrodite, the Cyprus Tourism Organization has built a cafeteria where you can eat while taking in the beautiful view over Petra tou Romiou. Meaning "Rock of Romios", the name Petra tou

Romiou also commemorates the legendary Greek hero Digenis Akritas, also known as Romios. He lived during the Byzantine era and, during an Arab raid by Saracen corsairs on Cyprus, hurled huge boulders into the sea to destroy the Arab ships. According to legend, the rocks here are the stones thrown by Romios.

Environs
A few kilometres east of Petra tou Romiou is the small resort community of **Pissouri**, surrounded by orchards. There is a large resort here, as well as some smaller hotels, as well as a long, sandy beach. Nearby are two golf courses: Secret Valley and Aphrodite Hills.

❷ Palaipafos

Road Map A4. In Kouklia village, 14 km (9 miles) east of Pafos, by the Pafos–Limassol road. 632 from Ktima Pafos. **Tel** 264 32155. **Open** 8:30am–7:30pm daily (to 5pm winter).

Just north of the large village of Kouklia are the ruins of the famous Palaipafos (Old Pafos), which was the oldest and most powerful city-state on the island in ancient times. According to tradition, it was founded by Agaperon – a hero of the Trojan Wars and the son of the King of Tegeia in Greek Arcadia. Palaipafos was also the site of the **Temple of Aphrodite**, the most important shrine of the goddess in the ancient world, but now only of specialist interest. Archaeological evidence points to the existence of a much older town

Aphrodite

The cult of Aphrodite arrived in Cyprus from the East; she was already worshipped in Syria and Palestine as Ishtar and Astarte. She was also worshipped by the Romans as Venus. In Greek mythology Aphrodite was the goddess of love, beauty and fertility who rose from the sea foam off the shore of Cyprus. She was married to Hephaestus, but took many lovers, including Ares and Adonis. She was the mother of Eros, Hermaphrodite, Priap and Aeneas, among others. The main centres for her cult of worship were Pafos and Amathous. The myrtle plant is dedicated to her, as is the dove.

Marble statue of Aphrodite from Soloi

on this site, dating back to the Bronze Age. Legend says that Pygmalion, a local king and also a brilliant sculptor, carved many statues, including one of an extraordinarily beautiful woman with whom he fell madly in love. Aphrodite, moved by his love, turned the cold statue into a living woman. Their union produced a son, Pafos, who gave the town its name.

The most famous figure of Pafos was Kinyras, ruler of the city and great priest of Aphrodite, who introduced many religious mysteries and gave rise to the dynasty that ruled the city for centuries.

A large **centre of worship** devoted to Aphrodite was established here in the 12th century BC, at the end of the Bronze Age. All that is left now are its foundations and fragments of the walls. The sanctuary was destroyed during an earthquake and rebuilt in the 1st century, during Roman times. At this place of worship, the goddess was represented by a black stone shaped as a cone, symbolizing fertility. For centuries, crowds of pilgrims flocked to Pafos from all over the ancient world. Adorned with flowers, the pilgrims walked into the temple where they were met by the temple courtesans. Aphrodite was worshipped through ritual sexual intercourse between the pilgrims and Aphrodite's priestesses – young Cypriot women who were obliged to offer their virginity to the goddess by giving

The small stone church of Agios Constantinos near Kouklion

themselves to a pilgrim man within the temple area. These orgiastic rites were mainly held in the spring, and elements have survived in the form of the spring flower festival – the Anthistiria.

Palaipafos was not always peaceful. It took part in the rebellion of the Ionian cities against the Persians. In 498 BC, the Persians laid siege to the city and, following a fierce battle, forced entry by scaling the ramparts, the remains of which can still be seen. In 325 BC, following a devastating earthquake that destroyed Palaipafos, its last king, Nikikles, moved the city to Nea Pafos (present day Kato Pafos), but Aphrodite's sanctuary retained its importance until the end of the 4th century, when Emperor Theodosius banned pagan cults within the

Panagia Chrysopolitissa inscription

empire. The sanctuary is now a site of excavations by Swiss archaeologists.

Standing on the hill is a Gothic structure known as the **Lusignan Court**, built in the times of the Crusaders and subsequently remodelled by the Turks. It is built on a square floor plan, and leading on to a square yard is an old tower gate. The rooms in the east wing contain a museum that exhibits locally discovered ceramics, stone idols, bronze articles and the black stone worshipped by followers of Aphrodite. On the ground floor there is an impressive Gothic hall with cross vaulting.

In the nearby Roman villa, known as the **House of Leda**, archaeologists have uncovered a 2nd-century AD floor mosaic of the Spartan Queen Leda with Zeus in the guise of a swan.

Adjacent to the sanctuary is the small 12th-century church of **Panagia Chrysopolitissa**, which was built over the ruins of an Early Byzantine basilica. It is dedicated to the early Christian Madonna, whose cult derives directly from Aphrodite the pagan goddess of love. As part of a tradition stemming from Cypriot folklore, women came here to light candles to the Virgin Mary – Giver of Mother's Milk. This church contains interesting 14th-century frescoes, and some of the colourful mosaics that covered the floor of the basilica have been preserved.

Ruins of the Sanctuary of Aphrodite

Folk Art Museum in Geroskipou

❸ Geroskipou

Road Map A4. 3 km (1.8 miles) east of Pafos. 🚌 601, 606, 612, 613, 631, 632, 633, 634, 636. 🎭 Agia Paraskevi (Jul).

The name Geroskipou (hieros kipos) means "sacred garden" in Greek. This testifies to the fact that this former village (now a suburban district bordering Pafos) was built on the site of a forest dedicated to Aphrodite. To this day, it is notable for its many flowers and fruit trees, especially citrus and pomegranate trees – symbols of the goddess.

The main street is lined with workshops producing the local delicacy – loukoumia (Cyprus delight). Made from water, sugar and citrus juice, thickened through evaporation, the resulting jelly is cut into cubes and coated with icing sugar. The workshops are open to visitors, who can view the production process and, while there, also buy other sweets including sugar-coated almonds and delicious halva – made of nuts, honey and sesame seeds. The tree-shaded main square of the town is surrounded by colourful shops selling baskets, ceramics and the celebrated loukoumia; there are also numerous cafés serving coffee and pastries.

Standing at the southern end of the market square is **Agia Paraskevi**, one of the most interesting Byzantine churches on the island. Built in the 9th century, this stone church features five domes arranged in the shape of a cross. The sixth one surmounts the reliquary located under the 19th-century

belfry. Originally, the church was a single-nave structure. Its interior is decorated with beautiful 15th-century murals depicting scenes from the New Testament, including the lives of Jesus and Mary, and the Crucifixion. The frescoes were restored in the 1970s.

The vault of the central dome has been decorated with the painting of the Praying Madonna. The three images opposite the south entrance – The Last Supper, The Washing of the Feet and The Betrayal – can be dated from the Lusignan period, due to the style of armour worn by the knights portrayed. Opposite are The Birth and Presentation of the Virgin, The Entry into Jerusalem and The Raising of Lazarus.

Another attraction, close to the market square, is the 19th-century historic house once home of the British Consul, Andreas Zamboulakis.

The stone church of Agia Paraskevi in Geroskipou

Now the building houses the **Folk Art Museum**, one of the most impressive on the island, including a collection of local folk costumes, textiles, embroidery and toys, as well as decorated gourds, furniture and domestic items.

🏛 **Agia Paraskevi Church**
Tel 26 961 859. **Open** Apr–Oct: 8am–1pm, 2–5pm Mon–Sat; Nov–Mar: 8am–1pm, 2–4pm Mon–Sat.

🏛 **Folk Art Museum**
Leondiou. **Tel** 26 306 216. **Open** 8:30am–4pm daily. ♿

❹ Pafos

See pp52–5.

Reconstructed Chalcolithic houses in Lempa's Experimental Village

❺ Lempa

Road Map A4. 4 km (2.5 miles) north of Pafos. 🚌 607, 642 from Ktima Pafos.

Set among citrus groves between the villages of Chlorakas and Kissonerga just a short distance from the sea, Lempa is home to the **Cyprus College of Art**. The artists, craftsmen and students here have studios in restored village houses. The road to the college is lined with sculptures. The independent pottery workshops are worth visiting.

Lempa was home to the earliest islanders, who settled here more than 5,500 years ago. West of the village centre you can see the **Lempa Experimental Village** – a partially reconstructed settlement dating from the Chalcolithic (bronze) era (3500 BC). British archaeologists have rebuilt four complete houses from that era. The clay, cylindrical dwellings are covered with makeshift roofs.

Agios Neofytos monastery, founded in the 12th century

Ⅲ Cyprus College of Art
Tel 24 254 042.. **W** artcyprus.org

♞ Lempa Experimental Village
Open dawn–dusk daily.

Environs
In the centre of the nearby village of Empa, some 2 km (1 mile) southeast of Lempa, is the 12th-century monastery church of **Panagia Chryseleoussa**. Inside it are the remains of frescoes that were initially destroyed by an earthquake in the mid-1900s, and later damaged by a bad restoration job.

❻ Agios Neofytos

Road Map A4. 9 km north of Pafos, 2 km NW of Tala. 🚌 604. **Open** 9am–1pm, 2–6pm daily (to 4pm Nov–Mar). 🚫🚫 25 Jan & 28 Sep.

This monastery was founded in the 12th century by a monk named Neofytos, one of the main saints of the Cypriot church. He was a hermit and an ascetic, author of philosophical treatises and hymns, who spent dozens of years here. Some of his manuscripts survive, including the *Ritual Ordinance*, a handbook of monastic life, and a historic essay on the acquisition of Cyprus by the Crusaders.

The future saint dug three cells in the steep limestone rock with his bare hands. The murals covering its walls are reputed to have been painted by Neofytos

A woman potter

himself. This, the oldest part of the monastery, is called the *Enkleistra* (hermitage). In two of the caves, murals depict the final days of the life of Christ – *The Last Supper*, *Judas's Betrayal* and the *Deposition from the Cross*, featuring Joseph of Arimathea whose face is thought to be a portrait of the saint. The dome, hewn from the soft rock, features the Ascension. The cell of the saint has bookshelves, benches and a desk at which St Neofytos used to work, all carved in the rock, as well as his sarcophagus presided over by an image of the Resurrection.

The main buildings, which are still inhabited by monks, include an inner courtyard, a small garden with an aviary, and a *katholikon* – the monastery church with a terrace dedicated to the Virgin Mary.

❼ Coral Bay

Road Map A4. 8 km (5 miles) north of Pafos. 🚌 615, 616.

This fine sandy beach between two promontories has a tropical air. All summer long it is covered by rows of sunbeds for hire. It offers soft sand and safe swimming for families, and there is a wide choice of watersports. There are many bars, restaurants and hotels, as well as a campsite for more thrifty visitors. Live pop concerts are held here on summer evenings. This beach is popular with young Cypriots from Larnaka and Limassol, especially on summer weekends.

On the northern headland archaeologists discovered **Maa Paleokastro** – a fortified Achaian settlement dating from the Bronze Age. The site now houses the **Museum of the Mycenean Colonization of Cyprus**.

Environs
Opposite the village of Chlorakas on the road to Pafos is the **Church of St George**, which commemorates the landing of General George Grivas at this spot in 1954. The local museum has a boat that was used by EOKA guerrillas for weapons smuggling.

Several kilometres inland lies the Mavrokolympos reservoir. Above the car park are the **Adonis Baths**, whose main attraction is its 10-m- (32-ft-) high waterfall. The road running along the Mavrokolympos river leads to more waterfalls.

The region also features numerous vineyards and banana plantations.

The picturesque crescent-shaped Coral Bay

❹ Pafos

Pafos is the name given to the twin towns of Pano Pafos (Upper Pafos, known as the Old Town or Ktima by locals) and Nea Pafos or Kato Pafos (Lower Pafos) *(see pp56–7)*. During the Byzantine era, when coastal towns were threatened by Arab raids, the town was moved inland to its present hilltop location. This is now the modern regional centre of trade, administration and culture, while the lower town is the site of fine Roman ruins and the majority of tourist facilities.

Exploring Pafos

Ktima is best explored on foot. Most of its major historic buildings and interesting sites, except for the Archaeological Museum, are within walking distance. The tourist area in the Old Town has been carefully restored. The main shopping street is Makarios Avenue, where you will find a wide choice of jewellery, clothing and footwear. After strolling along the streets of the Old Town it is worth stopping for a rest in the green district, to the south of town, near the acropolis and the Byzantine and Ethnographic Museums. The eastern part of town sports wide avenues lined with classical public buildings, schools and libraries. The western part is a maze of narrow streets and traditional architecture.

🅒 Grand Mosque

(Cami Kebir) Namik Kemil.
The Grand Mosque is a relic of the past Turkish presence in this area. Standing in the Mouttalos district, it had been the Byzantine church of Agia Sofia before being turned into a mosque.

The façade of Agios Kendas church, which was built around 1930

🅐 Agora

Agoras street.
In the centre of the Old Town is an ornamental covered market hall building, dating from the early 20th century. Sweet and souvenir sellers have replaced the fruit and vegetable vendors, who now trade in the outside market.

🅑 Mehmet Bey Ebubekir Hamam (Turkish Baths)

Militiathou, next to the covered bazaar (agora).
Among the trees south of the Agora are the Turkish baths. Originally this dome-covered stone structure probably served as a church. After serving as the Turkish baths, some of the rooms were used to house the municipal museum, but when this moved to new premises, the building stood empty. A period of neglect followed, but the building has been restored to its former glory. It now houses a coffee shop.

🅐 Agios Kendas

Leoforos Archiepiskopou Makariou III.
Built in 1930, the exterior is not particularly exciting, but the interior is well worth a visit. Here you will find a carved wooden iconostasis, a bishop's throne and a number of 19th-century icons.

🅓 Town Hall

Plateia 28 Octovriou.
The single-storey Neo-Classical building standing on the edge of the Municipal Garden, redolent of ancient Greek architecture, houses the Town Hall and the Registry Office. This is a popular wedding venue. On the opposite side, behind the slender Ionian column in the middle of the square, is the one-storey municipal library.

The Neo-Classical Town Hall and Registry Office of Pafos

🅐 Agios Theodoros (St Theodore's Cathedral)

Andrea Ioannou.
Built in 1896, Agios Theodoros is the oldest church in Ktima and is as important for the Orthodox community as St John's Cathedral (Agios Ioannis) in Nicosia.

Close to the square stands a column commemorating the victims of the Turkish slaughter of 1821 that claimed the lives of the Bishop of Pafos, Chrysanthos, and numerous other members of the Greek clergy.

Agora covered market, Pafos

Display in the Ethnographic Museum

🏛 Geological Exhibition

Ayios Theodoros 2. **Open** 9am–4pm
Mon–Sat (summer).

One of a few places on the
island where you can learn
about the geology of Cyprus,
this is a small private collection
of rocks and minerals. On
display are sedimentary rocks
with fossils; volcanic rocks from
the Troodos Mountains and the
Akamas peninsula; and metallic
minerals, particularly copper
and asbestos that have been
mined here for millennia.

🏛 Bishop's Palace and Byzantine Museum

Andrea Ioannou 5. **Tel** 26 931 393.
Open 9am–3pm Mon–Fri,
9am–1pm Sat. 🚫

This beautiful Byzantine-style
building is the residence of the
Bishop of Pafos and the most

important ecclesiastical building
after Agios Theodoros. It was built
in 1910 by Iaskos, the Bishop of
Pafos. Bishop Chrysostomos
subsequently extended the
palace, furnishing it with beautiful

The Dormition of the Virgin Mary,
the Byzantine Museum

arcades and allocating part of it
to the Byzantine Museum. The
museum houses a collection of
icons, including the oldest on the
island – the 9th-century *Agia
Marina*, and the 12th-century
Panagia Eloussa from the Agios
Savras monastery. There are also
religious books, including a 1472
Bible and a collection of documents produced by Turkish sultans.

🏛 Ethnographic Museum

Exo Vrysis 1. **Tel** 26 932 010.
Open 10am–5:30pm Mon–Sat,
10am–1pm Sun. 🚫

This privately run museum
houses collections of coins, folk
costumes, kitchen utensils,
baskets and ceramics as well as
axes, amphorae and carriages.
In the sunken garden is a wood-
burning stove from an old bakery
and an authentic 3rd-century
stone sarcophagus.

Pafos Town Centre

① Grand Mosque
② Agora
③ Loutra (Turkish Baths)
④ Agios Kendas
⑤ Town Hall
⑥ Agios Theodoros
　　(St Theodore's Cathedral)
⑦ Geological Exhibition
⑧ Bishop's Palace and
　　Byzantine Museum
⑨ Ethnographic Museum

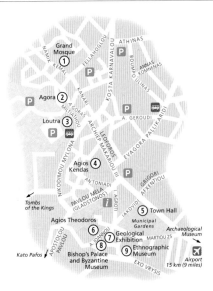

0 metres　　　200
0 yards　　　　200

For key to symbols *see back flap*

🏛 Tombs of the Kings
Leoforos Tafon ton Vasileon.
Tel 26 306 295. **Open** 8am–5pm daily
(to 6pm Apr, May, Sep & Oct; to
7:30pm Jun–Aug). 🅿 🚌 615.

The necropolis is a fascinating
system of caves and rock tombs
dating from the Hellenic and
Roman eras (the 3rd century BC
to 3rd century AD). Situated
north of Kato Pafos, beyond the
old city walls and close to the
sea, it consists of imposing
tombs carved in soft sandstone.

Eight tomb complexes have
been opened for viewing; the
most interesting are numbers 3,
4 and 8. Stone steps lead to
underground vaults. Some
tombs are surrounded by
peristyles of Doric columns,
beyond which you can spot
burial niches. Others have been
decorated with murals.

The architectural style of many
tombs, particularly those in the
northern section, reveals the
Egyptian influence; they were
inspired by the Ptolemy tombs in
Alexandria. One funerary custom
that has been documented is
that on the anniversary of the
death, relatives of the deceased
would gather around the tomb
for a ceremonial meal,
depositing the leftovers by the
actual sepulchre. Similar customs
prevail to this day in some Greek
Orthodox communities.

Over the following centuries
the tombs were systematically

The 12th-century stone church of Agia Kyriaki

plundered. One of the more
notorious looters was the
American consul from Larnaka,
Luigi Palma de Cesnola, who
plundered many sites in Cyprus,
including Kourion and the
Tombs of the Kings in Pafos.
These sites were built when
there were no longer
kings on Cyprus,
and they were
probably used to
bury prominent
citizens of Pafos,
civil servants and
army officers;
nevertheless, in
view of their
opulence they became known
as the Tombs of the Kings.

During times of persecution
they were used by Christians as
hiding places. Later the site was
used as a quarry. The place has a
unique atmosphere, best experienced in the morning.

Inscription on one of the stones
in Agia Kyriaki

🏛 Agia Kyriaki
Odos Pafias Afroditis.
Open daily.

The 12th-century stone
church of Agia Kyriaki,
with a later small belfry
and dome, is also known
as Panagia Chrysopolitissa
(Our Lady of the Golden
City). It was built on the
ruins of an earlier seven-
aisled Christian Byzantine
basilica, the largest in
Cyprus. A bishop's palace
also stood nearby. Both
buildings were destroyed
by the Arabs, but the
parts that have survived
include 4th-century
religious floor mosaics.
The road to Agia Kyriaki
leads along a special

platform built over the
archaeological digs, from where
you can see several single
columns. One of them has been
dubbed "St Paul's Pillar". The
apostle came to Cyprus to
preach Christianity, but was
captured and led before the
Roman governor,
Sergius Paulus, who
sentenced him to
flogging. St Paul
blinded his accuser,
Elymas, thus
convincing Sergius
of his innocence to
such an extent that
the governor
converted to Christianity.

Agia Kyriaki is used jointly
by the Catholic and
Anglican communities.

The beautiful church standing
nearby, built on a rock which
forms part of the Kato Pafos defence walls, is called *Panagia Theos-
kepasti* – "guarded by God". It is
apocryphally told that during a
scourging Arab attack a miraculous cloud enveloped the church,
concealing it from the enemy.

🏛 Catacombs of Agia Solomoni and Fabrica Hill
Leoforos Apostolou Palou.
Open dawn–dusk.

Inside a former tomb, is a subterranean church dedicated to
Solomoni, a Jewess, whose seven
children were tortured in her
presence, and who is now regarded by the Cypriots as a saint.

In Roman times the site was
probably occupied by a
synagogue, and earlier on by a
pagan shrine. Steep steps lead
down to the sunken sanctuary.
The adjacent cave contains a
tank with what is believed to

The Tombs of the Kings necropolis

be miraculous water. Similar catacombs on the opposite side of the street are called Agios Lambrianos.

Beyond Agia Solomoni, to the right, is the limestone Fabrica Hill containing carved underground chambers. They were created during Hellenic and Roman times but their purpose is unknown.

On the southern slope of the hill, Australian archaeologists have unearthed a Hellenic amphitheatre hewn out of the living rock. Nearby are two small cave churches, Agios Agapitikos and Agios Misitikos. Tradition has it that when dust collected from the floor of Agios Agapitikos is placed in someone's house, it has the power to awaken their love (*agapi* means "love"), while dust collected from Agios Misitikos will awaken hate (*misos*).

Fabric-festooned tree near the Catacombs of Agia Solomoni

A relief from the Hellenic era, Archaeological Museum

🏛 Archaeological Museum

Leoforos Georgiou Griva Digeni 43. **Tel** 26 306 215. **Open** 8am–3pm Mon–Fri (to 2:30pm Mon, to 5pm Wed), 9am–3pm Sat. **Closed** Sun. 🏛 💻 📷 📷

Housed in a small modern building outside the city centre, along the road leading to

Geroskipou, this is one of the more interesting archaeological museums in Cyprus. The collection includes historic relics spanning thousands of years from the Neolithic era through the Bronze Age, Hellenic, Roman, Byzantine and medieval times, and up until the 18th century AD.

Particularly interesting are the Chalcolithic (copper age) figurines. There are steatite idols, a skeleton from Lempa, a 3rd-century AD mummy of a girl and an array of Hellenic ceramics, jewellery and glass. There are also ancient sarcophagi, sculptures, a coin collection, clay pots used for hot water and a set of Roman surgical instruments – evidence of the high standard of ancient medicine. There are also numerous exhibits from Kato Pafos and from Kouklia, site of the ancient city-kingdom Paliapafos and the Sanctuary of Aphrodite. The Archaeological Museum is one of the destinations featured in the

Aphrodite Cultural Route, an initiative by the Cyprus Tourist Organisation (CTO) that aims to guide visitors to key places of interest associated with the goddess. A booklet with useful information on the route is available from CTO offices.

🏖 Beaches

Pafos itself has only a few small beaches in front of hotels; these offer excellent conditions for watersports. A pleasant municipal beach is situated by Leoforos Poseidonos, at the centre of Kato Pafos, close to the Municipal Garden. Somewhat out of the way, to the north of the archaeological zone, lies the sandy-pebbly Faros Beach.

Good pebble beaches can be found north of Pafos. About 8 km (5 miles) along the coast is a small beach in the bay of Kissonerga fringed by banana plantations. The loveliest, most popular sandy beach is situated at Coral Bay, 10 km (6 miles) north of town (*see p51*). All the usual beach facilities are offered here, together with most watersports.

There are also several beaches to the east, including Alikes, Vrysoudia and Pahyammos. A beautiful place for bathing is the beach near the Rock of Aphrodite, covered with smooth stones. The water here is crystal-clear and the environs truly enchanting. Facilities include a restaurant, toilets and a shower near the car park. Come either early in the morning for some quiet reflection or in the evening to enjoy the beautiful sunset.

Coral Bay beach, Paphos, Cyprus

Kato Pafos

The most accessible and inspiring archaeological park on the island, the ruins at Kato (Lower) Pafos were unearthed in 1962, shedding new light on Cyprus under the Roman Empire. In ancient times, this was the capital of Cyprus. Now a UNESCO World Heritage Site, the remains found here span over 2,000 years. The lavish mosaics found on the floors of four Roman villas indicate that this was a place of ostentatious wealth.

★ House of Dionysos
Some 2,000 sq m (21,500 sq ft) of magnificent mosaics can be viewed from wooden platforms.

House of Aion
This villa, with its interesting mosaics, was destroyed by an earthquake. It takes its name from the god Aion, whose image was once to the left of the entrance.

House of Theseus
The palace of the Roman governor contains a set of interesting mosaics portraying the myth of Theseus and Ariadne. The opulent villa discovered underneath dates from the Hellenic era.

Medieval Castle
The medieval Lusignan castle remodelled by the Turks now houses a museum; its flat roof affords a lovely view over the town and the harbour.

KEY

① **The East Tower,** was a defence structure, guarding the town against attacks by Arab pirates in the early Middle Ages.

② **Panagia Limeniotissa**, the Byzantine basilica of Our Lady the Protectress of Harbours, was destroyed in the 7th century by Arab raids.

③ **The Hellenic theatre** is located near the agora

0 metres	25
0 yards	25

Lighthouse
The small, white lighthouse on top of the hill is not related to the Roman ruins below.

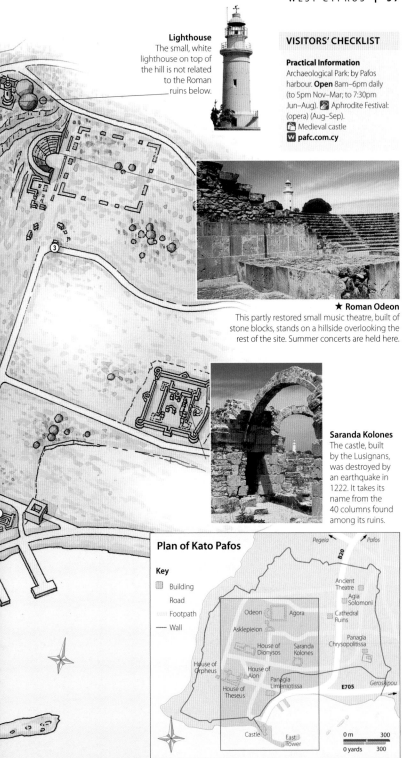

★ **Roman Odeon**
This partly restored small music theatre, built of stone blocks, stands on a hillside overlooking the rest of the site. Summer concerts are held here.

Saranda Kolones
The castle, built by the Lusignans, was destroyed by an earthquake in 1222. It takes its name from the 40 columns found among its ruins.

Plan of Kato Pafos

Key
- Building
- Road
- Footpath
- — Wall

Pegeia   Pafos   B20

Ancient Theatre
Agia Solomoni
Odeon   Agora   Cathedral Ruins
Asklepieion
Panagia Chrysopolitissa
House of Dionysos   Saranda Kolones
House of Orpheus
House of Aion
Panagia Limeniotissa
House of Theseus
E705   Geroskipou

Castle   East Tower

0 m   300
0 yards   300

For map symbols *see back flap*

Tree-lined avenue in the village
of Pegeia

❽ Pegeia

Road Map A3. 19 km (12 miles) south
of Pafos. 🚌 607, 616.

This small, picturesque hillside
village, 5 km (3 miles) inland
from Coral Bay, is the last sizeable
settlement before entering the
wilderness of Akamas. Pegeia,
meaning "springs", was founded
during the Byzantine era. It is
famous for its abundant spring
water – a great blessing in sun-
parched Cyprus.

Soak up the village atmosphere
in the pretty cobbled central
square with its fountains, and try a
bottle of the local Vasilikon wine.

Environs
On the hilltops to the north of
Pegeia, at an altitude of some
600 m (1,970 ft), are the villages
of the Laona region – **Ineia**,
Drouseia, **Arodes** and **Kathikas**.
Their lofty perches offer
sweeping views of the
surrounding area. In Ineia you
can visit the Ineia Folk Art
Museum; the local school in
Kathikas houses the Laona
information centre.

❾ Agios Georgios

Road Map A3. 🚌 616.

During Roman times **Cape
Drepano**, north of Coral
Bay, was the site of a late
Roman and early Byzantine
town and harbour. The
remains of a 6th-century
early-Christian basilica have
been unearthed here,
revealing some well-
preserved floor mosaics of
sea creatures, a semi-
circular bishop's throne
and several columns.

The coastal cliffs contains
several caves that served as
hiding places for the local
population during enemy raids.
Atop one craggy section is the
picturesque **Church of St
George** (Agios Georgios
Pegeias) built in the Byzantine
style in 1928. St George, its
patron saint, champions
animals and those who are
unlucky in love.

Close by there are several
taverns and fishermen's
cottages. The location affords a
lovely view over the fishing
harbour below, and the
nearby island of Geronisos
with its remains of a Neolithic
settlement. There are also
remains of a small temple that
was used during Greek and
Roman times.

Environs
North of Agios Georgios is the
Avakas Gorge. This deep ravine
has steep craggy banks, a dozen
or so metres high, and the river
Avgas runs through the base of
it. Avakas Gorge is a legally
protected area.

The picturesque Church of St George

❿ Lara

Road Map A3.

This sandy crescent is home
to two of the most attractive
beaches in southwest Cyprus.
To the south lies nearly
2 km (1 mile) of uncrowded
sand, while to the north
there is a shallow bay with a
half-moon stretch of fine
white sand frequented by
sea turtles.

This is one of the few
remaining Mediterranean
nesting grounds for the
rare green and loggerhead
varieties. During breeding
season (June to September)
staff from the Lara Turtle
Conservation Project
close access to the beach.
They arrange occasional
night-time walks along
the beach, when you can see
the turtles struggling ashore.

Although marine animals,
sea turtles lay their eggs on
dry land, crawling out onto
beaches during summer
nights to do this. Females
lay about 100 eggs at a
time, which they bury up i
n the sand up to half a
metre (one and a half feet)
deep. After laying, the eggs
are carefully removed to
a protected area on the
beach where they are safe
from dogs, foxes and
other predators.

After seven weeks the
eggs hatch and the
hatchlings head immediately
for the water. Turtles reach
maturity at about the age of
20, and the females return to
lay eggs on the same beach
where they were born.

The sandy beach at Lara Bay – a nesting ground for rare sea turtles

⓫ Baths of Aphrodite

Road Map A3. 8 km (5 miles) west of Polis, towards Akamas peninsula.
🚌 622, 644.

A path from the car park leads to the Baths of Aphrodite – a pool in a grotto shaded by overgrown fig trees. According to legend it was here that Aphrodite met her lover Adonis, who stopped by the spring to quench his thirst. It is said that bathing in this spot restores youth, but, sadly people are no longer allowed in the water.

Walking trails lead from the front of the Cyprus Tourism Organization (CTO) pavilion through the Akamas peninsula. The trails of Aphrodite, Adonis or Smigies will take you to the most interesting corners of the northwestern tip (see pp60–61). Detailed descriptions of the trails can be found in the Nature Trails of the Akamas brochure published by the CTO.

Situated a few kilometres further west is another magnificent spring, the Fontana Amorosa (Fountain of Love). It was once believed that whoever took a sip of water from the spring would fall in love with the very first person they encountered afterwards.

Environs

On the way to the Baths of Aphrodite you will pass Latsi (also known as Lakki and Latchi),

Akamas peninsula – the westernmost point of Cyprus

a small town with a fishing harbour. It was once a sponge-divers' harbour, and is now also the base for pleasure boats that offer tourist cruises along the Akamas peninsula. Latsi has numerous *pensions* and hotels; the harbour features several restaurants, where you can get tasty and inexpensive fish and seafood dishes. The town has pebble and coarse sand beaches.

⓬ Akamas Peninsula

Road Map A3. 18 km (11 miles) north of Agios Georgios.

Stretching north of Agios Georgios and Pegeia is the wilderness of the Akamas peninsula. The hillsides and headlands form the island's last undeveloped frontier, a region of spectacular, rugged scenery, sandy coves, clear water and hillsides covered with thick woodlands of pine and juniper. Its name comes from the legendary Akamas, son of Theseus, who arrived here on his triumphant return from the Trojan War and founded the town of Akamatis. Archaeologists are still searching for this site.

The peninsula's westward plain has rocks jutting out of the arid landscape, which is overgrown with tangles of trees and bushes.

Spring flowers

In the valleys and ravines the vegetation is lush due to more abundant water. The shoreline is characterized by steep cliffs dropping vertically into the sea, particularly around **Chrysochou Bay**.

Nowadays this area is practically deserted, inhabited only by wild animals and herds of goat, but this was not always so. In ancient times, the region had Greek towns, and later Roman and Byzantine towns, that bustled with life. On **Cape Drepano** you can see the ruins of a Roman harbour and a Byzantine basilica; in **Meleti Forest** you can visit the ruins of a Byzantine church, and tombs carved in rocks; and in the **Agios Konon region** archaeologists have discovered an ancient settlement. The Roman settlement, which once stood on the shores of the Tyoni Bay, is now submerged in water.

The only way to travel around the wild countryside of Akamas is by a four-wheel-drive vehicle or by a cruise along the coast from Latsi.

The westernmost point of the peninsula, and of the entire island, is **Cape Arnaoutis**, where you can see an unmanned lighthouse and the wreck of a ship that ran aground. The Cape is a magnet for divers, who will find vertical crags and caves where octopuses hide; fantastic arch-shaped rocks; or even come eye-to-eye with a barracuda.

The Baths of Aphrodite

Walking in the Akamas Peninsula

This is the wildest region of Cyprus, practically uninhabited and covered with forests. Its rich flora (over 500 species, including scores of orchid varieties) and fauna, the diverse geological features, the beautiful coastline and the legends and myths associated with this fascinating country make it a paradise for ramblers and nature lovers. The shortage of surfaced roads means that many places on the peninsula can be reached only on foot.

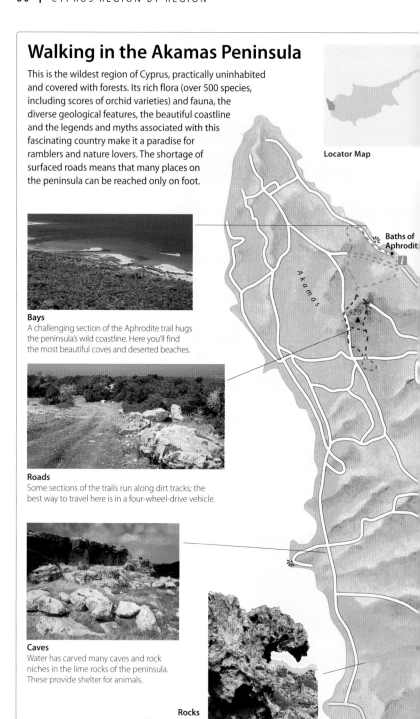

Locator Map

Baths of Aphrodite

Akamas

428 m

Bays
A challenging section of the Aphrodite trail hugs the peninsula's wild coastline. Here you'll find the most beautiful coves and deserted beaches.

Roads
Some sections of the trails run along dirt tracks; the best way to travel here is in a four-wheel-drive vehicle.

Caves
Water has carved many caves and rock niches in the lime rocks of the peninsula. These provide shelter for animals.

Rocks
Rocks, carved in fantastic shapes by wind and water, are a distinctive feature of the peninsula's landscape.

Neo Chorio

A stone church has survived here. There are plenty of places to stay in the village, as well as a few restaurants. To the south is the Petratis Gorge, famous for its bats' grotto.

Tips for Drivers

Length of trails: From 2 to 7.5 km (1 to 5 miles) long.
Where to stay: Accommodation can be found in Neo Chorio, Polis, Drouseia and at the Polis-Baths along the Aphrodite trail.
Additional information: Bring adequate food and water when walking. The best starting point for trails 1–4 is the Baths of Aphrodite; for trail 5, start in the village of Kathikas.

Lizards

Lizards, particularly the wall lizard, are common on the island. You may be lucky enough to encounter the Agana, the largest Cypriot lizard (30 cm/12 in long).

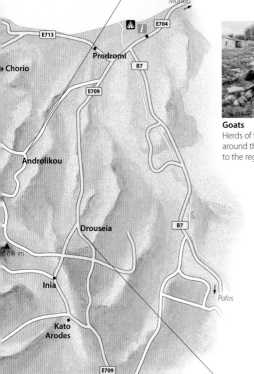

0 kilometres 2
0 miles 1

Mordou

E704

E713

Prodromi

B7

Chorio

E709

Androlikou

Drouseia

B7

568 m

Inia

Pafos

Kato
Arodes

E709

Kathikas

E711

E709

681 m

Pegeia

Pafos

Goats

Herds of free-ranging goats wander around the peninsula, presenting a threat to the region's natural environment.

Key

- ═══ Main road
- ══ Other road
- ▪▪▪ 1. Aphrodite trail (7.5 km)
- ▪▪▪ 2. Adonis trail (7.5 km)
- ▪▪▪ 3. Smigies trail (7.5 km)
- ▪▪▪ 4. Pissouromouttis trail (3 km)
- ▪▪▪ 5. Kathikas trail (2 km)
- ≋ River

Drouseia

This picturesque hilltop village with its stone houses is increasingly popular among the expatriate community. There is a taverna and accommodation here.

For additional map symbols *see back flap*

The 16th-century church of Agios Andronikos in Polis

⓭ Polis

Road Map A3. 35 km (22 miles) north of Pafos. 🚐 1,890. 🛈 Vasileos Stasioikou 2, 26 322 468. 🚌 645. 🎪 Summer Cultural Festival (Jul, Aug).

This small town, known as Polis Chrysochou (Town of the Golden Land), stands on the site of the ancient city-state of Marion, surrounded by extensive orange groves. Polis provides an excellent base for exploring the Akamas peninsula and the wilderness of Tilliria. In the centre of Polis is the 16th-century **Agios Andronikos** church, featuring some fine frescoes. Under Ottoman rule the church was turned into a mosque. The interior of the **Agios Rafael**, a Byzantine-style church, is decorated with colourful frescoes.

Polis is one of the most attractive and fastest-growing sea-side resorts of Cyprus. Popular with both backpackers and families, it offers a range of apartment complexes and a handful of small hotels, along with several campsites, including one on the beach.

Environs

Close to the town are some of the most beautiful beaches on the island, including a sand and-pebble beach stretching eastwards along Chrysochou Bay, a 15-minute walk from Polis. There are also picturesque villages and interesting churches, including the 16th-century Agia Aikaterini and 15th-century Panagia Chorteni.

Carved decoration above the entrance to Agios Andronikos in Polis

⓮ Marion

Road Map A3.

Founded in the 7th century BC by Greeks, the city-state of Marion was a major trading centre during the Classical and Hellenic eras. It owed its rapid development to the nearby copper mines. In 315 BC Marion was destroyed by the Egyptian king, Ptolemy I Soter. His son, Ptolemy II, rebuilt Marion under the name Arsinoe, but the town never regained its former power.

Up to now archaeologists have managed to unearth only a small portion of the ancient town, with a burial ground dating from the Hellenic period. An interesting collection of artifacts from the site can be seen in the **Marion-Arsinoe Archaeological Museum**. Of special note are the amphorae decorated with images of people, animals and birds, as well as with geometric patterns. Growing near the museum is an olive tree, over 600 years old, which still bears fruit.

🏛 Marion-Arsinoe Archaeological Museum

Polis. Leoforos Makariou III. **Tel** 26 322 955. **Open** 8am–2:30pm Mon, 8am–3pm Tue, Thu & Fri, 8am–5pm Wed, 9am–3pm Sat. 🎟

⓯ Panagia Chrysorrogiatissa

Road Map A3. 40 km (25 miles) northeast of Pafos, take a right turn before the village of Stroumpi. 1.5 km (1 mile) south of Pano Panagia. **Tel** 26 722 457. **Open** summer: 9:30am–12:30pm, 1:30–6:30pm daily; winter: 10am–12:30pm, 1:30–4pm daily. Donations welcome. 🎪 15 Aug.

In a beautiful setting 830 m (2,723 ft) above the sea, the Chrysorrogiatissa monastery is dedicated to "Our Lady of the Golden Pomegranate". It features an unusual triangular cloister built of reddish stone.

The monastery was founded in 1152 by Ignatius, who came across an icon with the image of the Virgin Mary. The Virgin appeared and told him to build a monastery. The icon is kept in a special casket. It was supposedly painted by St Luke the Evangelist. Several other icons are also stored here; the most famous being an 18th-century image of Mary and Jesus covered with a

Entrance to Panagia Chrysorrogiatissa monastery

cloak. Other objects include old Bibles, sculptures, manuscripts and crosses.

Environs
The single-aisle **Agia Moni** church, about 2 km (1.2 miles) from the monastery, is one of the oldest in the island. Dedicated to St Nicholas, it was built in the 4th century on the site of an old pagan temple of the goddess Hera.

The nearby village of **Panagia** is the birthplace of Archbishop Makarios III, the statesman and politician, who was born the son of a shepherd here on 13 August 1913. In 1960 the Archbishop was elected president of the republic. He died on 3 August 1977 and was buried at Throni near Kykkos, overlooking his village.

🏛 **Makarios's Family Home**
Pano Panagia. **Open** daily (key available from info centre). Donations welcome.

Tomb of Archbishop Makarios at Throni above Panagia

⑯ Xeros Valley
Road Map B4.

The Xeros river flows from the western slopes of the Troodos mountains through this scenic valley. The river initially flows through Pafos Forest and Cedar Valley, which is the main home of the cedars of the local *cedrus brevifilia* species. The area, which has been declared a nature reserve, is also home to the moufflon.

A car is needed to explore the valley. Following the old road from Pafos, turn left in the village of Timi, opposite the airport, to reach **Asprokremmos** reservoir, a mecca for anglers, as it is fed by the Xeros river. The valley of Xeros (which in Greek

means "dry") was devastated by the tragic earthquake of 1953. At the heart of the valley, away from the main roads, is the abandoned stone **Panagia tou Sinti** monastery. It can be reached via local roads from the village of Pentalia or Agia Marina. Further on, the road leads through hillside villages and vineyards.

Beyond the village of Vretsia the road steadily deteriorates, but after driving for a few more kilometres you can cross the Xeros river near the historic Venetian bridge of Roudia. The deserted village of **Peravasa** marks the start of the road leading south, towards the scenic Diarizos river valley.

Sheep in the Diarizos Valley

⑰ Diarizos Valley
Road Map B3.

Greener and better irrigated than the arid Xeros valley, the Diarizos valley is studded with medieval churches, farming villages and arched Venetian bridges. The clear-flowing river trickles southwest and, like the Xeros, feeds the Asprokremmos reservoir.

The village of **Nikokleia**, near Kouklia *(see p48)*, is an ancient settlement named in honour of King Nikokles, who transferred his capital to what is now Kato Pafos. The village is scenically located on the banks of the river. The old church contains

fascinating icons. On the opposite side of the river, near the village of Souskiou, archaeologists unearthed a Chalcolithic settlement. In it they found pendants and figurines, as well as statues and ancient tombs. In the village of Agios Georgios are rock tombs.

Further northeast are the remains of a former monastery, **Agios Savvas tis Karonos**, built in the early 12th century and restored by the Venetians.

Above Kithasi the road climbs upwards and the views become increasingly beautiful. On the left side of the road is the restored church of **Agios Antonios**. The church in Praitori houses 16th-century icons. Above the village, the road climbs towards the resort of **Platres** and the peaks of the Troodos mountains.

The arid Xeros valley, a scenic, rugged nature reserve

SOUTHERN CYPRUS

The southern region of Cyprus features Neolithic settlements and ancient towns, medieval castles and monasteries, and the island's most beautiful beaches, around Agia Napa. Other attractions include charming hilltop villages and the ports of Limassol and Larnaka. The region is full of reminders of famous past visitors to Cyprus, including Zeno of Kition, Saint Helena, Richard the Lionheart and Leonardo da Vinci.

The coast from Pissouri to Protaras is famous for its beautiful scenery and historic sites. It has the largest ports on the island and many crowded beaches, but just a short distance inland life flows at a gentle, lazy pace.

This southern region was the site of powerful city-states, including Kition (present-day Larnaka), Kourion – of which only magnificent ruins are left, and Amathous.

Among the oldest traces of man on Cyprus are the Neolithic settlements around Choirokoitia and Kalavasos. There are reminders of subsequent settlers, too. There was a Phoenician presence at Kition; there are temples and stadia attesting to the Greek presence;

and villas and theatres from the Romans. The Byzantine legacy includes mosaics in vast basilicas, churches with beautiful murals, and monasteries – including the mountain-top Stavrovouni monastery and the cat-filled St Nicholas monastery on the Akrotiri peninsula.

The medieval castle in Limassol was used by the Crusaders; Richard the Lionheart married Berengaria of Navarre and crowned her Queen of England here; and from the Gothic castle in Kolossi knights oversaw the production of wine and sugar cane. A reminder of the Arab raids is the tomb of the Prophet's aunt at the Hala Sultan Tekke, on the shores of the salt lake near Larnaka, which attracts flamingoes, swans and pelicans.

Scenic village of Kato Lefkara

◀ The popular Nissi beach in Agia Napa

Exploring Southern Cyprus

The best-preserved ancient town in Southern Cyprus is the Greco-Roman Kourion, with a beautifully located theatre, interesting mosaics, baths, a Byzantine stadium and the nearby Sanctuary of Apollo Ylatis. The best beaches for swimming and sunbathing are in Agia Napa and Protaras, with their enchanting clear water and lovely sandy beaches. They also offer the greatest number of attractions for young people. When exploring this part of the island be sure to visit Lefkara, a charming Cypriot village where women produce beautiful lace by hand and men make silver jewellery. Nature lovers often head for the salt lakes around Limassol and Larnaka, and are rewarded with the sight of hundreds of birds.

Stavrovouni monastery, founded by St Helena, mother of Constantine the Great

Sights at a Glance

Doorway of Panagia Chrysopolitissa church in Larnaka

Getting There

Most visitors to Cyprus arrive by air, and the biggest airport in the southern part of the island is outside Larnaka, serving a number of international flights. Motorways provide fast and safe travel links with Limassol and Agia Napa, as well as with Nicosia and Pafos. Alternatively, you can travel to Limassol by ship from Piraeus (Greece), Egypt, Lebanon and Syria. Most of the historic sites of Limassol and Larnaka are best explored on foot. Public transport in the form of buses and service taxis between major cities is good, but to reach smaller or more distant places a rental car is the best option for exploring Southern Cyprus.

The craggy coastline of Cape Gkreko

Key

- ▬▬ Motorway
- ▬▬ Major road
- ▬▬ Minor road
- ▬▬ Scenic route
- ▬ ▬ Track
- ▬▬ Regional border
- ▬■▬ Green Line

For additional map symbols *see back flap*

❶ Cape Aspro

Road Map B4. 4 km (2.5 miles) south
of Pissouri.

Cape Aspro is the highest point
along the virtually deserted
coast that stretches from
Kourion to Pafos. Most of the
coast along this, the
southernmost point of the
island (excluding the Akrotiri
Peninsula), is as flat as a
pancake. Towering over the
cape is the **Trachonas Hill**,
which affords magnificent views
over Episkopi Bay, the southern
slopes of the Troodos
mountains, the small town of
Pissouri and the monastery
church Moni Prophitis Ilias.

The area around **Pissouri** is
famous for its orchards and
vineyards; the fertile lime soil
yields abundant crops of sweet
grapes. The modern
amphitheatre, which was built
in 2000 with seating for a
thousand people, affords a
beautiful view over the sea and
the southern coast. During the
summer, plays and concerts are
staged here.

The town of Pissouri has a
pleasant little hotel – the Bunch
of Grapes Inn – in a restored
century-old home; there are
also several rustic tavernas that
offer typical local cuisine.

The rugged coastal cliffs rise
to a height of 180 m (590 ft).
They can be seen very clearly
from the air, as planes usually
approach Pafos airport from
this direction. To the east of
Cape Aspro is the pleasant and
clean sandy-pebbly Pissouri
beach with its clear,
blue water.

Ruins of the Sanctuary of Apollo Ylatis near
Kourion

❷ Sanctuary of Apollo Ylatis

Road Map B4. 3 km (2 miles) west of
Kourion. **Tel** 25 991 049. **Open**
8am–5pm daily (to 6pm Apr, May, Sep
& Oct; to 7:30pm Jun–Aug).

In ancient times the Sanctuary
of Apollo Ylatis (also known as
Hylates), was an important
shrine. Stone fragments and
toppled columns mark the site
of this 7th-century BC shrine to
the sun-god Apollo in his role
as "Ylatis", or god of the woods
and forests. The present ruins
date from early Roman times.
It was in use until the 4th
century AD, when Emperor
Theodosius the Great declared
a battle against pagans.

The sanctuary was
surrounded by a holy garden,
featuring laurel trees, myrtle
and palms, and was home to
deer. When pilgrims arrived
through the Curium and Pafian
gates, they placed votive
offerings by the residence of
the Great Priests, which were
then sent to the treasury.
When the treasury became
full, the priests stored the
offerings *(tavissae)* in a nearby
holy well. This hiding place
was discovered centuries later
by archaeologists, and the
ancient offerings can be seen
at the Kourion Archaeological
Museum at Episkopi and in the
Cyprus Museum in Nicosia.

Close by were baths and a
palaestra (gymnasium),
surrounded by a colonnaded
portico and used as a venue
for wrestling. Standing in one
corner of the *palaestra* is a
fragment of a large clay jug,
which was used for storing
water for the athletes. The
remaining buildings of the
complex include storehouses
and pilgrims' dormitories.

The former pilgrims' inn
marked the start of the holy
procession route leading to the
sanctuary. At the heart
of the sanctuary there was a
small temple with a pillared
portico, devoted to Apollo.
As reported by the ancient
geographer Strabo, any
unauthorized person who
touched the altar was hurled
from it to the sea, to placate
Apollo. The front of the
temple, with its two columns,
a fragment of the wall and
tympanum, has been partially
reconstructed.

Earthquakes, the spread of
Christianity and Arab raids all
played a role in destroying the
sanctuary, and now all that
remains are the romantic ruins.

Some 500 m (1,640 ft) east of
the sanctuary is a large, well-
preserved Roman stadium that
could hold 6,000 spectators.
Pentathlon events – consisting
of running, long jump, discus
and javelin throwing, and
wrestling – were staged here.
The athletes appeared naked,
and only men were allowed to
watch. In the 4th century the
stadium was closed, regarded as
a symbol of paganism.

The craggy coast of Cape Aspro

❸ Kourion

See pp70–71.

❹ Kolossi

Road Map B4. 14 km (9 miles) west of Limassol. **Tel** 25 934 907. 🚌 17. **Open** 8am–5pm daily (to 6pm Apr, May, Sep & Oct; to 7:30pm Jun–Aug). 🏛

The best-preserved medieval castle in Cyprus is situated south of the village of Kolossi. In 1210 the land passed to the hands of the Knights of St John of Jerusalem, who built a castle here to be used as the Grand Master's headquarters.

At the turn of the 14th and 15th centuries the castle was sacked several times by the Genoese and Muslims.

Kolossi castle in its present shape was built in 1454 by the Grand Master, Louis de Magnac. It is a three-storey structure, laid out on a square plan, 23 m (75 ft) high with walls over 2.5 m (8 ft) thick. Entry is via a drawbridge, with the entrance further guarded by a machicolation above the gate, which permitted the pouring of boiling water, oil or melted tar over attackers.

The entrance led to the dining room, whose walls were once covered with paintings. You can still see a scene of the Crucifixion with Louis de Magnac's coat of arms underneath. The adjacent room used to be the castle kitchen; stores were kept on the lower floor, and above were the living quarters; you can see stone fireplaces and windows. From here a narrow staircase leads to the flat roof surrounded by battlements. From here it was possible to supervise the work on plantations and in vineyards, and to spot enemy ships in the

The medieval Kolossi castle, used by the Knights of Jerusalem

distance. Next to the castle is a large vaulted stone building, once a sugar refinery. To the north are the remains of a mill, formerly used for grinding the sugar, and the small 13th-century church of St Eustace, used as the castle chapel by the Knights Templar and the Knights of St John of Jerusalem.

❺ Agios Nikolaos ton Gaton (St Nicholas of the Cats)

Road Map B4. Cape Gata, 12 km (7.5 miles) from the centre of Limassol. **Tel** 25 952 621. **Open** 8am–5pm daily.

The monastery of Agios Nikolaos ton Gaton stands on the Akrotiri peninsula, between the salt lake and the military airport. According to tradition it was founded by St Helena, mother of Constantine the Great, who visited Cyprus while returning from the Holy Land. Appalled by the plague of snakes, she sent a ship full of cats to the island to deal with them. The monks fed the cats and rallied them to fight by the

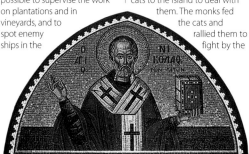

Image of St Nicholas of the Cats

ringing of the bell. Another reference to the cats is the naming of the nearby Cape Gata – the Cape of Cats.

The monastery was founded in 325, but the buildings we see now are the result of remodelling that occurred during the 14th century. At the heart of the monastery is an old church with Gothic walls and Latin coats of arms above the entrance. Candles inside the dark church illuminate the gilded iconostasis and the elongated faces on the icons, which appear to come to life.

A small section of the salt lake on the Akrotiri peninsula

❻ Akrotiri Peninsula

Road Map B4. 🚌 22.

Akrotiri is the southernmost point of Cyprus. Most of the peninsula is occupied by a sovereign British base – Akrotiri-Episkopi, which includes an air force base and a radio communications station. This base, along with a second one at Ohekelia, is a relic of the island's colonial past, when Cyprus was governed by the British.

The central part of the peninsula is occupied by a salt lake (one of the two on the island), a vantage point for watching flocks of water birds including swans, flamingoes and pelicans. Running along the east coast is the wide beach known as Lady's Mile, which was named after a mare used by an English army officer for his regular morning ride.

❸ Kourion

Ancient Kourion (or Curium) was a major centre of cultural, political and religious life. It was home to the centuries-old site of the Sanctuary of Apollo and later the seat of a Christian bishop. Perched on a bluff, the town was founded in the 12th century BC by Mycenaean Greeks, and was a large centre in the days of the Ptolemies and the Romans. Its trump card was its defensive location, and the control it wielded over the surrounding fertile land. Kourion was destroyed by two catastrophic earthquakes in the early 4th century.

Achilles' House
This takes its name from the 4th-century mosaic discovered inside the colonnade.

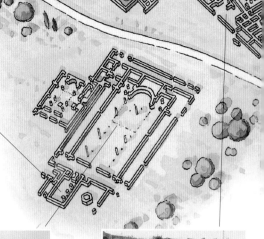

Baptistry & Bishop's Palace
Adjacent to the basilica and close to the bishop's palace was a large baptistry. Its remains include floor mosaics and some columns.

Basilica
The impressive triple-aisle building, erected in the 5th century AD on the site of a pagan temple, was destroyed by Arabs.

Nymphaeum
This imposing complex of stone fountains was built close to the public baths, on the spot where the aqueduct brought water to the city of Kourion.

Map of Kourion

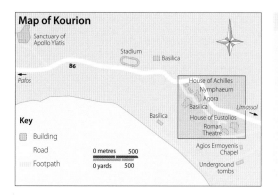

Sanctuary of
Apollo Ylatis

Stadium

Basilica

B6

Pafos

House of Achilles
Nymphaeum
Agora
Basilica
Basilica

Limassol

House of Eustolios
Roman
Theatre

Agios Ermoyenis
Chapel

Underground
tombs

Key

Building

Road

Footpath

0 metres   500

0 yards   500

VISITORS' CHECKLIST

Practical Information
Road Map B4. Kourion Archaeological Museum: 19 km
(12 miles) west of Limassol.
16 from Limassol. **Tel** 25 934
250. **Open** 8am–5pm daily (to
6pm Apr, May, Sep & Oct; to
7:30pm Jun–Aug). Sanctuary
of Apollo Ylatis: 3 km (2 miles)
west of Kourion. **Tel** 25 991 049.
Open 8am–5pm daily (to 6pm
Apr, May, Sep & Oct; to 7:30pm
Jun–Aug).

Roman Theatre
The theatre, built in the 2nd century BC, enjoys a
magnificent location overlooking the sea as well
as boasting excellent acoustics.

Baths
These baths form part of the House of
Eustolios, a late 4th-century AD private
residence. The best mosaic depicts Ktissis
as a woman holding a Roman measure, a
personification of architectural art.

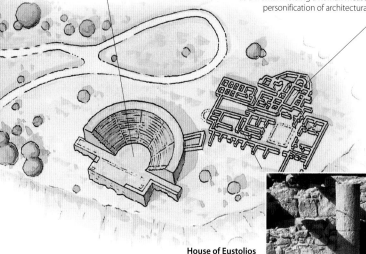

KEY

① **The House of the Gladiators**
was so named after the discovery of
two mosaics depicting gladiator fights.

② **Public baths**

House of Eustolios
Built in the early Christian
period, this house had
some 30 rooms arranged
around a colonnaded
courtyard with mosaic
floors. The inscription by
the entrance reads "Step
in and bring happiness
to this house".

❼ Limassol (Lemesos)

Limassol is a major centre of trade, business and tourism, and has the biggest harbour in southern Cyprus. It is probably the most fun-filled city on Cyprus in terms of the number of fairs and festivals held here. The year starts with a riotous carnival; May marks the Flower Festival; and September brings the famous Wine Festival. Hotels, restaurants and nightclubs are clustered mainly along the beach.

Strolling along the seaside promenade

Exploring Limassol

It is best to start from the medieval castle, the town's most interesting historic site. Nearby in the restored Carob Mill is the Carob Museum, where visitors can learn about this important Cypriot export. A covered bazaar and a mosque are also close by.

The area has many restaurants with Cypriot and international cuisine, a wine bar and a brewery. From here it is not far to the old harbour, now used by fishing boats and pleasure craft. You can enjoy an extended walk along the seaside promenade, passing the Orthodox Agia Napa cathedral. More material distractions can be found just inland from here, along the main

Colourful stalls of fruit and vegetables at the Central Market

shopping street, Ayiou Andhreou, which runs parallel to the coast.

🏛 Central Market

Saripolou, in the old district near the town hall. **Open** 6am–3pm Mon–Sat.

The Central Market, housed in a graceful arcaded building dating from the British era in the early 20th century, is a great place to shop for handmade reed baskets, olive oil, *loukoumia* (Cyprus delight) and other Cypriot delicacies, as well as fruit, vegetables, cheeses and meats. The stone market hall, its roof supported by metal pillars is of particular note, featuring two arched gates with Doric columns. It has been refurbished to a design by Penelope Papadopoulou. The market is surrounded by old tavernas that make a welcome change from the modern eating-places and souvenir shops in the city's resort area. The stone-paved square in front of it is used as a venue for shows and fairs.

🏛 Cyprus Handicraft Centre

Themidos 25. **Tel** 25 305 118.
Open 7:30am–2:30pm Mon–Fri (also 3–6pm Thu except Jul–Aug).

At this centre you can buy locally made gifts and souvenirs, including jewellery, lace, ceramics, mosaics and woodcarvings produced by Cypriot craftspeople using traditional methods.

All stock is government-vetted and the fixed prices offer a good gauge of how much visitors should spend on products elsewhere.

🏛 Town Hall

Archiepiskopou Kyprianou.
🌐 **limassolmunicipal.com.cy**

The town hall is situated in the centre of Limassol, on a narrow street opposite the post office and near Agia Napa Cathedral. It was built to a design by the German architect Benjamin Gunzburg, based on the ancient Greek style of civic architecture. The columns by the entrance are redolent of the Tombs of the Kings in Pafos.

🏛 Agios Andronikos Church

Agiou Andreou. 🕐 6:30pm (in summer); 4:30pm (in winter) Sat; prayers Sun (times vary).

The Church of Agios Andronikos and Athanosis (in Greek *athanosis* means immortality) was built in the 1870s in Neo-Byzantine style. For a while it served as the town's cathedral. The church is accessible only from the waterfront. It is

Town Hall, dating from Colonial times

separated from the sea by the promenade, near the Agia Napa Cathedral.

Seaside Promenade

Perfect for an evening stroll, Limassol's palm-fringed promenade stretches for nearly 3 km (2 miles) along the shoreline, starting at the old harbour and continuing eastward towards St Catherine's Church. It is lined with well-kept greenery and benches, from where you can

The Orthodox cathedral of Agia Napa

admire the seascape and watch the ships awaiting entry to the harbour.

🏛 Agia Napa Cathedral
Genethliou Mitella.
On the fringe of Limassol's old quarter, this vast Byzantine-style structure was built in the early 20th century on the ruins of a Byzantine church. It was consecrated in 1906, and today it serves as Limassol's Orthodox cathedral.

The Greek architect Georgios Papadakis of Athens designed the cathedral, which represents Greek Orthodox religious architecture at its florid and grandiloquent best. This large stone church, sporting a twin-tower façade, is covered with a dome resting on a tambour over the intersection of the nave with the transept.

The cathedral was consecrated with the veil of St Veronica, with the imprinted image of Christ's face (the *veraikon*).

🅶 Grand Mosque
Genethliou Mitella. **Open** vary. Donations welcome.
The area around the harbour and castle was once inhabited mainly by Turks, and there are some remaining Turkish in scriptions and street names. The Grand Mosque – Cami Kebir – is still used by the handful of Turkish Cypriots resident in the city, and by Muslim visitors. The city's largest mosque with a graceful minaret is squeezed between old buildings behind the Turkish Bazaar.

🏛 Limassol Castle
See pp76–7.

The Grand Mosque with its distinctive pointed minaret

🏛 Carob Museum
Vasilissis 1, by Limassol Castle.
Tel 25 342 123. **Open** daily (times vary so call ahead).

This museum is located in a renovated former mill close to the medieval castle, in an area that is known for its art exhibitions and stylish cafés.

The Carob Museum shows how the carob is harvested, what it is used for and its relevance to the island's economy. The carob can be used in the production of honey, sweets and chocolate. Derivatives are also used for making paper, photographic filmplates and medicines. Historic machinery used to store and process the fruit is displayed alongside utensils and useful information.

Limassol Town Centre

① Central Market
② Cyprus Handicraft Centre
③ Town Hall
④ Agios Andronikos Church
⑤ Seaside Promenade
⑥ Agia Napa Cathedral
⑦ Grand Mosque
⑧ Limassol Castle
⑨ Carob Museum

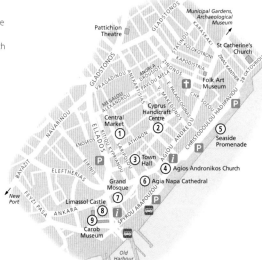

0 metres 400
0 yards 400

For key to symbols *see back flap*

Artifacts in the Archaeological Museum

Further Afield

Outside the city centre are a number of sights worth visiting, including St Catherine's Catholic Church, the Municipal Gardens and mini-zoo, the District Archaeological Museum and Folk Art Museum, as well as a theatre, municipal art gallery and – among the best of the local attractions – the wineries. Stretching beyond the municipal beach to the east is the extensive tourist zone with dozens of hotels, tavernas, pubs, restaurants, souvenir shops and clubs.

🏛 St Catherine's Catholic Church

28 Oktovriou 259. **Tel** 25 362 946. 🕆 6:30pm daily (English & Greek); 8am (Greek), 9:30am (Greek), 11am (Latin) & 6:30pm (English) Sun.

This twin-tower church stands opposite the beach, near the end of Limassol's palm-lined promenade. Consecrated in 1879, it is one of several Catholic churches in this part of the island.

🏛 District Archaeological Museum

At the junction of Kanningos and Vyronos, next to the Municipal Gardens. **Tel** 25 305 157. **Open** 8am–4pm Mon–Fri, 9am–3pm Sat. 🗺

At the entrance to this museum is a mosaic depicting the bath of Eros and Aphrodite. The museum's collection includes artifacts found in excavations of the ancient city-states of Kourion and Amathous, as well as Neolithic tools and jewellery.

The highlights of the collection are the statue of the Egyptian god Bes – the god of harvest depicted in the guise of a dwarf; the statue of Hathor, Egyptian goddess of heaven, music and dance; the statue of Zeus discovered at Amathous; and the head of Zeus from Fasoula, carved from limestone. Other exhibits include collections of glass and terracotta artifacts.

🏛 Municipal Gardens and Mini-Zoo

28 Oktovriou, on the seafront. **Open** summer: 9am–7pm; winter: 9am–4pm. 🗺

The charming Municipal Gardens feature ponds and fountains. Shaded by trees, they are full of exotic greenery and flowers. The gardens include an amphitheatre and a small zoo and aviary. Zebras, cheetahs and moufflon are among the animals here. In early September the Municipal Gardens become the venue for the famous Wine Festival. As well as grape trampling and folk dances, the crowds are treated to free wine from local producers.

🏛 Folk Art Museum

Agiou Andreou 253. **Tel** 25 362 303. **Open** 8:30am–3pm daily. 🗺

The Folk Art museum is housed in an attractive historic building dating from 1924. Arranged over six rooms is a good collection of 19th- and 20th-century Cypriot folk art.

The exhibition includes country tools, domestic utensils, wooden chests, traditional folk costumes, jewellery, tapestries and handcrafted products such as net curtains, bedding and bedspreads, which were traditionally stored in *sentoukia* – decorative trunks used as a bride's dowry.

Costume from the Folk Art Museum

🏛 Wineries

F. Roosevelt. **Tel** 25 362 756. **Open** year-round. 🗺 🗺

Wine has been produced for over 4,000 years in Cyprus, with wine-growing a long-established tradition in the area surrounding Limassol. Along the avenue leading from the old town to the harbour are the largest wineries in Cyprus, belonging to KEO, SODAP, ETKO and LOEL. These are open to the public for both tours and tastings. You can visit the vaults themselves to see the huge barrels used to age and mellow the sweet dessert wine, Commandaria, which has been produced in Cyprus for over 800 years. At the end of the tour you will be offered a chance to taste and buy the wines. Other distilleries produce *zivania*, a spirit distilled from grape seed

The leafy, pleasantly shaded Municipal Gardens

For hotels and restaurants in this region see pp162–5 and pp170–77

left over from the production of wine and sherry. "Five Kings" brandy, commemorating a medieval banquet attended by five kings, including the King of Cyprus, is also produced here.

Pattichion Theatre

Agias Zonis. **Tel** 25 343 341.
Musicals, drama and ballet productions are staged at the Pattichion, the oldest theatre in Limassol. The theatre was purchased by the Nicos and Despina Pattichi Foundation, then rebuilt and reopened in 1986. It is sponsored by the Limassol Municipality.

The theatre holds up to 760 people; backstage there are dressing rooms for 80 artists. The Pattichion theatre has hosted the Vienna Philharmonic Orchestra, the Athens Chamber Music Ensemble, the Vivaldi Orchestra from Moscow and Jazz Art Ballet from Paris.

Municipal Art Gallery

28 Oktovriou 103. **Tel** 25 586 212.
Open 7:30am–2:30pm Mon–Fri.
The Municipal Art Gallery houses works by Cypriot painters, including early artists such as Diamantis, Kashialos, whose famous work *Chariot Drawn by Two Donkeys* is displayed, Kanthos and Frangoudis. Contemporary painters are also represented. The gallery, designed by Benjamin Gunzburg (who also designed the Town Hall), was built in the 1930s.

Lady's Mile beach and the new harbour in Limassol

Fasouri Watermania Waterpark

Near Trahoni village, Limassol–Pafos Road. **Tel** 25 714 235. **Open** May–Oct: 10am–5pm daily (to 6pm Jun–Aug). **fasouri-watermania.com**
This popular waterpark has many water attractions including swimming pools, slides and artificial waves. Great for families and kids of all ages.

New Port

4 km (2.5 miles) west of city centre. **Tel** 25 819 200. 30.
The new port in Limassol is the largest in Cyprus. It was enlarged after 1974, when Famagusta port fell under Turkish occupation. Besides the commercial port, it includes a terminal for passenger ferries as well as cruise ships.

The old harbour, situated near Limassol castle, is now used by fishing boats and pleasure craft. The modern yachting marina at the St Raphael resort, is situated around 12 km (7.5 miles) east of the city centre, in the tourist zone, near Amathous.

Beaches

Although long and wide, the municipal beach in Limassol is not among the island's most attractive beaches; it is covered with compressed soil and pebbles, and is located near a busy street.

Better beaches can be found further afield. Beyond the new harbour, in the eastern part of the Akrotiri peninsula, is Lady's Mile – a long and relatively quiet sandy beach (*see p69*). To the west, about 17 km (10.5 miles) from the city centre, Kourion beach enjoys a lovely location at the foot of the hill where ancient Kourion once stood. You can reach it by public transport from Limassol. Avdimou beach, a further 12 km (7.5 miles) along, has nice sand and a pleasant restaurant, although no shade.

The most pleasant sandy beach is found near Pissouri, some 44 km (27 miles) from Limassol. Here you can hire a deck chair and an umbrella, and nearby are several pleasant tavernas and restaurants.

The pre-war building of the Municipal Art Gallery

King Richard the Lionheart

The English king, famed for his courage, was passing near Cyprus on his way to the Crusades when a storm blew one of his ships, carrying his sister and fiancée, to the shore. The ruler of Cyprus, the Byzantine Prince Isaac Komnenos, imprisoned both princesses and the crew. The outraged Richard the Lionheart landed with his army on the island, smashed the Komnenos army, imprisoned Komnenos and occupied Cyprus. In May 1191, in the chapel of Limassol castle, he married Princess Berengaria. Soon afterwards he sold the island to the Knights Templar.

English king Richard the Lionheart

Limassol Castle

This stronghold at the centre of the Old Town, near the harbour, was built by the Lusignan princes on foundations erected by the Byzantines. Later Venetian, Ottoman and British occupiers strengthened its defences. In 1191 the castle chapel was the venue for the wedding of Richard the Lionheart to Princess Berengaria of Navarre. The Turks later rebuilt the castle as a prison. During World War II it served as British Army headquarters. Nowadays it houses the Medieval Museum.

Castle Roof
The flat, stone roof of Limassol Castle was once used by its defenders. Today visitors come here to admire the panoramic view – the best in town.

The Reliefs
The section devoted to Byzantine art houses not only numerous beautiful reliefs and mosaics from the oldest Christian basilicas, but also a number of religious icons.

Grape Press
This grape press is among the stone artifacts in the castle gardens.

Knights' Hall
The first-floor hall, in the south wing of Limassol Castle, houses two suits of armour and a collection of rare, antique coins.

Main Hall
The Main Hall houses a large collection of Byzantine, Gothic and Renaissance sculptures, carvings and reliefs. Among them are carved images of the Lusignan kings from the portal of Agia Sofia Cathedral.

VISITORS' CHECKLIST

Practical Information
Irinis. Close to the old harbour.
Tel 25 305 419. **Open** 9am–5pm
Tue–Sat, 10am–1pm Sun.
There are cafés, restaurants and souvenir shops close by the castle, though none inside.

Main Lobby
Leading to the most opulent room, the lobby houses sculptures and coats of arms as well as photographs of Gothic and Renaissance architecture.

Fragment of a Portal
This fragment from Agia Sofia Cathedral forms part of the medieval stonemasonry exhibits in the museum collection.

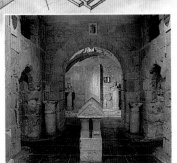

Sarcophagi chamber
A chamber hidden in the shadowy recesses of the castle contains a collection of sarcophagi and tombstones.

Main Entrance
The castle is entered through a small bastion located on the east side of the castle.

The ruins of ancient Amathous, scenically located along the coast

❽ Amathous

Road Map C4. 12 km (7.5 miles) east of Limassol city centre. **Open** 8am–5pm daily (to 6pm Apr, May, Sep & Oct; to 7:30pm Jun–Aug). 🚌 30.

Located on a high hill east of Limassol are the stone remains of the ancient port of Amathous. Named after its legendary founder Amathus, son of Aerias and king of Pafos, this once major commercial centre was founded between the 10th and 8th centuries BC.

Amathous was the first of the island's city-states. Over the centuries it was inhabited by Greeks, Phoenicians, Egyptians and Jews.

After the arrival of Christianity on Cyprus, St Tychon founded a church here and became the first bishop of Amathous. He became the patron saint of the town.

The town existed until the 7th century AD when, together with other coastal centres, it was destroyed in Arab raids.

In later times the site was used as a quarry; huge stones were transported to Egypt for use in the construction of the Suez Canal. The American consul (and amateur archaeologist) Luigi Palma di Cesnola destroyed large areas of the city while treasure hunting.

The best-preserved part is the agora (marketplace), with a dozen remaining columns. In the

Large stone vessel from Amathous

north section are parts of the aqueduct system and the site of a bathhouse. Standing on top of the hill was the acropolis, with temples to Aphrodite and Hercules, the remains of which can still be seen. Close by, archaeologists have unearthed the ruins of an early Christian, 5th-century Byzantine basilica. Fragments of powerful defence walls can be seen on the opposite side of the road.

The coastal part of the town collapsed during an earthquake. Its ruins stretch a great distance into the sea.

❾ Agios Georgios Alamanos

Road Map C4.

The buildings of the Agios Georgios Alamanos monastery can be seen from the Nicosia-Limassol motorway. Although the monastery, just like the new Byzantine-style church, is not of great architectural merit, it is interesting to watch the local monks painting icons.

In the nearby village of Pentakomo, on the opposite side of the motorway, are surviving stone houses. Close to the church is a pleasant café, where there are occasional concerts and plays.

❿ Kalavasos

Road Map C4. 40 km (25 miles) from Larnaka, 1.5 km (1 mile) from exit 15 on the motorway. 🚌 95 from Limassol, 401 from Larnaka.

Up until the 1970s the inhabitants of this village were involved in mining copper ore from the neighbouring mountains. A symbol of this industrial past is the local steam engine, which was once used here. The Cyprus Agrotourism Company has restored some of the houses for the use of tourists.

Environs

Close by archaeologists have unearthed the Neolithic settlement of **Tenta**. Smaller than the neighbouring Choirokoitia, part of it is covered by a huge tent. The settlement, which was encircled by a defensive wall, featured a roundhouse and beehive huts built from clay and stone.

The nearby village of **Tochni** is one of the most popular agrotourism sites in Cyprus. Situated in a valley, amid olive trees and vineyards, the peaceful village is built around a small church. Picturesque narrow alleys lead to stone houses.

The Neolithic settlement of Tenta

⑪ Choirokoitia

Road Map C4. 40 km (25 miles) from Limassol, 1.5 km (1 mile) from exit 14 on the motorway. ▣ 401, 402, 403 from Larnaka. **Tel** 24 322 710. **Open** Apr, May, Sep & Oct: 8am–6pm daily; Jun–Aug: 8am–7:30pm daily; Nov–Mar: 8am–5pm daily. 🅰

In the village of Choirokoitia, close to the motorway that runs between Limassol and Nicosia, archaeologists discovered the ruins of a large Neolithic settlement surrounded by a stone wall. One of the oldest settlements in Cyprus, it existed as early as 6,800 BC.

It was sited on the slope of a hill, close to the river Maroni. Its inhabitants, who numbered close to 2,000 at the peak of its development, lived in beehive huts built of stone and clay. Many of the houses unearthed by archaeologists contained under-floor graves with gifts and personal effects. The dead were laid to rest in an embryonic position, with heavy stones placed on their chests to prevent them from returning to the world of the living.

The population of Choirokoitia formed a well-organized farming community. They cultivated the fertile local soil, hunted, bred goats, spun and weaved, and produced clay figurines and other objects. The artifacts uncovered at this site include flint sickle blades, stone vases and primitive triangular fertility gods. The women wore beautiful necklaces made of shells or imported red cornelian.

The foundations of several dozens of houses have been unearthed. Some of these have been reconstructed, providing a glimpse into how the earliest Cypriots lived. Many of the items found here are exhibited in the Cyprus Museum in Nicosia.

The settlement was abandoned suddenly, and then repopulated around 4,500 BC. These later inhabitants introduced clay pots, some of which have been unearthed. The Choirokoitia archaeological site has been declared a UNESCO World Cultural and Natural Heritage Site.

Lefkara's Lace and Silverware Museum

⑫ Agios Minas

Road Map C4. Close to Lefkara. **Tel** 24 342 952. **Open** May–Sep: 8am–noon, 3–5pm daily; Oct–Apr: 8am–noon, 2–5pm daily.

Agios Minas, a small monastery located in a scenic mountain setting, was founded in the 15th century and renovated in the mid-18th century. Subsequently abandoned, it was taken by a convent in 1965. The nuns are involved in painting icons, growing flowers and fruit, and keeping bees. They sell the delicious honey.

The 15th-century convent church, which was built by the Dominicans, features wall frescoes depicting St George slaying the dragon and the martyrdom of St Minas.

Environs

The nearby village of **Vavla** has lovely stone houses, some of which are being renovated for use by tourists.

⑬ Lefkara

Road Map C4. 40 km (25 miles) from Larnaka. ▣ 405 from Larnaka.

This village, set amid picturesque white limestone hills (*lefka ori* means white hills), is famous for the lace-making skills of its womenfolk. In the Middle Ages Lefkara was a health resort visited by Venetian ladies. While staying here they busied themselves with embroidery, which they taught the local women. One story tells of Leonardo da Vinci supposedly coming to the island in 1481 to order an altar-cloth for Milan cathedral. The lace patterns are predominantly geometric, with crosses or diamonds and occasionally flowers, birds or butterflies. While the women busy themselves with embroidery, the local men produce jewellery and other objects from silver and gold.

The village buildings, with their yellow walls and red roofs, stand in attractive contrast with the natural surroundings. At the centre of Lefkara is the 16th-century Churchw of the Holy Cross containing a carved and gilded wood iconostasis and a precious sacred relic – a fragment of the True Cross on which Christ was crucified. The beautiful stone Patsalos building houses the **Lace and Silverware Museum**.

Ⅲ Lace and Silverware Museum
Pano Lefkara. **Tel** 24 342 326. **Open** 9:30am–5pm daily. 🅰

Reconstructed houses at Choirokoitia archaeological site

⑭ Pyrga

Road Map C3. 35 km (22 miles) from Nicosia. 🚌 455 from Larnaka.

This village is home to the Gothic **Chapel of St Catherine**, also known as the "Chapelle Royal". Erected by the Lusignan King Janus for his wife Charlotte de Bourbon, the chapel is built of volcanic rock on a square floorplan. It has three doors and, on the altar wall, three Gothic windows. The interior features fragments of the original frescoes. These depict the *Crucifixion*, with King Janus and Queen Charlotte by the cross; the *Raising of Lazarus*; the *Last Supper*; and the Lusignan coats of arms.

Close by is the Marini river on whose banks in 1426 the Egyptian Mamelukes smashed the Cypriot army, capturing King Janus and taking him prisoner to Cairo. The king regained his freedom two years later, after a ransom was paid.

Gothic chapel of St Catherine in Pyrga

Environs
The village of **Kornos**, to the west, is famous for its oversized ceramic products, such as storage jars.

⑮ Stavrovouni Monastery

Road Map D3. 40 km (25 miles) from Larnaka, 9 km (5.5 miles) from motorway. **Tel** 22 533 630. **Open** Apr–Aug: 8am–noon, 3–6pm daily; Sep–Mar: 7–11am, 2–5pm daily. 🚫 No women allowed 🏛 14 Sep.

Stavrovouni (Mountain of the Cross) monastery was built on a steep, 750-m (2,460-ft)

Agia Varvara (monastery of St Barbara) at the foot of Stavrovouni

mountain. In ancient times the mountain was called Olympus, and it was the site of a temple to Aphrodite.

According to tradition, the monastery was founded in 327 by St Helena, mother of Constantine the Great. On her journey back from the Holy Land, where she found the True Cross of Christ, she stopped in Cyprus and left behind fragments of the precious relic. These can be seen in a large silver reliquary in the shape of a cross. Over the following centuries the monastery fell prey to enemy raids and earthquakes. In 1821, during the Greek independence uprising, it was burned to the ground by the Turkish governor of Cyprus. The present monastery is the result of 19th-century restoration. The small **church** contains a lovely iconostasis and a wooden cross dating from 1476, carved with scenes

from the life of Jesus. Around the church are the monks' cells and other monastic quarters. The monastery also houses a collection of monks' skulls, with the name of the deceased written on each forehead.

Today the monks produce exquisite cheeses and sultanas, and also keep honey bees.

At the foot of Stavrovouni is the **monastery of St Barbara** (Agia Varvara), known for the local monks' icon painting. Their most celebrated artist was Father Kallinikos.

⑯ Kiti

Road Map D4. 7 km (4.5 miles) southwest of Larnaka. **Open** church: 7am–6:45pm daily (from 9:30am Sun).

The **Panagia Angeloktisti** ("Built by Angels") church, in the northwestern end of the village of Kiti, consists of three parts. The first is the 14th-century Latin chapel with the coats of arms of knights above the entrance. The second part is the 11th-century dome-covered church, built on the ruins of an early Byzantine basilica, whose apse has been

The Stavrovouni monastery towering over the district

For hotels and restaurants in this region see pp162–5 and pp170–77

incorporated into the present building. The 6th-century apse mosaic is the church's main attraction. It depicts Mary holding the Christ Child, flanked by the Archangels Michael and Gabriel, with peacock-feather wings.

The third part of the church is a small 12th-century chapel dedicated to Saints Cosmas and Damian (patron saints of medicine) and decorated with 15th-century murals.

Environs
The 15th-century watchtower, one kilometer (half a mile) from Kiti lighthouse, features a statue of a lion – the symbol of the Venetian Republic.

Panagia Angeloktisti church in the village of Kiti

⑰ Hala Sultan Tekke

Road Map D3. 5 km (3 miles) SW of Larnaka. **Open** 8am–5pm daily (to 6pm Apr, May, Sep & Oct; to 7:30pm Jun–Aug).

On the shores of a salt lake, surrounded by cypress, palm and olive trees, the Hala Sultan Tekke is a major Muslim sanctuary. It includes an octagonal 1816 mosque built by the Turkish governor of Cyprus, and a mausoleum with the tomb of Umm Haram.

Umm Haram, paternal aunt of the Prophet Mohammed, was killed after falling off a mule while accompanying her husband in a pillage raid on Kition in 649. The mosque has a modest interior and the mausoleum contains several sarcophagi covered with green cloth. After Mecca, Medina and Jerusalem, the Hala Sultan Tekke is among the holiest sites for Muslims.

To the west of the car park archaeological excavations continue, unearthing a late-

Mosque and Hala Sultan Tekke mausoleum on the shores of the Salt Lake

Bronze Age town. Many items found here originated from Egypt and the Middle East.

Environs
The Salt Lake, close to the mosque, is one of two such lakes on Cyprus. In winter and early spring it provides a gathering point for thousands of flamingoes, swans, pelicans and other migrating water birds. The lake lies below sea level and in winter is filled with water seeping from the sea through the lime rocks. In summer it dries out, leaving a thick deposit of salt. Until the 1980s it yielded 3 to 5 thousand tons of salt annually.

According to legend, the Salt Lake was created after Lazarus landed on this shore. Hungry and thirsty, he asked a local woman in the vineyard for a handful of fruit. She tersely refused to give him anything, so the saint, in revenge, turned her vineyard into a salt lake.

⑱ Larnaka

See pp82–5.

⑲ Kellia

Road Map D3. 5 km (3 miles) north of Larnaka. 🚌 442 from Larnaka.

Standing to the west of Kellia, formerly a Turkish Cypriot village that derives its name from the cells of early Christian hermits who once made this their home, is the small **Church of St Anthony** (Agios Andonios), where cells are carved into the rocks.

It was first built in the 11th century, but the subsequent remodelling works have all but obliterated its original shape. The layout resembles a cross inscribed into a square, with the three aisles terminating in an apse and a 15th-century narthex.

Restoration efforts have revealed some beautiful murals. The most interesting of them is the *Crucifixion*, painted on the southeast pillar, one of the oldest paintings on the island. Other notable paintings are on the pillars and on the west wall of the church, including the *Assumption of the Virgin Mary*, *Judas' Betrayal* and *Abraham's Sacrifice*.

Zeno of Kition (kitium)

Born in 334 BC, this Greek thinker founded the Stoic school of philosophy (named after Stoa Poikale – the Painted Colonnade on the Athenian agora where he taught). Zeno's philosophy embraced logic, epistemology, physics and ethics. The Stoics postulated that a life governed by reason and the harnessing of desires was of the highest virtue, leading to happiness. Stoicism left a deep mark on the philosophy and ethics of the Hellenic and Roman eras.

Bust of Zeno of Kition

⑱ Larnaka

Larnaka stands on the site of ancient Kition. It takes its name from the Greek *larnax*, meaning "sarcophagus" (there were many ancient and medieval tombs in the district). The city has an international airport, a port, several interesting museums and a seaside promenade lined with numerous cafés and restaurants. The tourist zone has luxurious hotels, tavernas, nightclubs and souvenir shops.

Larnaka's seaside promenade lined with palm trees

Exploring Larnaka

The best place to begin is ancient Kition, followed by the Archaeological and Pierides Museums. From here continue with the church of St Lazarus (Agios Lazaros) and the Byzantine Museum, then proceed towards the sea, visiting the Turkish fort and mosque. The seaside promenade leads to the marina and beach.

🏛 Kition

0.5 km (0.3 mile) NE of Archaeological Museum. **Open** 8am–2:30pm Mon–Fri (to 5pm Wed).

The ancient city of Kition (Kitium) lies in the northern part of Larnaka. According to tradition it was founded by Kittim, grandson of Noah. Archaeological excavations indicate, however, that the town was founded in the 13th century BC. Soon afterwards the Mycenaeans landed on the island; they reinforced the city walls and built a temple. The Phoenicians, who conquered the city in the 9th century BC, turned the temple into a shrine to the goddess Astarte. Kition was a

major trade centre for copper, which was excavated in mines near Tamassos.

🏛 Mycenaean Site

Leoforos Archiepiskopu Kyprianou. The main archaeological site (dubbed Area II) is near the cemetery for foreigners. There are wooden platforms from where you can view the dig. The defence walls dating from the late Bronze era were later strengthened by the Mycenaeans, who added fortifications built of stone and clay bricks.

🏛 Acropolis

Leontiou Kimonos. Situated on top of Bamboula hill (immediately behind the Archaeological Museum) was the acropolis, which had its own defence walls. In the late 1800s the hill was plundered by British soldiers, who used the rubble to cover malaria-breeding swamps. In the 1960s archaeologists stumbled upon ancient tombs filled with ceramics and jewellery, as well as alabaster sculptures and stone fragments.

A figurine from Pierides Museum

🏛 Archaeological Museum

Kalograion. **Tel** 24 304 169. **Open** 8am–3pm Mon–Fri (to 2:30pm Mon, to 5pm Thu), 9am–3pm Sat. 🅿

The Archaeological Museum displays vases, sculptures and cult statues from Larnaka and the surrounding area. It has a collection of ceramics (mostly Mycenaean), votive terracotta figurines and glass objects from Roman times. There is also an interesting exhibition of Cypriot-Minoan inscriptions, as yet undeciphered. There are also sculptures in the garden.

Interior staircase of Larnaka's Pierides Museum

🏛 Pierides Museum

Zinonos Kitieos 4. **Tel** 24 814 555. **Open** 9am–4pm Mon–Thu, 9am–1pm Fri & Sat. 🅿
🌐 pierides foundation.com.cy

This museum contains the largest private collection in Cyprus. Comprising some 2,500 relics assembled by five generations of the Pierides family, the collection spans from the Neolithic era to medieval times. It was started in 1839 by Cypriot archaeologist Demetrios Pierides, who committed part of his fortune to the preservation of artifacts

Excavations of the ancient city of Kition

For hotels and restaurants in this region see pp162–5 and pp170–77

Natural History Museum in the municipal park

VISITORS' CHECKLIST

Practical Information
Road Map D3. 🗺 143,000.
ℹ Plateia Vasileos Pavlou, 24 654
322. 🎪 Kataklysmos Fair (50 days
after Easter), Flower Festival (May).

Transport
🚌 Arrive/depart at the end of
Leoforos Athinon promenade,
close to the marina.

pillaged from ancient tombs by treasure hunters such as the American consul in Larnaka, Luigi Palma di Cesnola.

The most precious objects include Neolithic stone idols and 3,000-year-old ceramic vessels. There are also terracotta figurines dating from the archaic era; miniature war chariots and cavalry soldiers; amphorae and goblets in geometric and archaic styles decorated with images of fish and birds; and Hellenic statues. Of particular note is the striking astronaut-like figure jumping on springs, painted on an archaic ceramic vessel. Other exhibits include weaponry and a set of historical maps of Cyprus and of the eastern Mediterranean. In the rooms at the back of the

building is a collection of handicrafts, including jewellery, embroidery, everyday items and richly carved furniture. There are also works by the primitive artist Michael Kashialos, who was murdered by the Turks in his studio in 1974.

🏛 Museum of Natural History

Leoforos Grigori Afxentiou.
Tel 24 652 569.
Open 9am–4pm Mon–Fri,
10am–1pm Sat.

Located in the municipal park, this small building houses a diverse collection of exhibits illustrating the natural environment of Cyprus. Arranged across eight

rooms displays shows specimens of plants, insects and animals (from both land and sea), many of which are now rare in the wild.

There are also interesting geological exhibits. Besides the collection of copper minerals – the main source of the island's wealth since ancient times, you can see minerals belonging to the asbestos group. The large open mines from which these minerals came are located near Amiantos, on the southeastern slopes of the Troodos mountains. Other exhibits include fossils from the island's limestone.

Fountain in front of the town hall

Larnaka Town Centre

① Kition
② Mycenaean Site
③ Acropolis
④ Archaeological Museum
⑤ Pierides Museum
⑥ Museum of Natural History
⑦ Agios Lazaros Church
⑧ Agia Faneromeni
⑨ Büyük Cami
⑩ Larnaka Fort and Medieval Museum
⑪ Beaches

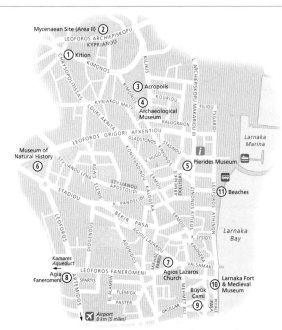

0 metres 400
0 yards 400

For key to symbols see back flap

St Lazarus Church dating from the 10th century

⬆ Agios Lazaros Church

Plateia Agiou Lazarou. **Tel** 24 652 498.
Open 8am–12:30pm, 2–6:30pm daily
(to 5:30pm Sep–Mar).

The Church of St Lazarus (Agios
Lazaros) stands in the southern
part of Old Larnaka. It was
constructed in the early 10th
century on the site of a
church dating from 900
AD, which was built to
house the saint's tomb.
   Its architectural style
reveals the influence of
both eastern and
western trends.
Following its retrieval
from the hands of the
Turks in 1589, the church
was used by Roman
Catholic and Orthodox
communities for 200
years, as evidenced by
inscriptions on the
portico. The interior is built
around four vast pillars supporting
a roof with three small domes. Its
main features are the Rococo
pulpit, around 300 years old,
and a small icon depicting
Lazarus emerging from his tomb,
an image reverently paraded
through the church at Easter. The

Icon from the
Byzantine Museum

magnificently carved
iconostasis includes a
number of precious
icons; the best of
these dates from the
17th century and
portrays Lazarus
rising. On the right
side of the central
nave is a large gilded
reliquary containing
the skull of the saint.
The crypt houses
several stone sarcop-
hagi. One of them
supposedly housed
the relics of St Lazar-
us. The tomb bore the Greek inscription: "Lazarus, friend of Jesus".
   The graves in the courtyard are
mainly British consuls, civil
servants and merchants.
   Larnaka has other notable
places of worship, including the
metropolitan cathedral, Agios
Chrysotrios, built in 1853;
Agios Ioannis, featuring
a beautiful iconostasis
from the beginning of
the 17th century; and
the Roman Catholic
church Terra Santa. Also
of note is the
19th-century "Clown
Mosque" (Zahuri Cami),
with its double dome
and truncated minaret.

▥ Byzantine Museum

Plateia Agiou Lazarou.
Tel 24 652 498. **Open** 8:30am–
12:30pm, 3–5:30pm Mon–Sat.
Closed Wed & Sat pm.

Entry to this museum is from the
courtyard of Agios Lazaros church.
The collection consists of icons
and other objects associated with
the Orthodox religion, including
chasubles and Bibles.

A previous, extensive collection
vanished during the turbulent
period between 1964 and 1974.
It was kept in the fort, which fell
into the hands of the Turks. When
it was regained by the Greeks,
many items had vanished.

⬆ Agia Faneromeni

At the junction of Leoforos
Faneromeni and Artemidos.

This subterranean chapel is a
two-chambered cave hewn into
the rock. Its structure suggests a
pagan tomb, probably dating
from the Phoenician era. The
chapel was famed for its magical
properties. The sick would circle
it twice, leaving behind anything
from a scrap of clothing to a lock
of hair in the hope that they
were also leaving behind their
illnesses. Girls, whose boyfriends
were far away, would come here
to pray for their safe return.

▦ Amphitheatre

Leoforos Artemidos.

The open-air amphitheatre,
used for staging events during
the July Festival, is situated
opposite the Zeno of Kition
Stadium, close to the Agia
Faneromeni chapel.

☪ Büyük Cami

Leoforus Athenon. **Open** daily.

Standing beyond the fort, at the
border between the Greek and
Turkish districts, is the Grand
Mosque (Büyük Cami). Originally
the church of the Holy Cross,
this building now serves Muslim
visitors mostly from the Middle
East. Modest attire is required,
and before entering you must
remove your shoes. For a small
fee you can climb the narrow,
steep stairs that lead to the top
of the minaret. From here there

Saint Lazarus

Lazarus, brother of Martha and Mary, was
resurrected by Jesus four days after his
death at Bethany. He moved to Cyprus,
becoming Bishop of Kition. After his final
death he was buried here; his tomb was
discovered in 890. Emperor Leo VI helped to
build St Lazarus church, in exchange for
which some of the saint's relicts were
transferred to Constantinople, from where
they were stolen in 1204. Today they are in
Marseille Cathedral.

Painting showing the resurrection of Lazarus

is a lovely, panoramic view of Larnaka and the nearby Salt Lake. Stretching beyond the fort, right up to the fishing harbour is a large district that once belonged to the Turks. Its streets still bear Turkish names, but it is now inhabited by Greek Cypriot refugees from the area around Famagusta and the Karpasia peninsula.

The imposing mid-18th-century aqueduct

A variety of yachts moored in Larnaka marina

🚢 Larnaka Harbours

The southern part of town has a small but picturesque fishing harbour. Larnaka marina is situated several hundred metres to the north of the coastal promenade, beyond a small beach. Only boat crews are allowed entry, but you can stroll along the breakwater. Beyond the marina there are cargo and passenger terminals; the passenger terminal is the second largest in Cyprus.

🏰 Larnaka Fort and Medieval Museum

On the seashore, by the south end of the coastal promenade. **Tel** 24 304 576. **Open** 9am–5pm Mon–Fri (to 7:30pm Jun–Aug).

The fort in Larnaka was built by the Turks around1625 on the site of a medieval castle which had been destroyed by Mamelukes two centuries previously. When ships sailed into the harbour (which no longer exists), they were welcomed by a gun salute fired from the castle.

During the Byzantine period, the fort was used as a police headquarters, prison and execution site. In 1833, it was partially destroyed by a lightning strike. Today the fort houses a small Medieval Museum with arms and armour dating from Turkish times, and treasure troves unearthed in Kition and at the Hala Sultan Tekke. The crenellated wall, with menacing guns and cannons, is now a viewing platform. During summer the castle yard serves as a venue for concerts, occasional plays and other cultural events.

🏖 Beaches

The sandy municipal beach by the Finikoudes promenade, in the neighbourhood of the marina, owes its popularity mainly to a double row of shade-giving palm trees. Another

A cannon at Larnaka's Fort

municipal beach is situated to the south of the fishing harbour. Although the beach itself is small, it is popular with locals due to its water-sports facilities and the numerous restaurants and cafés in the vicinity. The best sandy public beach in the area is located some 10 km (6 miles) east of the city and is run by the Cyprus Tourism Organization. About 10 km (6 miles) south of Larnaka, near Kiti, there is a rocky cove with patches of sand; this area is undeveloped and relatively free of people.

There are other beaches, some of them sandy, located a few kilometres north of Larnaka, within the tourist zone. However, your enjoyment of them may be hampered by the smell emanating from the nearby oil refinery.

🏛 Aqueduct (Kamares)

3 km (1.9 miles) from Larnaka.

On the outskirts of Larnaka, by the road leading to Limassol, are the remains of an aqueduct that once supplied the town with water taken the River Thrimitus. The aqueduct was built in 1745 by the Turkish governor, Elhey Bekir Pasha, and functioned until 1930. Some 75 spans of this impressive structure still stand; they are illuminated at night.

Larnaka beach in high season

Octagonal fountain in the courtyard of Agia Napa monastery

⓴ Agia Napa

Road Map E3. 🚌 201 Agia Napa Circle Line. 🏨 3,200. 🛈 Leoforos Kryou Nerou 12, 23 721 796. 🎭 Kataklysmos.

Until the 1970s Agia Napa was a quiet fishing village with a scenic harbour. However, following the Turkish occupation of Varosha – the Greek Cypriot neighbourhood of Famagusta – Agia Napa assumed the role of Cyprus's prime bathing resort. Now a teeming holiday resort especially popular with British and Scandinavian young people, the town centre has scores of hotels, nightclubs and cafés that have given Agia Napa its reputation as the second most entertaining playground in the Mediterranean, after Ibiza.

An interesting historic relic of Agia Napa is the 16th-century Venetian **Monastery of Agia Napa**, enclosed by a high wall. According to legend, in the 16th century a hunter's dog led him to a spring in the woods where he found a sacred icon of the Virgin that had been lost 700 years earlier. (A church had been built here as early as the 8th century, hacked into the solid rock and named Agia Napa – Holy Virgin of the Forest). The spring was thus believed to have healing powers and the monastery of Agia Napa was built on the site. Soon after, Cyprus fell to the Turks and the Venetian

monks fled, but villagers continued to use the beautiful **monastery church**.

The only church on the island with a free-standing belfry, it is built partly underground in a natural grotto. The route to its gloomy, mysterious interior leads through an entrance crowned with an arch and a rosette. Inside is a complex maze of grottoes, niches and shrines. From April until December, the church celebrates Anglican mass every Sunday at 11am and Roman Catholic mass at 5pm. At the centre of the monastery's arcaded **courtyard** is an octagonal Renaissance fountain decorated with marble reliefs and topped with a dome resting on four columns. Nearby, water supplied by a Roman aqueduct flows from the carved marble head of a wild boar.

Fountain detail, Agia Napa monastery

The monastery was restored in the 1970s and now houses the **World Council of Churches Ecumenical Conference Centre.**

The **Thalassa Museum of the Sea** in Agia Napa is designed to show the impact of the sea on the history of the island. It features a replica of the "Kyrenia Ship" dating from the times of Alexander the Great, which sank off the coast of Kyrenia some 2,300 years ago.

The majority of the museum's exhibits come from the private collection of naturalist George Tomaritis. They include a range of preserved marine fauna as well as a collection of shells and maritime exhibits.

Beautiful sandy beaches can be found in the surrounding area. One of them is **Nissi Beach**, with its small island. Neighbouring **Makronissos Beach** is linked to the town centre by bicycle routes. Nearby, on a craggy peninsula, are 19 Hellenic tombs hacked into the rock. Two kilometres (1 mile) west is a sandy beach, **Agia Thekla**, with a small chapel and an old church in a rock cave.

🏛 **Thalassa Museum of the Sea**
Leoforos Kryou Nerou. **Tel** 23 816 366. **Open** summer: 9am–1pm Mon, 9am–5pm Tue–Sat, 3–7pm Sun; winter: 9am–1pm Mon, 9am–5pm Tue–Sat, closed Sun. 🅿
🌐 pieridesfoundation.com.cy

㉑ Cape Gkreko

Road Map E3. 🚌 101 from Famagusta and Paralimni.

This headland at the south-eastern tip of Cyprus rises in a steep crag above the sea. The neighbouring coves with their clear water are a paradise for scuba divers and snorkellers.

Popular sandy beach in Agia Napa

The rugged coast of Cape Gkreko with its limestone cliffs

The entire area, with its limestone rock formations, is a **protected nature reserve**.

Archaeologists discovered the remains of two **temples**: the Hellenic temple of Aphrodite, and the Roman temple of Diana. The cape is surrounded by underwater **shipwrecks**, including a Genoese ship filled with looted treasure, which sank in the 15th century.

Walking along the shore towards Protaras you will come across a rock bridge over a small bay protruding inland, a Roman quarry, and a little further on, the **Agii Anargyri Church** above a grotto hidden in a craggy cliff underneath. The area affords magnificent views over Konnos Bay and the clifftop hotel.

㉒ Protaras

Road Map E3. 101 from Famagusta and Paralimni. Leoforos Protaras Cape Gkreko 356, 23 832 865.

Protaras is a conglomeration of hotels, tavernas, cafés, watersports centres and an excellent place to spend a holiday. In summer, its beautiful sandy beaches attract crowds of tourists ready to enjoy watersports, or to go for a cruise on one of the local pleasure boats.

The area is dominated by a rocky hill with the picturesque **chapel of Prophitis Elias** (the Prophet Elijah) affording a magnificent panoramic view of Protaras and nearby Varosha.

Further north are more beaches including Pernera, Minas and Agia Triada with a small church, situated in a coastal cove. Near the latter, close to the roundabout on the road to Paralimni, is **Ocean Aquarium**, with crocodiles, penguins and other marine life.

🔲 Ocean Aquarium
Paralimni, Protaras Ave. **Open** 10am– 6pm daily. **Tel** 23 741 111.

Environs
The area encompassing Agia Napa, Paralimni and the tourist region of Protaras is known as **Kokkinohoria** (red villages) due to its red soil, rich in iron compounds. The scenery is dominated by windmills that drive pumps, which draw water from deep underground.

After 1974, the old village of **Paralimni** became the administrative centre of the district. Situated close to the occupied, northern part of Cyprus, it received a great many refugees after the invasion and now its population numbers about 11,000.

The village skyline is dominated by three churches. The oldest of these is Panagia (Virgin Mary) dating from the 18th century and lined with porcelain tiles typical of the period. It also houses a small Byzantine museum. Paralimni is famous for delicacies such as smoked pork (pasta) and pork sausages (loukanika).

The neighbouring farming village of **Deryneia** perches atop a hill, right by the "Green Line". From here there

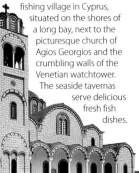

Statue of a diver in Protaras

are views of Varosha's abandoned houses, the former tourist district of Famagusta now resembling a ghost town, and the Gothic Cathedral of St Nicholas, which has been turned into a mosque.

Deryneia has three pretty churches – 15th-century Agia Marina, 17th-century Agios Georgios and the church of the Panagia.

The village of **Liopetri** is famous for the potatoes that are grown here, as well as the woven baskets used to collect them. You can still see local basket weavers at work. The 15th-century village church of Agios Andronikos has a carved iconostasis with lovely icons and paintings in the apses.

The Akhyronas barn is Cyprus's national memorial. It was here that four EOKA fighters were killed in a battle with the British in 1958.

Potamos Liopetriou, to the south, is the most beautiful fishing village in Cyprus, situated on the shores of a long bay, next to the picturesque church of Agios Georgios and the crumbling walls of the Venetian watchtower. The seaside tavernas serve delicious fresh fish dishes.

The 18th-century church in Paralimni

TROODOS MOUNTAINS

Stretching some 120 km (75 miles) over southwestern Cyprus, the Troodos mountain region is truly astonishing and completely different from the rest of the sun-baked island. In winter and early spring, the peaks are often capped with snow, and the forests fill the cool air with the scent of pine and cedar. The mountain villages and monasteries hidden in the forests seem a world away from the crowded coastal areas, even during the peak holiday season.

The shady valleys and lofty peaks of the Troodos mountains have long been a refuge for people in search of calm and tranquillity, including the monks who came here looking for a place where they could be closer to God and farther from temptation.

Mount Olympus, the island's highest peak at 1,951 m (6,400 ft), rises above the other mountains in the mighty massif, crowned with the distinctive radar domes of the British army. In winter, its slopes swarm with skiers eager to enjoy a sport that is rare in this part of Europe.

The southern slopes are perfectly suited to growing the grapes used to produce the island's famous wine, the sweet Commandaria.

Almost half of the 144 species of plants unique to Cyprus grow in the Troodos region. The central section has been declared a nature reserve.

Travelling through the Troodos mountains brings visitors into contact with quiet, friendly villages, where the local people produce sweets of fruit and nuts soaked in grape juice (soujouko), as well as excellent wine and flavourful goat cheese (halloumi).

No trip to the region is complete without seeing the Byzantine painted churches. The austere architecture of these Orthodox sanctuaries, hidden in remote valleys and glens, hides a wealth of amazingly rich murals (commonly referred to as frescoes) depicting scenes from the Bible.

A church hidden in the mountains – a distinctive feature of the region

◀ The Royal Kykkos Monastery in the Troodos mountains

Exploring the Troodos Mountains

Among the highlights of a visit to the Troodos mountains are the many painted churches, some dating from the Byzantine period. Ten of these isolated churches have been listed as UNESCO World Cultural Heritage Sites. The tomb of Archbishop Makarios, the first president of Cyprus, lies near Kykkos Monastery at Throni. The Commandaria region's villages have produced the famous Cypriot dessert wine since the 12th century. The true treasures of the Troodos mountains are their waterfalls hidden among lush greenery – unusual in the eastern Mediterranean.

Theotokos Archangelos Church, one of the many small churches in the region

Sights at a Glance

1. Tilliria
2. Cedar Valley
3. Kykkos pp94–5
4. Agios Ioannis Lampadistis
5. Panagia tou Moutoulla
6. Pedoulas
7. Mt Olympus (Chionistra)
8. Troodos
9. Trooditissa
10. Platres
11. Omodos
12. Potamiou
13. Vouni
14. Koilani
15. Lofou
16. Monagri
17. Timios Stavros
18. Pelendri
19. Agios Nikolaos tis Stegis
20. Kakopetria
21. Panagia tis Podithou
22. Panagia Forviotissa
23. Panagia tou Araka
24. Stavros tou Agiasmati

For hotels and restaurants in this region see pp162–5 and pp170–77

Winding roads and arid landscape typical of the region

Getting There

From Larnaka airport, follow the motorway signs toward the Troodos mountains, and then take the B8 road. The B9 road from Nicosia passes through Kakopetria. The best route from Pafos is along the scenic Diarizos valley. Leave the motorway at Mandria and turn towards Nikoklea. The mountain roads are of good quality, but winding and steep in places.

→ Morfou

Astromeritis

Nicosia →

B9

Nikitari   Vyzakia

LEFKOSÍA

Evrychou

Atsas

Adhelfi Forest

Xyliatos

🔵 **22** PANAGIA
FORVIOTISSA

akies

alopanagiotis

21 PANAGIA TIS
PODITHOU

Kapoura

🔵🏠 **4** AGIOS IOANNIS
LAMPADISTIS

AGIA TOU
OUTOULLA **5**

20 KAKOPETRIA

🏠🌲 **6** PEDOULAS

🏠 **19** AGIOS NIKOLAOS
TIS STEGIS

Kourdali   Saranti

STAVROS TOU
24 AGIASMATI

Marathassa

Prodromos

Spilia

Mt Adhelfi
1612m

🏠 **23** PANAGIA
TOU ARAKA

Platanistasa

MOUNT OLYMPUS **7**

Chandria

Pitsillia

8 TROODOS

aminaria

9

TROODITISSA

Fini

Troodos

Pano
Amiantos

Kyperounta

Agridia

Alona

Agros

PELENDRI **18**

PLATRES **10**

L E M E S O S

17 TIMIOS
STAVROS

Pera Pedi

11 OMODOS

14 KOILANI

Trimiklini

POTAMIOU
12

Silikou

13 VOUNI

B8

15 LOFOU

Laneia

alia

Agios
Therapon

16 MONAGRI

*Panagia tis
Amasgou*

↓ Limassol

Key

━━━ Secondary road

┈┈┈ Minor road

━━━ Scenic route

– – Track

▬▬▬ Regional border

■ ▪ Green Line

△ Summit

For additional map symbols *see back flap*

❶ Tilliria

Road Map B3.

Tilliria is a desolate region east of Polis, on the northwestern slopes of the Troodos mountains. Its forested hills extend behind the former monastery, Stavros tis Psokas, in the direction of the Turkish enclave of Kokkina, Pyrgos, Kato and the sea. This region has never been inhabited, although people came here to work the long-since defunct copper ore mines. It is ideal for experienced hikers.

In ancient times, Cyprus was overgrown with dense forests, which were cut down to build ships and fire the furnaces in the copper-smelting plants.

Under British rule of the island, action was taken to restore the former character of the Cypriot forests. The extensive Pafos Forest was created in the western region of the Troodos mountains.

The wooded hills of the remote Tilliria region – a hiker's paradise

❷ Cedar Valley

Road Map B3.

This valley, set in the midst of the forest backwoods, contains most of the island's trees of the local *cedrus brevifolia* variety, different from the better known Lebanese cedar. The valley is a nature reserve, and with a bit of luck visitors will see the moufflon – a wild Cypriot sheep. In the early 20th century, when the British declared these animals a protected species, only 15 of them remained in the wild;

now the forests of Cyprus are home to over 1,500 of them. The male displays powerful, curled horns. The moufflon is a symbol of Cyprus and appears on its coins.

Environs
Standing in the midst of the Pafos Forest is the abandoned 19th-century monastery of **Stavros tis Psokas**, now used by the Forestry Commission. It contains a restaurant, several guest rooms and a campsite. The locals claim it to be the coolest place on the island. Close to the campsite is an enclosure containing moufflon.

The Forestry Commission building is the starting point for hiking trails to the nearby peaks of Tripylos and Zaharou. Starting from the car park by the spring and the junction with the road leading towards the sea, you can walk or drive to Mount Tripylos – one of the highest peaks in the district at 1,362 m (4,468 ft), which offers a magnificent panorama of the Pafos and Tilliria hills.

❸ Kykkos

See pp94–5.

❹ Agios Ioannis Lampadistis

Road Map B3. Kalopanagiotis.
Tel 22 952 580. **Open** 9am–12:30pm, 2–5pm daily (Nov–Apr: 9am–noon, 1–4pm). Donations welcome.

The monastery of St John of Lampadou (ancient Lambas) is one of the most interesting in Cyprus and has been awarded

Kalopanagiotis village, scenically located on a mountain slope

UNESCO World Heritage status. The old monastery complex includes three churches covered with one vast roof. The oldest one, dedicated to St Irakleidios, dates from the 11th century and is decorated with over 30 12th- and 15th-century frescoes illustrating key events in the life of Jesus. The painting on the dome depicts Christ Pantocrator. Others show the Sacrifice of Abraham, the Entry into Jerusalem and the Ascension. The 15th-century series of paintings seen on the vaults, arches and walls depicts various scenes from the New Testament.

The second church, of **Agios Ioannis (St John) Lampadistis**, dating from the 11th century, is dedicated to the saint who was born in Lampadou. He renounced marriage in favour of the monastic life, went blind, died at the age of 22, and was canonised soon afterwards. His tomb is inside the church and the niche above contains a silver reliquary with the saint's skull. The church interior is

Monastery buildings of Agios Ioannis Lampadistis

decorated with 12th-century paintings. The richly gilded iconostasis dates from the 16th century. The narthex (portico) common to both churches, which was added in the 15th century, includes a cycle of paintings depicting the miracles of Christ.

The **Latin chapel**, added in the second half of the 15th century, is decorated with 24 magnificent Byzantine wall paintings with Greek texts written in about 1500.

Environs

The mountain village of **Kalopanagiotis** is scenically located in the Setrachos Valley. It has existed since medieval times and has retained its traditional architecture, cobbled streets, and many churches and chapels. The village is now a small health resort with therapeutic sulphur springs (with beneficial properties for rheumatic conditions and gastric ailments). It is also known for its beautifully carved breadbaskets called *sanidha*. Kalopanagiotis is believed to be descended from ancient Lambas, which produced the local saints, Ioannis and Irakleidios. Nearby is an arched medieval bridge.

❺ Panagia tou Moutoulla

Road Map B3. 3 km (1.8 miles) from Pedoulas. Moutoullas. **Open** vary. Donations welcome.

The village of Moutoulla, situated in a valley below Pedoulas, is renowned for its mineral water spring and its tiny church of **Our Lady of Moutoulla** (Panagia tou Moutoulla) built in 127980.

This is the oldest of the Troodos mountain painted churches. Its most interesting features are the pitched roof and finely carved entrance door. Beyond these doors is another set of equally beautiful doors (wood carving has been a local speciality for centuries). Above them is the image of *Christ Enthroned*, flanked by *Adam and Eve*, and *Hell and Paradise*, with a procession of

Panoramic view of Pedoulas in the Marathassa valley

saints marching into Heaven. The cycle of paintings inside the church, illustrating key events in the life of Jesus and Mary, are similar to the wall paintings in the nearby Church of the Archangel Michael. The most distinctive of these faded paintings include *Mary with the Christ Child* in a cradle, and *St Christopher and St George Fighting the Dragon* with the head of a woman in a crown. There is also a portrait of the church founder, Ioannis Moutoullas, with his wife Irene.

Remains of a wall painting in Panagia tou Moutoulla

❻ Pedoulas

Road Map B3. 190.

This sizeable village is located in the upper part of the Marathassa valley. The Setrakhos River that drains it flows down towards Morfou Bay. Pedoulas is famed for its surrounding orchards, gentle climate, bracing air and bottled spring water, which you can buy in most shops in Cyprus. The most beautiful

season here is spring, when the houses are completely enveloped by a sea of flowering cherry trees.

The most significant site in the village is the **Church of the Archangel Michael** (Archangelos Michail), dating from 1474. It is one of ten mountain churches listed as UNESCO World Cultural Heritage Sites, due to its magnificent interior wall paintings.

The paintings are unusually realistic. The north side of the tiny reading room is decorated with a painting of the Archangel Michael.

The renovated paintings are notable for their realistic images, including the *Sacrifice of Abraham*, the *Baptism in the Jordan River*, the *Kiss of Judas* and the *Betrayal of Christ in the Garden of Gethsemane*. The apse, usually decorated with an image of Christ Pantocrator, includes the Praying Mary *(Virgin Orans)* and the *Ascension*. Seen above the north entrance is the figure of the founder, Basil Chamados, handing a model of the church to the Archangel Michael.

Environs

The neighbouring village of Prodromos, which numbers only 150 inhabitants, is perched on top of a mountain range at an elevation of 1,400 m (4,593 ft). It is the highest village in Cyprus, and also, thanks to its decent accommodation facilities, a good base for starting to explore the Marathassa valley.

❸ Kykkos

This is the largest, most imposing and wealthiest of all the monasteries in Cyprus. Built in the middle of magnificent mountains and forests, away from human habitation, its most precious treasure is the icon of the Most Merciful Virgin, claimed to have been painted by St Luke and credited with the power to bring rain. The holy image is kept in the monastery museum.

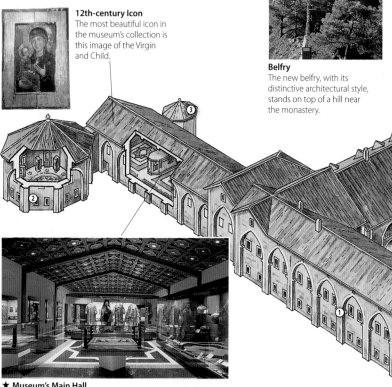

12th-century Icon
The most beautiful icon in the museum's collection is this image of the Virgin and Child.

Belfry
The new belfry, with its distinctive architectural style, stands on top of a hill near the monastery.

★ Museum's Main Hall
The monastery museum contains some important treasures: gold and silver liturgical vessels, holy books, and embroidered vestments, as well as beautiful and precious icons.

KEY

① **The main wing** of the monastery is home to the monks' cells.

② **The rotunda** has a darkened room housing the museum's most precious exhibits – the ancient, beautiful icons.

③ **A collection of manuscripts, documents and books**

General View
The hills surrounding Kykkos afford memorable views over the small monastery church and belfry, flanked by one-storey buildings with red roof tiles.

Small Courtyard
The church courtyard leads to the monastery buildings that used to house the museum.

VISITORS' CHECKLIST

Practical Information
Road map B3. Monastery, church & museum: **Open** Jun–Oct: 10am–6pm daily; Nov–May: 10am–4pm daily. 🅿 🛒 🖂
Ⓦ kykkos-museum.cy.net

★ Royal Doors
Inside the church is a richly decorated iconostasis incorporating the Royal Doors.

Church Entrance
The *katholicon*, or monastery church, is entered via a doorway decorated with lovely mosaics.

Main Monastery Entrance
This small, but wonderfully decorated entance is covered in beautiful mosaics.

Main Courtyard
The cloisters running along the edge of the main courtyard are decorated with mosaics depicting the history of Kykkos Monastery.

❼ Mount Olympus (Chionistra)

Road Map B3. 45 km (28 miles) north of Limassol. 🚌 bus from Nicosia in the summer.

Chionistra, the traditional name of Olympus, means "the snowy one". The slopes of the 1,950-m (6,400-ft) mountain are covered with umbrella-shaped pine trees interspersed with cedars and junipers. The most beautiful season here is spring, when wildflowers are in bloom. In good weather the view from the top extends as far as the coast of Turkey.

In winter the mountain is covered with a layer of snow up to 3 m (nearly 10 ft) deep, making Mount Olympus popular with downhill skiers. The ski runs on the southern slopes of Sun Valley are short and easy, while the northern runs are much longer and considerably more difficult. There are also two cross-country trails. Equipment hire and lessons are available.

The nearest hotel and restaurant facilities are in Troodos and Pano Platres.

Ski Station
Open Jan–Mar. 🌐 cyprusski.com

Umbrella pines on the slopes of Mount Olympus

❽ Troodos

Road Map B3. 🚌 64 from Limassol. 📷 15. 🛈 25 421 316. **Open** 8:15am–3:45pm Mon–Fri (2nd week of month: to 3pm Mon–Fri, 9am–2pm Sat). 📷

This small resort offers a few restaurants, souvenir shops and tourist car parks. In the summer there are horse and donkey rides, while hikers have a

The iconostasis in Trooditissa church with the miraculous icon of Mary

choice of several trails. The **Troodos National Park Museum** has a collection of local natural specimens. There is also a walk along a 300-m- (984-ft-) long botanical-geological path and a short film about the natural environment of Troodos.

Hidden in the forest a few kilometres south is the former residence of the British governor of Cyprus, now the summer villa of the president of the Republic of Cyprus. The overseer who helped to build it in 1880 was Arthur Rimbaud, the famous French poet.

❾ Trooditissa

Road Map B3. 8 km (5 miles) west of Pano Platres. **Closed** to the public.

This monastery is surrounded by pine forests on the southern slopes of the Troodos mountains, a few kilometres west of Platres. It was founded in 1250 on the site of an old sanctuary. During the Iconoclastic Wars of the 8th century, a monk brought here an icon of the Virgin Mary which, according to tradition, was painted by St Luke. The icon remained hidden in a cave until 990, when it was discovered, thanks to the miraculous light emanating from it.

The present **monastery church** dates from 1731. Its carved wooden

iconostasis is covered with gold leaf. The miracle-working icon – the magnificent image of the Panagia, Queen of Heaven, is to the left of the Royal Doors, covered with a curtain of silver and gold.

The monastery, whose austere regime is similar to that of Stavrovouni (see p80), is home to a dozen or so monks.

Environs
The nearby village of **Fini** (Foini) is renowned for its traditional handicrafts, now limited to pottery studios and a workshop producing distinctive Cypriot chairs.

The private **Pilavakion Museum**, run by Theofanis Pilavakis, displays vast ceramic jugs for storing olive oil. Adjacent to Iliovasilema bar is a small shop producing the local delicacy – *loukoumi* (Cyprus delight) said to be the best in Southern Cyprus.

Between Fini and the monastery, on a small stream running through a deep ravine where British soldiers practice climbing skills, is the picturesque **Chantara waterfall**.

Panoramic view of Fini, known for handicrafts

⑩ Platres

Road Map B3. 37 km (23 miles) NW of Limassol. 🏔 350. 🚌 62 from Limassol. 🏛 25 421 316.

The most famous mountain resort in Cyprus, Platres lies on a steep bank above the Kyros stream. The location and surrounding forests give it an excellent climate, making it a favourite holiday spot for Limassol and Nicosia residents.

Several colonial-style villas serve as reminders of British rule, and the few hotels and restaurants have all been designed in the same style. The town centre consists of a single street with a post office and a square next to the tourist information office, from where buses depart for Limassol *(see p203)*.

Platres is the starting point for several walking trails, including "Caledonia" that runs from the Psilodendro restaurant, past the Caledonia waterfall and ending at the former residence of the British governor; and "Pouziaris", which leads to a mountain of the same name.

⑪ Omodos

Road Map B4. 8 km (5 miles) from Pano Platres. 🏔 300. 🚌 40 from Limassol.

Scattered over the southern slopes of the Troodos mountains are the Krassochoria vine-growing villages, of which Omodos is the capital. Established in the 11th century, the settlement is famous for its

Courtyard of the Timiou Stavrou Monastery, in Omodos

production of wine, as well as for specialized *papilla* lace making.

Timiou Stavrou Monastery (Monastery of the Holy Cross) stands in the centre of the village. Built around 1150, it acquired its present shape in the 19th century. Timber-roofed monastic buildings surround the three-hall basilica, which contains a carved wooden iconostasis dating from 1813. According to legend, St Helena (mother of Emperor Constantine) left here a piece of the rope with which Christ was tied to the cross. The venerated relic is kept in a vast silver cross-shaped reliquary. Another holy relic St Philip's skull, kept in a silver casket.

There are no more monks in the village. The shops and stalls sell local *papilla* lace, silver

Famous Omodos *papilla* lace

jewellery, wine, honey and the ring-shaped *arkatena* bread typical of this village.

Environs

Vasa, a few kilometres west of Omodos, is a pleasant village. The Knights Hospitaller of St John, from the Kolossi commandery, were drawn to the village to escape the unbearable summer heat. The knights stayed in the monastery, which once stood here. Its 14th-century church, **Agios Georgios**, survives to this day together with its interesting frescoes. The small church museum in Vasa has religious icons and liturgical objects rescued from various abandoned churches.

Vasa has pretty white houses with red-tiled roofs and a spring flowing with pure mineral water. The village and the surrounding area offer several good restaurants, where you can get simple Cypriot dishes.

The Cypriot poet Dimitris Lipertis (1866–1937) has associations with Vasa. The house in which he lived has been made into a small museum.

The nearby archaeological site has yielded several Roman tombs, and the artifacts found in them – including amphorae and jewellery – can be viewed in Nicosia at the Cyprus Museum.

🏛 **Timiou Stavrou Monastery**
Omodos. **Open** sunrise to sunset daily.

Kingdom of Alashia

For more than 100 years scientists have been searching for the mysterious Kingdom of Alashia. According to texts preserved on clay tablets in el-Amama, its kings corresponded with the Egyptian pharaohs. Analysis of the texts has established that the copper-rich kingdom was situated at the foot of the Troodos mountains, close to present-day Alassa, where equipment for smelting and processing copper has been discovered.

Tablet from el-Amarna describing Alashia

The Donkey Sanctuary west of Vouni

⓬ Potamiou

Road Map B4. 3.5 km (2 miles) south
of Omodos.

This backwoods hamlet, reached via Omodos or Kissousa, is on an architectural par with the neighbouring village of Vouni. In summer its red-roofed stone houses vanish from view, swamped by creeping vines. The pride of the village is its small 16th-century church, Agia Marina, and the ruins of a Byzantine church standing near the Khapotami stream.

⓭ Vouni

Road Map B4. 4 km (2.5 miles) south
of Koilani.

In the mid-1990s this extraordinarily picturesque, partly deserted village was declared a legally protected historical site. Turned into an open-air

museum, its life now centres around a handful of *kafeneia* (local cafés) and restaurants.

One of the main attractions is the **Vouni Donkey Sanctuary**, to the west of the village, which is run by the charitable foundation "Friends of the Cyprus Donkey". Mary and Patrick Skinner founded the sanctuary in 1994 with just six donkeys; today they care for about 120 elderly, sick and abandoned animals. During the grape-harvest season, strong and healthy animals are hired out to the local farmers to help them collect the grapes. Children visiting the sanctuary can enjoy donkey rides. Membership of the "Friends of the Cyprus Donkey" society is open to all.

🖂 **Donkey Sanctuary**
Vouni. **Tel** 25 945 488. **Open** 8:30am–4:30pm Mon–Fri.
Ⓦ donkeysanctuarycyprus.org

⓮ Koilani

Road Map B4.

Another tiny mountain village built on lime soil, Koilani has excellent conditions for growing grapevines and fruit trees. The scenic location, surrounded by lush vineyards, makes up for its shortage of historic sites.

A small two-room **museum** set up behind the Neo-Byzantine church of Panagia Eloussa houses a collection of icons and other religious objects gathered from old churches in the area. For a period during the 17th century, the Limassol archbishopric was based in Koilani.

Close to the village in the valley of the Kyros stream, on the site of a former monastery, is the 12th-century domed **chapel of Agia Mavra**, which was subsequently extended. Its interior, including the domed vault, is decorated with rather unsophisticated wall paintings.

Men whiling away the afternoon in the centre of Koilani

⓯ Lofou

Road Map B4. 26 km (16 miles) northwest of Limassol.

This gorgeous village lies hidden amid the vineyards that cover the hillsides of the Commandaria region. The south-facing slopes and the abundance of water from the nearby Kourris and Kyros rivers produce local grapes that are large and sweet.

Lofou village spreads atop a limestone hill (*lofos* means hill). Its buildings represent the traditional stone-and-timber architecture typical of Cyprus mountain villages.

The Wines of Cyprus

"The sweetness of your love is like Cyprus wine", wrote Mark Antony, offering Cyprus to Cleopatra as a wedding present. To this day vintage brands, including the sweet Commandaria, are produced on the island and continue to enjoy a good reputation. Many of the best wines are produced in monasteries, based on old recipes. The majority of white wines are of the dry variety; the most widely known are Palomino, White Lady, Aphrodite and Arsinoe. Popular red wines are Othello and Semele. The wines drunk in the north include white and red Kantara varieties.

Wine barrels in Koilani

Towering above the village is the white silhouette of the **Church of the Annunciation**, with a tall, slender belfry. The present church was built in the late 19th century. Inside, among many beautiful icons, is a 16th-century image of the Mother of God.

References to Lofou appear in records dating from the Lusignan period, when it was called Loffu, but the village is probably much older, existing already in the Byzantine era.

Lofou can be reached from the north, via Pera Pedri village, or by a rough track (suitable only for four-wheel-drive vehicles) from Monagri, to the east.

Environs
The attractions of **Silikou** village, situated further north, include an olive press museum and some interesting examples of 14th-century frescoes in the Timios Stavros church.

⑯ Monagri

Road map B4. 21 km (13 miles) from Limassol.

Rising above the vine- covered hills and the Kouris valley are the walls of the **Archangelos monastery**. Built in the 10th century on the ruins of an ancient temple, the monastery was rebuilt in the mid-18th century after a tragic fire. The monastery church features a number of lovely wall paintings, some of them by Filaretos – the creator of the magnificent paintings adorning the cathedral church of John the Theologian (Agios Ioannis) in Nicosia. There are also reminders of Turkish times, when the new rulers converted the church into a mosque, including the geometric *mihrab* decorations, unique in

View of the hilltop Lofou village

Cyprus. The two Corinthian columns that support the portico date probably from the Roman era. The church has a carved, painted iconostasis.

Environs
A few kilometres downstream from Monagri, on the west bank of the river, is the 12th-century convent church of **Panagia tis Amasgou**, one of several Byzantine churches in the Kouris valley, near Limassol. It features beautiful but unrestored frescoes, created between the 12th and 16th centuries. These can be viewed, thanks to the generosity of the resident nuns.

The **Kouris dam**, down the river, is one of the largest structures of its kind in Cyprus; the reservoir collects rainwater used for domestic supplies and for irrigating fields and vineyards.

Situated along the main road leading from Limassol to the Troodos mountains is **Trimiklini** village. Hidden behind its church is a charming, tiny old stone chapel in a cemetery.

On the east side of the road, amid vineyards, lies another vine-growing village, **Laneia** (Lania). Its well-preserved and lovingly maintained old houses are set along narrow winding streets. Standing in the village centre is a white church with a tall belfry; next to it are two cafés. Laneia and its surrounding villages are home to local artists.

🏠 **Monastery of Archangelos**
Monagri. **Tel** 25 362 756.
Open by prior arrangement.

🏠 **Panagia tis Amasgou**
Tel as above. **Open** as above.

Neo-Classical school building in Lofou

⓱ Timios Stavros

Road Map B3. 8 km (5 miles)
west of Agros. **Open** vary.
Donations welcome.

The design of Timios Stavros
(Holy Cross) church is different
from that of other Cypriot
churches. Standing on the
lakeshore, at the southern end
of the village, this three-aisled
edifice was built on a square
plan and topped with a slender
dome on four columns.

Opposite the entrance are
the portraits of the church's
founders, as well as their coats-
of-arms, and the figure of the
apostle, Doubting Thomas.
The painting to the right depicts
the lineage of Jesus. The series
of 14 preserved paintings above
the pulpit illustrates the life of
Mary, including the *Nativity* and
the *Presentation of Jesus at the
Temple*, with figures dressed in
Lusignan period costumes.

The iconostasis includes a
silver reliquary containing
fragments of the True Cross, for
which the church is named.

⓲ Pelendri

Road Map B3. 8 km (5 miles) west of
Agros, 32 km (20 miles) from Limassol.
🚌 60, 66 from Limassol.

In the Middle Ages, this village
on the southern slopes of the
Troodos mountains was the seat

Fragment of a painting in Timios Stavros Church

of Jean de Lusignan, son of Hugo
V (the Franconian King of Cyprus).

At the centre of the village is
the **Panagia Katholiki Church**,
dating from the early 16th
century, which has Italian-
Byzantine-style paintings.

It is worth spending some
time visiting the nearby **Tsiakkas
Winery**, which produces local
wines using traditional methods.
The visit must be arranged in
advance (**Tel** 25 991 080).

⓳ Agios Nikolaos tis Stegis

Road Map B3. 3 km (2 miles) NW of
Kakopetria. **Open** 9am–4pm Tue–Sat,
11am–4pm Sun. Donations welcome.

This stone church, built
in the form of a cross,
supports a double roof,
giving it the name, St
Nicholas of the Roof. The
oldest section of the
building dates from the
11th century; the dome
and narthex were added
a hundred years later,
and in the 15th century
the entire structure was
covered with a huge
ridge roof. This outer
roof was designed to
protect the building
from snow, which falls
here occasionally.

The church once
served as the chapel of a
monastery, no longer in
existence. Inside, you can
see some of the oldest

wall paintings anywhere in the
Troodos mountain churches.
Painted over a period of about
500 years, between the 11th
and the 15th centuries, they
demonstrate the evolution
of Orthodox religious art,
making this church an excellent
place to study the development
of Byzantine wall painting.

Along with paintings
from the early Byzantine
period, known as "hieratic" or
"monastic" styles influenced
by the art of Syria and
Cappadocia, you can also
see typical Komnenos and
Paleologos art styles. During
the Komnenos dynasty
(1081–1180), the Byzantine
style, which had been rigid
and highly formalized up
to that point, began to
move towards realism and
emotional expression in the
figures and in their settings.

The artists who created the
wall paintings during the
Paleologos dynasty continued
to display similar attention to
the emotional and aesthetic
qualities of their art.

Paintings inside the church
illustrate scenes from the New
Testament. Among
the earliest paintings here
are the *Entry to Jerusalem*, and
the warrior saints George and
Theodore brandishing their
panoply of arms. The ceiling of
the main vault depicts the
Transfiguration of the Lord
on Mount Tabor and the
Raising of Lazarus from the

Interior of Timios Stavros Church

◀ Mountain village in Troodos at sunset

dead, conveying the startling impression the events made on the disciples of Jesus and the relatives of Lazarus.

The **Crucifixion** in the north transept shows the Sun and Moon personified weeping over the fate of the dying Jesus. A painting of the **Resurrection**, depicts the women coming to visit the grave and being informed of the Lord's resurrection by an angel at the empty tomb. The painting dates from the Lusignan period.

The **Nativity** in the south transept vault shows the Virgin Mary breast-feeding the Christ Child. Painted around it is an idyllic scene with pipe-playing shepherds and animals. Adjacent is a shocking 12th-century painting of the 40 **Martyrs of Sebaste** – Roman soldiers who adopted Christianity and were killed for it – being pushed by soldiers into the freezing waters of an Anatolian lake. In the dome vault is an image of **Christ Pantocrator**.

A picturesque narrow street in old Kakopetria

⑳ Kakopetria

Road Map B3. 80 km (50 miles) from Nicosia.

This old village in the Solea region, in the valley of the Kargotis River, displays interesting stone architecture. At an elevation of 600 m (1,968 ft), its climate is mild enough to allow the cultivation of grapes. Besides wine, Kakopetria was once renowned for its production of silk. Now it is a weekend retreat for Nicosia residents. The village derives its

Agios Nikolaos tis Stegis, featuring magnificent wall paintings

name "Accursed Rocks" from the rocks which, during an earthquake, once killed a great number of people.

The surrounding district has several intriguing churches and chapels, including the **Archangelos Church** which dates from 1514, covered with a ridge roof. It is decorated with paintings depicting the life of Jesus. The paintings in the **Agios Georgios church** are influenced by folk tradition.

㉑ Panagia tis Podithou

Road Map B3. Panagia tis Podithou: Galata. **Open** collect key from café on the village square. **Tel** 22 922 394. Donations welcome.

Dating from 1502, this church is also known as Panagia Elousa (Our Lady of Mercy). Originally, it was a monastery church dedicated to St Eleanor. Later, it belonged to the Venetian family of Coro. The wall paintings that decorate the church date from the Venetian period. Created by Simeon Axenti, their style betrays both Byzantine and Italian influences. They are an example of the strong influence that Western art exerted at that time on Cypriot decorative art. The poignant **Crucifixion** is particularly interesting, painted within a triangle and revealing Italian influences. Mary

Magdalene can be seen at the foot of the Cross, her hair loose, alongside a Roman soldier and the two crucified thieves. The **Communion of the Apostles** in the apse is flanked by the figures of two Kings: Solomon and David. The painting in the narthex depicts **Our Lady the Queen of Heaven**; painted below it is the image of the church's founder – Dimitrios Coro – with his wife.

It is worth spending some time visiting the early 16th-century church, **Agios Sozomenos**, with its cycle of folk-style wall paintings created in 1513, also by Simeon Axenti. Take a closer look at the painting depicting St George fighting the dragon, whose tail is entwined around the hind legs of the knight's horse, as well as the image of St Mamas riding a lion while carrying a lamb in his arms. The nearby church of **Agia Paraskevi** features the remains of some 1514 wall paintings, probably created by a disciple of Axenti.

The charming church of Panagia tis Podithou

Fresco in Panagia Forviotissa church

❷ Panagia Forviotissa (Panagia tis Asinou)

Road Map B3. 5 km (3 miles) SW of Nikitari village. **Tel** 99 830 329.
Open 9:30am–1pm, 2–4pm Mon–Sat, 10am–4pm Sun. Donations welcome.

Beyond the village of Nikitari, the road climbing towards the Troodos mountains leads through a dark forest and into a valley overgrown with pine trees. Here, on a wooded hillside, stands the small 12th-century church of Panagia Forviotissa, also known as Panagia tis Asinou. With its red tiled roof, this church dedicated to Our Lady of the Meadows is listed as a UNESCO World Cultural Heritage Site.

The church was founded in 1206 by Nikiforos Maistros, a high-ranking Byzantine official, portrayed on the paintings inside. At first glance the building, with its rough stone walls and simple ridge roof, does not resemble a church. However, this humble one-room structure hides a number of genuine treasures. There are frescoes dating from the 12th to the 16th centuries, which were restored in the 1960s and 1970s.

The wall and ceiling decorations are among the finest examples of Byzantine frescoes, starting with the *Christ Pantocrator* (Ruler of the World) on the vault of the narthex. There are also figures of the apostles, saints, prophets and martyrs. The following frescoes date from 1105: the *Baptism in the Jordan River*, the *Raising of Lazarus*, the *Last Supper*, the *Crucifixion* and the *Resurrection*.

They were painted by artists from Constantinople who represented the Komnenos style.

Altogether there are over 100 frescoes here, illustrating various religious themes. It is worth taking a closer look at the extraordinarily realistic painting covering the westernmost recess of the vault – the *Forty Martyrs of Sebaste*. Next to this are the *Pentecost* and the *Raising of Lazarus*.

The cycle of paintings in the nave illustrates the life of Jesus, from the Nativity to the Crucifixion and Resurrection. Seen in the apse is the *Communion of the Apostles*; Jesus offers the Eucharist to his disciples, with Judas standing aside.

The best paintings include the *Dormition of the Virgin*, above the west entrance, and the terrifying vision of the *Last Judgment*. Above the south entrance is a portrait of the founder, Nikiforos Maistros, presenting a model of the church to Christ.

The narthex offers further surprises. The moufflon and two hunting dogs on the arch of the door herald the arrival of the Renaissance; Byzantine iconography did not employ animals. Here, too, is another image of the church founders, praying to the Virgin and Child, with Christ Pantocrator surrounded by the Apostles. Between 1965 and 1976, the frescoes underwent a process of meticulous cleaning and restoration, under supervision by experts on Byzantine art from Harvard University.

Environs

The village of **Vyzakia**, some 6 km (4 miles) down the valley from Panagia Forviotissa, is worth visiting to see the small, wooden-roofed Byzantine **Church of the Archangel Michael** with its frescoes depicting the life and the martyrdom of Jesus. Dating from the early 16th century, these wall paintings reveal a strong Venetian influence.

The little 12th-century church of Panagia Forviotissa

❸ Panagia tou Araka

Road Map C3. Lagoudera. **Tel** 99 557 369. **Open** 9am–noon, 2–5pm daily. Donations welcome. 📷 Feast of the Birth of the Virgin (6–7 Sep).

The 12th-century church of Panagia tou Araka stands between the villages of Lagoudera and Saranti. Its interior is decorated with some of the island's most beautiful frescoes, painted in 1192 by Leon Authentou, who arrived from Constantinople and worked in

Panagia tou Araka Church, surrounded by mountains

Christ Pantocrator fresco in the
Church of Panagia tou Araka

the aristocratic Komnenos style.
This church contains some of
the most interesting examples of
pure Byzantine art in Cyprus.

The most magnificent of the
paintings depicts Christ
Pantocrator in a blue
robe, surrounded by
images of angels and
prophets. In the apse
are images of 12 early
Christian saints, inclu-
ding St Barnabas, the
patron saint of Cyprus.
Above them is the
Virgin Mary enthroned,
with the Child Jesus on
her knees, flanked by
the Archangels Gabriel and
Michael.

Relief from Panagia
tou Araka

Another interesting fresco is
the *Birth*, showing the Infant
Jesus being bathed, watched by
angels, shepherds, a flock of
sheep and a white donkey.

The small, richly carved and
gilded iconostasis contains only
four icons. On the right is a
larger-than-life painting of the
Madonna of the Passion
(*Panagia Arakiotissa*), to whom
the church is dedicated.

Environs
The mountain hamlet of **Spilia**
has a splendidly preserved oil
press housed in a stone building.
In the central square are
monuments commemorating
the EOKA combatants who
fought the British, blowing
themselves up in a nearby
hideout used to produce
bombs. Some 2 km (1.3 miles) to
the north of Spilia, in the village
of **Kourdali**, is a three-aisle
basilica, **Koimisis tis Panagias**,

which once belonged to a
former monastery. Inside, the
Italian-Byzantine wall paintings
depict figures dressed in
Venetian clothes. The Virgin,
fainting at the foot of the
cross, wears a dress with
exposed shoulders. Other
interesting paintings here
include: *Doubting Thomas*, the
Praying Virgin (Virgin Orans) and
the *Dormition of the Blessed Virgin*.
The best times to visit are 14–15
August, which are local feast days.

Another site worth visiting is
the diminutive **Church of
Timiou Stavrou** in Agia Eirini,
which contains more paintings
depicting the life and death of
Jesus. It also has a deisis – an
image of the Mother of God
and John the Baptist sitting on
both sides of Christ, who holds
in his hand the
prophecy
pronouncing him
the Messiah and
adjudicator on the Day
of the Last Judgment.
An attractive local walk
leads along the
Madhari ridge to the
top of **Mount Adhelfi**,
at 1,612 m (5,288 ft).
From here there is a
stunning panoramic view over
the Troodos mountain region.

㉔ Stavros tou Agiasmati

Road map C3. 6 km (3.7 miles) north
of Platanistasa. **Open** vary, collect key
from custodian in the coffee shop.
Donations welcome. 13 & 14 Sep.

A rough road leads to this small
church, in an isolated setting on
the mountainside of Madhari.
Originally built as the chapel for
an older monastery, its low

main door was designed to
prevent Arab and Turkish
invaders from entering on
horseback, a common way
of desecrating churches.

Inside Stavros tou Agiasmati
is the island's most complete
cycle of paintings illustrating
the Gospel. Some parts refer
to the Old Testament. Another
cycle of paintings illustrates
the story of the Holy Cross.
Together they form a fine
assemblage of 15th-
century frescoes.

The church's interior is
divided into two horizontal
zones of paintings: the lower
zone displays life-size figures
of the saints while the upper
zone has 24 scenes from the
New Testament.

Behind the iconostasis, the
apse features a magnificent
image of the Virgin uniting
Heaven and Earth. Some of the
paintings depict scenes not
known anywhere else, like the
fresco of the *Last Supper* in
which only Christ is present; or
the *Raising of Lazarus* in which a
group of Jews is clearly
offended by the smell of the
resurrected Lazarus. The fresco
of *Peter's Denial* includes a
shockingly large image of a
rooster. One of the niches in the
north wall features a series of
ten paintings that illustrate the
discovery of the Holy Cross by
St Helena, the mother of the
Emperor Constantine. The
frescoes are partly the work of
Philip Goul, a Lebanese artist
who is characterized by his
spare yet profound style.

Standing in the north wall
niche is a magnificently
decorated cross, which gives
Stavros tou Agiasmati (church
of the Holy Cross) its name.

Stavros tou Agiasmati church, in its remote mountainside location

CENTRAL CYPRUS

With the exception of the divided city of Nicosia, the heartland of Cyprus remains surprisingly unexplored by visitors. The plains are covered with colourful carpets of cultivated fields, crisscrossed by roads that link the small villages. They descend radially towards Nicosia *(see pp116–35)*, whose suburbs sprawl across the Pentadaktylos range. The eastern part of the Troodos mountains – the Pitsillia area is incorporated in this region.

The vast plain on Mesaoria (meaning "the land between mountains") is a gently undulating area dotted with small towns and old-fashioned villages. The watchtowers and fences occasionally seen from the road are reminders of the "Green Line" – the buffer zone border. The defunct airport to the west of Nicosia once provided international service.

Central Cyprus is the island's least developed region, from a tourist's point of view. It is almost devoid of hotels and restaurants, although here and there you can find a small agrotourism farm or a *kafeneion* – a local café. Tourists usually visit this region on their way to the beautiful Troodos mountains, or to the bustling seaside resorts in the south.

The most interesting historical sites of central Cyprus are the ruins of ancient Tamassos and Idalion. Tamassos, which was established around 4,000 BC, grew rich thanks to the copper ore deposits discovered nearby. Today, items made of this metal are among the most popular souvenirs from this region.

Also of interest are the Convent of Agios Irakleidios, the unusual subterranean Church of Panagia Chrysospiliotissa and Machairas Monastery on the northeastern slopes of the Troodos mountains, in the Pitsillia area. Nearby are the mountain villages of Fikardou, Lazanias and Gourri, and further south the town of Agros, which is famous for its roses.

Roadside vineyard in central Cyprus

◀ Panagia Tou Machaira monastery and church, Troodos

Exploring Central Cyprus

Central Cyprus, stretching south of Nicosia and covering the Pitsillia area of the eastern Troodos mountains, has limited facilities for visitors. Nevertheless, when travelling to the Troodos mountains or Nicosia it is worth exploring this region, especially the ruins of ancient Tamassos, the centre of the copper-producing area since the Bronze Age. Peristerona, home to one of the most beautiful Byzantine churches in Cyprus, as well as a fine mosque, is well worth a visit. Life proceeds slowly in the picturesque villages, with their bougainvillea-clad houses.

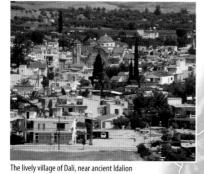

The lively village of Dali, near ancient Idalion

0 kilometres 5
0 miles 5

Getting There

Central Cyprus is easily accessible. From Larnaka airport the A2 motorway runs inland towards Nicosia. From the main port in Limassol, a motorway follows the coastline and branches off as the A1 road towards Nicosia. The route from Pafos airport leads through the mountains. The road is good, and you can combine the journey with a tour of the Troodos mountains.

Kyrenia

Famagusta

ammari

Agios Dometios

B10

Engomi

B9

NICOSIA
(Lefkosia)

B17

Strovolos

Aglandjia

**ARCHANGELOS
MICHAEL** ❷

A9

B9

Kato Lakatameia

*Athalassa
Forest*

Pano
Lakatameia

Latsia

Geri

**PANAGIA
CHRYSOSPILIOTISSA** ❸

A1

B1

Kato Deftera

LEFKOSÍA

Tseri

Agios
Sozomenos

Ergates

Psimolofou

Episkopeio

Pera

TAMASSOS ❺

Politiko

❹

Dali

❽ **POTAMIA**

❼ **IDALION**

**AGIOS IRAKLEIDIOS
MONASTERY**

PERACHORIO ❻

Agia Varvara

B2

Lympia

A2

Kapedes

Gialias

Alampra

Larnaka

achairas Forest

Lythrodontas

B1

A1

*Prophitis
Elias Monastery*

↓ *Limassol*

Peristerona Mosque, one of
the oldest and finest
mosques in Cyprus

Sights at a Glance

❶ Peristerona
❷ Archangelos Michael
❸ Panagia Chrysospiliotissa
❹ Agios Irakleidios Monastery
❺ Tamassos
❻ Perachorio
❼ Idalion
❽ Potamia
❾ Machairas
❿ Palaichori
⓫ Agros
⓬ Louvaras

Key

══ Motorway
▬▬ Major road
— Secondary road
┄┄ Minor road
— Scenic route
– – Track
▬▬ Regional border
■ ■ Green Line

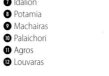

The gleaming Royal Doors in
Archangelos Michael church

For additional map symbols *see back flap*

❶ Peristerona

Road Map C3. 27 km (17 miles) west of Nicosia, along the road to Troodos.

Peristerona is the centre of Cyprus' watermelon-growing district. The village straddles a river that is usually dry, and features the beautiful five-domed **Church of St Barnabas and St Hilarion**, whose tall slender belfry is topped with a cross. This is a prime example of early 10th-century Byzantine architecture. The domes, resting on tall tambours with conical tips, are arranged in the shape of a cross. (A similar five-domed structure, the Agia Paraskevi Church, can be seen near Pafos, in the village of Geroskipou, *see p50*.) The proprietor of the neighbouring café holds the key to the church; it is worth gaining entry.

The narthex, which houses a vast chest depicting the siege of a castle, provides a view of the nave, which is separated by arches from the side aisles. The remains of the 16th-century wall paintings illustrate the life of King David, and there is also a vast reading room. The gilded iconostasis, beautifully carved in wood, dates from 1549.

The nearby **mosque**, one of the oldest and most magnificent anywhere on the island, was built on a square floor plan. Its tall, arched tracery-laden windows indicate that this was once a Gothic church. Now the mosque stands empty, with pigeons nesting inside. The proximity of the church belfry and the mosque's minaret are reminders of a time when both communities – Greeks and

Fresco from the Archangelos Michael church

Turks – coexisted peacefully here in the village. Today, Peristerona is inhabited only by Greek Cypriots, while their Turkish Cypriot neighbours have moved north, beyond the demarcation line several kilometres away.

Environs

The Mesaoria plain lies between the Pentadaktylos mountain range to the north and the Troodos massif to the south. The village of Orounta, a few kilometres south of Peristerona, is home to the **Church of Agios Nikolaos**, part of the long deserted monastery here. Similar to other villages scattered on the north slopes of the Troodos mountains, such as Agia Marina, Xyliatos and Vyzakia, this area is home to small mountain churches, as well as numerous taverns and *kafenia* (cafés) where you can savour an original *meze* or relax over a cup of Cyprus coffee.

❷ Archangelos Michael

Road Map C3. On the outskirts of south Nicosia.

The Byzantine church of the Archangel Michael on the bank of the Pediaios River was built by Archbishop Nikiforos, whose tomb can be seen in the northern section of the building. It was rebuilt in 1636 and again in 1713, when it was bought by Kykkos Monastery. The austere edifice, constructed from a yellowish stone with small windows and a simple portico, is covered with a shallow white dome resting on a tall tambour.

The church interior has a lovely wooden iconostasis and frescoes depicting, among others, the Archangel Michael. The frescoes are more lively than some of their rivals. Their colours were brightened by restoration in 1980 and include a range of Gospel and Old Testament scenes.

Environs

To the north is a complex of playing fields and a market site; next to these is the church of Panagia Makedonitissa. Nearby is a military cemetery. On the opposite side of the river, at the end of Athalassa Avenue is Athalassa forest, the largest wooded area in the vicinity of Nicosia. It features pine, cedar and eucalyptus trees. There is also a reservoir where permit holders are allowed to fish. All this makes it a pleasant place during high summer.

❸ Panagia Chrysospiliotissa

Road Map C3. 12 km (8 miles) southwest of Nicosia.

This rarely visited subterranean church, situated near the village of Kato Deftera, is dedicated to Our Lady of the Golden Grotto. Originally a series of ancient catacombs, these were converted

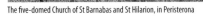

The five-domed Church of St Barnabas and St Hilarion, in Peristerona

into a church in the early Christian era. The interior of Panagia Chrysospiliotissa was once covered with beautiful frescoes, which are now severely damaged.

An apse, nave, narthex and a series of vestries are carved in the sandstone. This underground church is considered one of the earliest examples of a Levantine-style Christian monastery. This type of monastery, although rare in Cyprus, was common in the region that covers present-day Israel, Jordan, Lebanon and parts of Syria. On 15 August every year, a festival is held here to celebrate the monastery's name day.

Agios Irakleidios Monastery buildings

Inside the subterranean Panagia Chrysospiliotissa

❹ Agios Irakleidios Monastery

Road Map C3. 20 km (12 miles) SW of Nicosia. **Tel** 22 623 950. **Open** daily, hours vary (call to check).

St Heracleidius (Agios Irakleidios) Monastery stands close to the ruins of Tamassos. In the mid-1st century, in the course of their activities as missionaries on the island of Cyprus, the apostles Barnabas and Paul appointed a local man, Heracleidius, as the first Bishop of Tamassos. Bishop Heracleidius became famous for his many miracles; he was also a well-known exorcist. At the age of 60 he was killed by pagans and buried at this spot, where a small early Christian church and monastery were built. The monastery church, built in the 5th century, was repeatedly destroyed; the present building was erected in 1759.

Inside is a fresco depicting the baptism of Heracleidius administered by the apostles Paul and Barnabas, as well as beautiful geometric Byzantine mosaics and a monogram of Jesus. Relics of St Heracleidius – including his skull and forearm – are kept in a special silver reliquary.

From the side chapel to the south, a stairway descends to the catacombs, where Heracleidius spent his final years, and where he was buried.

The present buildings date from the late 18th century. The wall paintings of the period depict scenes from the life of St Heracleidius. At that time the monastery was famous for its icons, which were painted here. Now it is inhabited by a superfluity of nuns, who breed canaries and make delicious rose-petal jam and sugar-coated almonds.

❺ Tamassos

Road Map C3. 8 km (11 miles) SW of Nicosia. **Excavation site: Tel** 22 622 619. **Open** by appointment (**Tel** 99 218 525) Mon–Fri.

Near the village of Politiko, along the route leading to Machairas Monastery, archaeologists have unearthed the remains of the ancient town of Tamassos, founded by Trakofryges of Asia Minor c.4,000 BC. Around 2,500 BC, rich copper deposits were discovered here, which led to the town's growth and prosperity. Temesa (an alternative name for Tamassos) is mentioned in Homer's *Odyssey*; an excerpt describes Athena's journey to Temesa in order to trade iron for copper.

Later, in about 800 BC, the town was taken over by the Phoenicians. Their King, Atmese of Tamassos, along with other Cypriot Kings, paid tribute to the Assyrian rulers.

Alexander the Great gave the local copper mines as a present to King Protagoras of Salamis, in gratitude for his help during the siege of Tyre. In 12 AD, the Judaean King Herod the Great leased the local copper mines; many Jews arrived on the island to supervise the excavation of this valuable commodity. Archaeological works started in 1890 and continue to this day. The major discoveries are the subterranean royal tombs dating from 650–600 BC, which have long since been looted. Two of them survive in perfect condition. Other discoveries include a citadel, the site of copper processing and the Temple of Aphrodite (or Astarte). Many items discovered here are now in London's British Museum and Nicosia's Cyprus Museum.

Mosaic fragment from Tamassos

❻ Perachorio

Road Map C3. 17 km (10.5 miles) south of Nicosia.

The small village of Perachorio is the setting of the hilltop **Church of the Holy Apostles** (Agioi Apostoloi). This domed, single-aisle building has several side chapels.

The church, in a scenic setting, conceals fragments of beautiful 12th-century frescoes, in a style similar to those in the Panagia tis Asinou Church (see p104). Experts regard these as the best examples of the Komnenos style anywhere on the island. The most interesting are the images of angels in the dome, below the damaged painting depicting Christ Pantocrator. Another interesting painting shows two shepherds conversing casually, their shoulder bags hanging from a tree, while the infant Jesus is bathed. The apse features a picture of the Virgin, flanked by St Peter and St Paul. Also depicted are saints, martyrs, emperors and demons.

Nearby is the 16th-century church of Agios Dimitrios.

Church in Perachorio with lovely 12th-century paintings

❼ Idalion

Road Map D3. 20 km (12 miles) south of Nicosia. 🎭 Adonis Festival (spring).

The ancient Idalion, whose remains can be seen in the present-day village of Dali, was one of the oldest city-states on the island. According to legend, it was founded by King Chalcanor, a Trojan War hero.

The town is built on top of two hills; only a small portion of its ruins has so far been unearthed, including tombs along the road

A stone church in the Potamia area

to Larnaka. Idalion existed from the Bronze Age up to about 1,400 BC. The town had 14 temples, including those dedicated to Aphrodite, Apollo and Athena. Archaeological excavations are still under way. The best artifacts can be seen in the Cyprus Museum in Nicosia.

The remains of Idalion had already sparked interest in the 19th century. The American consul, Luigi Palma di Cesnola, plundered thousands of tombs in this area, robbing them of all their valuable items. Local farmers also found large numbers of votive figurines of Aphrodite while working in the fields, which indicates that this was a major site of the cult of Aphrodite, the most important Cypriot goddess.

Legend tells of Aphrodite's love for Adonis, son of Zeus and Hera. Ares, the jealous god of war, turned himself into a wild boar and killed Adonis in a nearby forest. Each spring, millions of red poppies and anemones cover the area, said to spring from his blood.

Ruins of the ancient city-state of Idalion, near present-day Dali

❾ Potamia

Road Map D3.

Situated close to the Green Line, the little village of Potamia is one of the few places in the south with a small Turkish community. The village has a history of coexistence and today elects both a Greek- and a Turkish-Cypriot mayor.

Not far from the village are the ruins of the Lusignan Kings' summer palace, and several Gothic churches.

Environs

The surrounding area is not of great interest, due to the many factories and industrial estates built in the immediate vicinity of Nicosia. To the southwest of the derelict village of **Agios Sozomenos** are the ruins of **Agios Mamas church**, built in the Franco-Byzantine style. This is one of the best Gothic historic sites on the island. Construction began in the early 15th century, in the Gothic style which was prevalent on the island at that time. However, it was never completed. Today visitors can see the walls of the three-apsed aisles, separated by intricate arcades, and the monumental portico.

The village of Agios Sozomenos was abandoned early in 1964, when Greek Cypriot police attacked the village inhabited by Turkish Cypriots in retaliation for the killing of two Greeks. Both sides suffered severe losses. The stone wall surrounding the village is a reminder of these events.

Cypriot Church Frescoes

The shady, forested valleys of the Troodos mountains hide small Byzantine churches; ten of these have been named UNESCO World Cultural Heritage Sites. Along with a few other churches and chapels throughout the island, they conceal frescoes representing some of the most magnificent masterpieces of Byzantine art. In keeping with Orthodox canons, the interior is divided according to theological order. The dome symbolizes Heaven, presided over by Christ Pantocrator, the Ruler of the World, usually surrounded by archangels and prophets. Below are the main scenes from the New Testament, including the saints and fathers of the Church. The apse behind the altar features an image of the Virgin with Child. The portico usually contains the Last Judgment, painted above the exit.

Christ Pantocrator
Often painted within the dome, the Omnipotent King of the World looks down from heaven. His right hand is raised in a gesture of benediction; his left hand holds a book as a symbol of the Law.

The Life of Jesus and Mary
The life of the Holy Family has been depicted in many frescoes, as illustrations of the New Testament.

Agios Mamas
Mamas is one of the most celebrated and popular of all Cypriot saints. His name has been given to many churches throughout the island.

The Praying Virgin (Virgin Orans)
Mary raises her hand towards heaven in a pleading gesture. Her eyes are turned towards the people, urging them to trust in Christ.

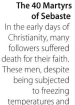

The 40 Martyrs of Sebaste
In the early days of Christianity, many followers suffered death for their faith. These men, despite being subjected to freezing temperatures and then fire, held to their faith and were martyred.

The Way of the Cross
The images of the way of the cross and the Lord's Passion are among the most dramatic subjects for fresco painters.

9 Machairas Monastery

Road Map C3. Near Deftera, 41 km (25 miles) SW of Nicosia. **Tel** 22 359 334 **Open** 8:30am–5:30pm daily (groups only 9am–noon Mon, Tue & Thu).

On the northern slopes of the Troodos mountains, in the area known as Pitsillia, stands one of Cyprus's most famous monasteries – Machairas (Panagia tou Machaira). The monastery rises like a fortress from the mountainside of Kionia, almost 800 m (2,625 ft) above sea level. Its name originates from the word *mahera*, which means "knife" and probably derives from the knife found next to an icon hidden in a cave. The locals believe that the icon, brought here by a monk from Constantinople, was painted by the Apostle Luke. Two hermits from Palestine found the icon in a cave, and then built a church dedicated to the Virgin Mary in 1148. In 1187, Emperor Manuel Komnenos provided the funds to build a bigger church; he also exempted it from the jurisdiction of the local bishop.

The monastery buildings in their present form date from the early 20th century. The beautiful church, surrounded by cloisters, houses the icon attributed to St Luke, which depicts the Holy Virgin pierced with a sword. It also contains numerous other beautiful and well-preserved icons and cult objects. The Gospel, printed in Venice in 1588, is held in the treasury. The monks are extremely pious; their vows are as severe as those taken by the brothers from Mount Athos in Greece.

For Cypriots, this place is associated with EOKA commander, Grigorios Afxentiou, who hid here disguised as a monk. British soldiers ambushed him in a nearby bunker. His comrades surrendered, but Afxentiou chose to fight and resisted the attacks of 60 British soldiers for several hours. Only flame-throwers could put an end to this heroic battle. On the spot where Afxentiou fell now stands a larger-than-life statue depicting the hero.

Environs
Beyond the village of Lythrodontas, where the paved road ends, is a small monastery dedicated to the Prophet Elijah (Prophitis Elias), hidden in the Machairas Forest.

10 Palaichori

Road Map C3.

The village of Palaichori lies in a deep valley, near the source of the Peristerona river. The village and the surrounding area feature several churches and chapels, but the most interesting of these is the **Metamorfosis tou Sotiros**

View of Palaichori village

chapel. Erected in the early 16th century, this small church is decorated with frescoes. On the south wall is the scene that gives the chapel its name. It shows a luminous figure of Christ, with prophets and disciples, atop Tabor Mountain at the time of the Transfiguration.

Lions are the predominant motif of the remaining paintings: in the den with Daniel, preparing to bury the body of St Mary the Beatified of Egypt and finally, St Mamas riding a particularly elongated predator.

Environs
The three picturesque villages of **Fikardou**, **Gourri** and **Lazanias** at the eastern end of the Pitsillia area form a legally protected conservation zone, due to their unique traditional architecture. The largest number of typical folk buildings have survived in Fikardou, which now looks more like an open-air museum than a village. The village has been declared a monument of national culture, being the best example of rural architecture from the past few centuries. It has narrow alleys paved with stone, and neat little timber houses, two-storeys high, with wooden

Courtyard of the Machairas Monastery

balconies. The old houses of Katsinioros and Achilleas Dimitri, which are some of the loveliest in the village, have been turned into a **Rural Museum** with a collection of tools and period furnishings. They include a loom, distillery equipment and an olive press.

🏛 **Rural Museum**
Fikardou. **Tel** 22 634 731.
Open 9am–5pm daily (Nov–Mar: 8am–4pm). 🅿

⑪ Agros

Road Map C3. 🚌 66 from Limassol.

Agros is a large village lying at an altitude about 1,000 m (3,280 ft) above sea level, in the picturesque Pitsillia area. The village is famous for its delicious cold meats, particularly its sausages and hams, as well as its fruit preserves and products made of rose petals. The locally cultivated Damask rose is said to have been brought here by the father of Chris Tsolakis, in 1948. Chris now owns a small factory of rose products, making rose water, liqueur, rose wine, rose-petal jam and rose-scented candles. Rose petals are harvested between late May and early June.

The charms of Agros and its environs are promoted enthusiastically by Lefkos Christodoulou who runs the largest local hotel – Rodon.

His efforts have resulted in the creation of numerous walking trails. The neighbourhood is home to several Byzantine churches decorated with frescoes. Agros itself has no historic sites. The old monastery, which stood here until 1894, was pulled down by the villagers in a dispute with the local bishop. Agros boasts an excellent climate, reputedly good for a long lifespan.

Interior of the chapel of St Mamas, Louvaras, with frescoes of Jesus' life

⑫ Louvaras

Road Map C4. 25 km (15.5 miles) north of Limassol.

Louvaras is a small village situated among the hills. The local attraction is the **Chapel of St Mamas**, decorated with exquisite late 15th-century frescoes depicting scenes from the life of Jesus. They include the

Detail of a colourful fresco from St Mamas Chapel

Teaching in the Temple, Meeting with the Samaritan Woman at the Well, and the Resurrection, in which the guards wear medieval suits of armour. The figures above the door, dressed in Lusignan clothes, are likely to represent the original donors.

St Mamas is one of the most popular Cypriot saints. He is portrayed on the north wall riding a lion while cradling a lamb in his arms. The scene is associated with an interesting legend. Mamas, a hermit, was ordered to pay taxes by the local governor. He refused to do so, claiming to live solely from alms. The governor lost patience and ordered Mamas to be thrown in jail. As the guards led Mamas away, a lion leapt from the bushes and attacked a lamb grazing peacefully nearby. The saint commanded the lion to stop, took the lamb into his arms and continued his journey on the back of the chastened lion. Seeing this miracle, the governor freed St Mamas, who became the patron saint of tax-evaders.

The village of Agros, scenically located among the hills

SOUTH NICOSIA

Near the centre of the island, Nicosia (Lefkosia in Greek) is Europe's only divided capital city. The numerous historic sites and traditional atmosphere of South Nicosia have been carefully preserved. The Old Town lies within an imposing defence wall erected by the Venetians in the 16th century. In the evenings, the narrow streets fill with strolling crowds of Cypriots and tourists alike who come to dine and socialize in the pedestrianized Laiki Geitonia district.

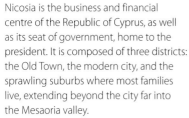

Nicosia is the business and financial centre of the Republic of Cyprus, as well as its seat of government, home to the president. It is composed of three districts: the Old Town, the modern city, and the sprawling suburbs where most families live, extending beyond the city far into the Mesaoria valley.

The charming Old Town, with its narrow, one-way streets, is surrounded by a Venetian wall stretching for 4.5 km (2.8 miles). The wall is punctuated by 11 bastions and three gates. The Porta Giuliana (Famagusta Gate) houses a Cultural Centre. Visitors heading for the border foot-crossing to Turkish-controlled North Nicosia (near the Ledra Palace Hotel) are greeted by the grim Pafos Gate,

near the demarcation line. Crossing the border is much easier these days thanks to the partial lifting of restrictions.

The Laiki Geitonia district, east of Eleftheria Square (Plateia Eleftherias), has narrow, winding alleys filled with restaurants, art galleries and boutiques set between traditional houses, typical of Cypriot urban architecture. Ledra Street is a prestigious pedestrian precinct with smart boutiques and garden restaurants. One of the crossings to North Cyprus is located here. At the heart of Nicosia stands the Archbishop's Palace.

South Nicosia has a range of museums to visit, including the wonderful Cyprus Museum.

Rooftop view of the tightly packed Nicosia area

◀ Laiki Geitonia in the old town area

Exploring South Nicosia

The majority of historical sites in Nicosia are found within the mighty town walls. The main attractions, not to be missed, are the Cyprus Museum, the Archbishop's Palace and St John's Cathedral. The latter contains pristine 18th-century frescoes on Biblical themes. The Cyprus Museum holds the island's largest collection of archaeological artifacts, gathered from many sites. The restored district of Laiki Geitonia makes a pleasant place to rest with its numerous cafés, as well as providing good shopping in the local stores. The Cyprus Tourism Organization also offers free tours of the capital *(see p125)*.

5th-century BC figurine from the Cyprus Museum

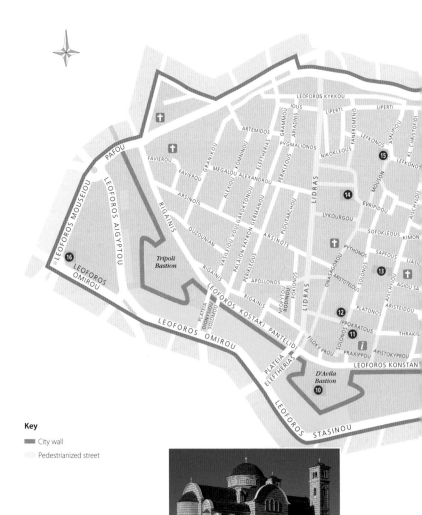

Key

■ City wall

▒ Pedestrianized street

Church along the border of South Nicosia

Getting There

You can reach South Nicosia via the A2 motorway from Larnaka International Airport, or the A1 motorway from Limassol Port. The town appears against the backdrop of the Pentadaktylos mountain range, situated on the Turkish side of the border. A good, wide road leads through the suburbs almost to the centre of Nicosia. You can cross the border to North Nicosia at the Ledra Palace Hotel and Ledra (Lidras) Street.

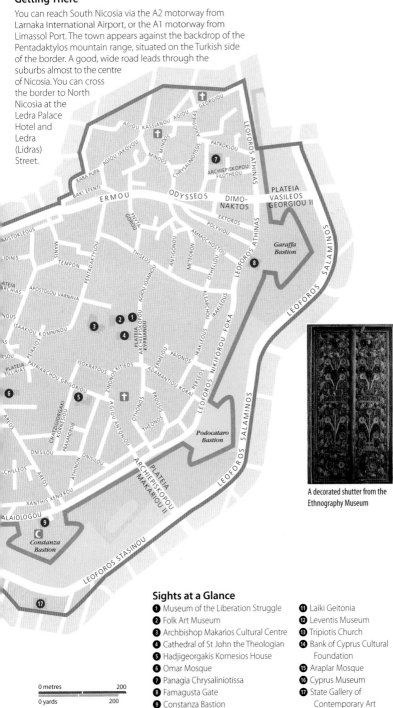

A decorated shutter from the Ethnography Museum

Sights at a Glance

1. Museum of the Liberation Struggle
2. Folk Art Museum
3. Archbishop Makarios Cultural Centre
4. Cathedral of St John the Theologian
5. Hadjigeorgakis Kornesios House
6. Omar Mosque
7. Panagia Chrysaliniotissa
8. Famagusta Gate
9. Constanza Bastion
10. Town Hall
11. Laiki Geitonia
12. Leventis Museum
13. Tripiotis Church
14. Bank of Cyprus Cultural Foundation
15. Araplar Mosque
16. Cyprus Museum
17. State Gallery of Contemporary Art

0 metres 200
0 yards 200

For additional map symbols see back flap

Street-by-Street: South Nicosia

South Nicosia is surrounded by Venetian defence walls and bastions, and has served as the capital since the 11th century. During the Lusignan era, this was a magnificent city, home of the Royal Palace and scores of churches. Today the area within the old walls is full of museums, sacred buildings and historical buildings, which help to recreate the atmosphere of bygone centuries. It is enjoyable to stroll along the streets of old Nicosia, stopping for coffee, or taking a shopping trip to the rebuilt district of Laiki Geitonia. The only drawback is the neglected zone of no man's land dividing the city.

❸ Archbishop Makarios Cultural Centre
The island's largest, most precious collection of magnificent icons and mosaics are housed here.

Richly decorated
19th-century houses are the pride of the southern part of the Old Town.

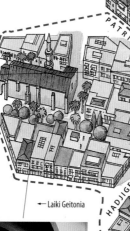

← Laiki Geitonia

PATRIARCHOU GRIGORIOU

ISOKRATOUS

ZINO

HADJIGEORGAKI KORNESIOU

ATHINON

AGIOU AN

The Archbishop's Palace was built in 1956-60 in Neo-Byzantine style.

❻ Omar Mosque
A former Augustinian church was converted into a mosque in 1571, following the capture of the city by Turks. It is the largest mosque in southern Cyprus.

❺ Hadjigeorgakis Kornesios House
This historic 18th-century building, a former home of the Turkish dragoman, was awarded the Europa Nostra Prize following its restoration. Now it houses a small Ethnological Museum.

❷ Folk Art Museum
The highlight here is the collection of 19th- and early 20th-century Cypriot folk art. The textiles, ceramics, wooden artifacts and folk costumes are housed in a former Bishop's Palace.

Locator Map
See pp118–19

❶ Museum of the Liberation Struggle
Here are documents, photographs and weapons associated with the struggle for independence from 1955 to 1959.

Liberty Monument
on the Podocataro Bastion symbolizes the liberation of the Cypriot nation.

❹ Cathedral of St John the Theologian
Erected by Archbishop Nikiforos, this small church contains beautiful 18th-century frescoes.

Key
— Suggested route

❶ Museum of the Liberation Struggle

Plateia Archiepiskopou Kyprianou.
Tel 22 305 878. **Open** 8am–2pm
Mon–Fri (3:30–5:30pm Thu). 🖼

Housed in a building just behind the Old Archbishop's Palace is the Museum of the Liberation Struggle. Its collection of photographs, documents, weapons and other objects chronicles the bloody struggle of the EOKA organization against the colonial British army from 1955 to 1959. The exhibits illustrate the guerrilla warfare tactics carried out by EOKA against the British and those Cypriots who objected to the armed struggle.

The collection also includes materials documenting British reprisals, including arrests, interrogations and torture. The museum is primarily intended for Cypriots and school groups.

Museum of the Liberation Struggle

The Folk Art Museum, housed in the old Archbishop's Palace

❷ Folk Art Museum

Plateia Archiepiskopou Kyprianou.
Tel 22 430 008. **Open** 8:30am–1pm
Mon–Sat (3–5:30pm Wed & Sat). 🖼

Behind the cathedral is the Old Archbishop's Palace, which now houses the Folk Art Museum. On display here is a diverse array of exhibits illustrating the culture of Cyprus. Outside, the main museum attractions are the wooden water wheel, olive presses and carriages. Inside are folk costumes dating from the 19th and 20th centuries, household furnishings and other domestic implements, ceramics, textiles, Lefkara laces and silver jewellery.

❸ Archbishop Makarios Cultural Centre

Plateia Archiepiskopou Kyprianou.
Byzantine Museum: **Tel** 22 430 008.
Open 9am–4:30pm Mon–Fri,
9am–1pm Sat. **Closed** Sat pm in Aug.
🖼 🌐 makariosfoundation.org.cy

This cultural centre, adjacent to the New Archbishop's Palace, houses several libraries, the School of Ecclesiastical Music and the Byzantine Museum, which was founded by Archbishop Makarios in 1982.

Also known as the Icon Museum, the Byzantine Museum contains the largest and most valuable collection of icons in Cyprus. Around 230 icons span the 8th to the 19th centuries. Through the exhibition you can follow the changing trends in the art of icon "writing", and see the idiosyncratic images of Jesus, the Virgin Mary, the saints and the apostles. The best exhibits include the 13th-century icon by the main door, portraying Prophet Elijah being fed by a raven, and the image of the Virgin holding the dead body of Christ – the equivalent of the Roman Catholic *Pieta*.

The reconstructed apse was rescued from the church of Agios Nikolaos tis Stegis in the Troodos mountains.

For several years the museum has displayed

Crown exhibit from the Byzantine Museum

6th-century Byzantine mosaics stolen during the 1970s from Panagia Kanakaria Church in Lythrangomi in the Turkish-occupied Karpasia peninsula. Following a lengthy court battle, the Cypriot government recovered the mosaics. They depicted various religious figures, including the Virgin Mary, the archangels Michael and Gabriel, and several apostles. The figure of Jesus, depicted in one of the mosaics clutching a scroll of parchment, has the appearance of a Hellenic god. All of the figures have unnaturally large eyes, a characteristic trait of early-Christian art.

In addition to mosaics and icons, the museum's collection includes ecclesiastical garments and books.

The New Archbishop's Palace was erected in 1956–60 in the Neo-Byzantine style to a design by Greek architect George Nomikos. Usually closed to visitors, it does open occasionally, when you can visit the bedroom of Archbishop Makarios, where his heart is kept. A giant statue of Makarios, the first president of the Republic of Cyprus, stands in front of the palace.

Located near the Makarios Cultural Centre, and housed in a former power plant, is the Municipal Arts Centre, a venue for major art exhibitions.

❹ Cathedral of St John the Theologian

Plateia Achiepiskopou Kyprianou. **Tel** 22 432 578. **Open** 8am–noon, 2–4pm Mon–Fri, 8am–noon Sat.

The small Cathedral of St John (Agios Ioannis) dates from 1662. Built of yellow stone and covered with a barrel vault, it stands on the ruins of a medieval Benedictine monastery. Its interior is decorated with magnificent paintings depicting Biblical scenes from the life of Jesus, from birth to crucifixion, including a striking Last Judgment above the entrance.

The four paintings on the right wall, next to the Archbishop's throne, show the discovery of the relics of the apostle Barnabas, founder of the Cypriot church. They also show the privileges granted by Byzantine Emperor Zeno to the Cypriot church, including *autokefalia* (independence from the Patriarch of Constantinople) and the right of the Archbishop to wear purple garments during ceremonies, to use the sceptre instead of the crosier, and to sign letters with red ink. The paintings tightly covering the walls and ceiling are by the 18th-century artist, Filaretos.

Among the furnishings are a fine carved and gilded iconostasis, and a pulpit with its double-headed eagle, a symbol of Byzantium.

To the right, by the door leading to the courtyard, stands a small marble bust of

A fragment of the decoration in the Hadjigeorgakis Kornesios House

Archbishop Kyprianos, who was hanged by the Turks in 1821 in retaliation for the outbreak of Greek national insurgence. Kyprianos founded the first secondary school in Cyprus. The Pancyprian Gymnasium, regarded as the most prestigious high school in the Greek part of the island, exists to this day. Its Neo-Greek building is on the opposite side of the street.

❺ Hadjigeorgakis Kornesios House

Ethnological Museum: Patriarchou Grigoriou 20. **Tel** 22 305 316. **Open** 8:30am–3:30pm Tue–Fri (to 5pm Wed), 9:30am–3:30pm Sat.

One of the town's most interesting buildings is the House of Hadjigeorgakis Kornesios, a well-preserved building from the late 18th century. Kornesios, a highly educated Greek Cypriot businessman and philanthropist, served from 1779 as a dragoman – a liaison between the Turkish government and the Greek Cypriot population. Despite serving the Turks for a

number of years, he was arrested and executed by them.

The opulent house is decorated with Anatolian-style columns and lattice-work. The bedroom and Turkish-style drawing room lined with carpets occupy the first floor. The ground floor contains servants' quarters and a *hammam* – Turkish bath. Part of the house holds a small ethnological exhibition.

Kornesios Patriarchou Grigoriou Street leads to the nearby Omar Mosque.

❻ Omar Mosque (Ömeriye Cami)

Trikoupi and Plateia Tylliria. **Open** daily, except during services. Donations welcome.

This mosque takes its name from Caliph Omar, who supposedly reached Nicosia in the course of the 7th-century Arab raids on Cyprus.

The site now occupied by this mosque was once home to a 14th-century church, which served the local Augustine monastery. The Church of St Mary drew pilgrims in great numbers from Cyprus and throughout Europe to visit the tomb of the Cypriot saint John de Montfort, a member of the Knights Templar.

The church was converted into a mosque after the town was captured by the Turks, led by Lala Mustapha Pasha, in the 16th century. On the floor of the mosque are Gothic tombstones, used by the Turks as building material.

The mosque is used by resident Muslims from Arab countries. It is open to visitors; please remove your shoes before entering. It is also possible to climb to the top of the minaret, from where there are lovely views of Nicosia.

Minaret of the Omar Mosque

The small, yellow-stone Cathedral of St John the Theologian

Chrysaliniotissa Church, renowned for its collection of icons

❼ Panagia Chrysaliniotissa

Chrysaliniotissas.

The Chrysaliniotissa church, the capital's oldest house of worship, is dedicated to Our Lady of the Golden Flax. It stands at the centre of the district bearing the same name, right on the Green Line. It was built in c.1450 by Helen, the Greek-born wife of the Frankish King John II. The church takes its name from a miraculous icon found in a field of flax.

This L-shape building, with two domes and a slender belfry, is famous for its collection of rare Byzantine icons.

Located nearby at Dimonaktos 2 is the small **Chrysaliniotissa Crafts Centre**. Various types of Cypriot art and handicrafts can be seen and purchased in this small crafts centre. Eight workshops, a café and a souvenir shop surround the central courtyard, which is modelled on a traditional inn.

Chrysaliniotissa church detail

Prior to the division of Nicosia the opposite side of Ermou Street, called Tahtakale Cami after the mosque that stood here, was home to many Turkish Cypriots. Based on the Nicosia Master Plan, the old houses are being renovated and new occupants are moving in. Thanks to the founding of the Municipal Cultural Centre in Famagusta Gate, the district is becoming more attractive.

❽ Famagusta Gate

Leoforos Athinon. **Tel** 22 430 877.
Open 10am–1pm, 4–7pm Mon–Fri, 4–7pm Sat & Sun.

One of three city gates, Famagusta Gate is situated in the Caraffa bastion of the Venetian defence walls. Low-built and comprising a log tunnel ending at a wooden gate, it resembles the Venetian gate from Iraklion, on Crete. The side facing town is decorated with six Venetian coats-of-arms.

The structure was thoroughly renovated in the 1980s. Now it houses the **Municipal Cultural Centre**. The main room is used for exhibitions, concerts and theatrical performances. The smaller side room is devoted to art exhibitions. Thanks to the Cultural Centre, this part of town has been transformed into a pleasant artists' district.

Environs
The medieval Venetian defence walls are the most distinctive

element of old Nicosia. They were erected during 1567–70 to a design by Italian architect Giulio Savorgnano. The present-day Famagusta Gate was originally called the Porta Giuliana, in honour of the architect.

The 5-km- (3-mile-) long Venetian walls contain 11 artillery bastions and three gates – the other two are called the Pafos and Kyrenia Gates, after the towns they face.

The defence walls fit in well with Nicosia's overall appearance. The bastions and the areas between them have been converted into car parks and market squares. The d'Avila bastion, near the Plateia Elefteria (Eleftheria Square), is the site of the town hall and the municipal library. The Podocataro bastion features the Liberty Monument, which depicts the goddess of Liberty clad in ancient robes, while two EOKA soldiers at her feet open prison bars from which a group of Cypriots emerges.

❾ Costanza Bastion

Leoforos Konstantinou Palaiologou.
🕌 Wed. Bayraktar Mosque closed to visitors.

One of the 11 bastions protruding from the Venetian walls encircling the old quarter of Nicosia, Costanza Bastion is the site of the Bayraktar mosque, which was erected to commemorate the Turkish soldier, who was killed as he scaled the defence wall during the siege of Nicosia. Every Wednesday, the area in front of the mosque turns into a colourful fruit and vegetable market.

Famagusta Gate, housing Nicosia's Municipal Cultural Centre

Entrance to the town hall building, resting on Ionian columns

⑩ Town Hall

Plateia Eleftheria (Eleftheria Square).

Built in the Classical Greek style, the single-storey town hall stands on the d'Avila bastion, next to the municipal library. An ornamental semicircular stairway leads to the portal, which rests on Ionian columns. **Plateia Eleftheria** (Eleftheria Square) opposite the town hall, has undergone a multi-million-euro renovation and is where Nicosians gather for public rallies.

Eleftheria Square is the starting point for the two main shopping streets of old Nicosia: **Onasagorou** and **Ledra**. Both are lined with dozens of shops selling shoes, clothes, textiles and souvenirs.

At the end of Ledra Street, whose name evokes the ancient town that once stood on the site of present-day Nicosia, is a checkpoint and crossing to North Nicosia, with a monument to those Greek Cypriots who disappeared during the Turkish invasion. There is a small museum here.

⑪ Laiki Geitonia

The pedestrianized Laiki Geitonia (Popular Neighbourhood) is a restored section of Old Nicosia near the brooding Venetian defence walls, the town hall and Ledra – South Nicosia's main shopping street. Clustered within a small area of narrow, winding alleys in prettily restored houses are numerous restaurants, shady cafés, handicraft workshops

and souvenir shops aimed primarily at tourists. Here you will also find tourist information offices, offering free maps and brochures.

The project to rebuild and restore the Laiki Geitonia district was honoured with the prestigious Golden Apple ("Pomme d'Or") Award, granted by the World Federation of Journalists and Travel Writers in 1988. The district has an inviting atmosphere, well suited to relaxing or a leisurely stroll.

Guided tours around South Nicosia start from outside the Cyprus Tourist Organization office located at 35 Odos Aristokyprou, in the Laiki Geitonia district. It is worth joining one of these tours, as they take visitors to many interesting sites that are normally closed to tourists.

⑫ Leventis Museum

Ippokratous 17, Laiki Geitonia. **Tel** 22 661 475. **Open** 10am–4:30pm Tue–Sun.

The fascinating Leventis Museum houses a collection devoted to the history of Nicosia, from ancient times to the 1970s.

Its creators have succeeded in putting together an intriguing exhibition showing the everyday life of Nicosia's residents. Visitors to the museum are particularly drawn to the exhibits relating to the times of the Franks and the Venetians, including medieval manuscripts and the opulent clothes of the city's rulers. Also of note are the documents and photographs dating from the colonial era.

The restored building which houses the museum was built in 1885 by a rich merchant for his daughter.

An exhibit from the Leventis Museum

Environs

The pedestrianized Ledra Street, which is full of shops, can be reached by walking from Plateia Eleftheria. The Cypriot military checkpoint here houses a small exhibition that is devoted to the island's northern territories, occupied by the Turks. Here, you can walk across the Green Line to the Turkish checkpoint and access North Nicosia.

Inside a souvenir shop in Laiki Geitonia

⓭ Tripiotis Church

Odos Solonos. **Open** 9am–5pm daily.

Dedicated to the Archangel Gabriel, Tripiotis Church is the loveliest of the surviving Gothic churches in south Nicosia. This three-aisle, square edifice topped with a small dome was built in 1695 by Archbishop Germanos. Designed in the Franco-Byzantine style, it has a rich and interesting interior with Gothic windows, while the exterior has a medieval stone relief depicting lions, mermaids and sea monsters. The pride of the church is its intricately carved iconostasis, which contains several old icons covered with silver revetments. The church takes its name from the district of Nicosia in which it stands. This was an area that was once inhabited by very wealthy families.

View of the three-aisled Tripiotis Church

⓮ Bank of Cyprus Cultural Foundation

Phaneromeni 86–90. **Tel** 22 677 134. **Open** 10am–7pm Mon–Sun. ⓦ boccf.org

One of Cyprus's most prominent private art collections, the George and Nefeli Giabra Pierides collection, is housed here. The Cultural Foundation is an institution that sponsors scientific research and conducts educational and cultural activities. The magnificent exhibits represent works from the early Bronze Age (2,500 BC) to the end of the Middle Ages, and are superbly displayed and illuminated in modern cabinets. The exhibits, numbering over 600 items, include ancient bronze and gold jewellery and Mycenaean amphorae and goblets. Also on display are terracotta figurines, anthropomorphic red-polished vases and realistic limestone

Jug, Bank of Cyprus Cultural Foundation

Hellenic statues depicting, among others, Apollo and Hercules. Glazed ceramics dating from the Middle Ages can also be seen.

Close to the Bank of Cyprus Cultural Foundation stands the **Agia Faneromeni church**, the largest church within the city walls, built in 1872 on the site of a former Greek Orthodox monastery. *Faneromeni* in Greek means "found through revelation". The church was built towards the end of Turkish rule on the island. Inside is a beautiful iconostas and a marble mausoleum containing the remains of the bishops and Greek priests who were murdered by the Turks in 1821.

Adjacent to the church is the imposing Neo-Classical building of the **Fanero-meni High School**.

⓯ Araplar Mosque

Odos Lefkonos.

Standing close to the Agia Faneromeni church, the Araplar Mosque was founded in the converted 16th-century Stavros tou Missirikou Church, which had been designed in the Gothic-Byzantine style.

Although the mosque is usually closed, it is sometimes possible to peek inside and see its imposing interior with the octagonal-drummed dome supported on columned arches.

⓰ Cyprus Museum

Leoforos Mouseiou 1. **Tel** 22 865 864. **Open** 8am–4pm Mon–Fri, 9am–4pm Sat, 10am–1pm Sun. 🅿

The island's largest and best archaeological museum occupies a late 19th-century Neo-Classical building. The 12 or so rooms house a range of exhibits illustrating the history of Cyprus, from the Neolithic Era (7,000 BC) to the end of Roman rule (395 AD).

The museum is arranged in chronological order. **Room 1** displays the oldest traces of mankind's presence on the island. There are objects from the mid-5th century BC, as well as objects from Khirokitia, stone bowls, primitive human and animal figures carved in andesite, limestone idols, and jewellery made of shells and cornelian (which would have been imported to Cyprus). There are also early ceramics, both without decoration and with simple geometric patterns, Bronze Age amulets and cross-shaped figurines carved in soft, grey steatite.

Room 2 contains clay bowls and vessels of sometimes bizarre shapes, decorated with figurines of animals. Here you will find a miniature model of a temple and a collection of ceramic vessels and figurines. **Room 3** houses a collection of ceramics up to

Roman times, including lovely Mycenaean vases and craters dating from the 15th century BC. Later, the ceramics became gradually more Greek in style. There is also a collection of several thousand terracotta figurines depicting smiling gods.

Room 4 holds a collection of terracotta votive figurines found in the Agis Eirini sanctuary near the Kormakitis peninsula, in the north of the island. The most interesting exhibits in the sculpture gallery, in **Room 5**, include the statue of Zeus, the God of Thunder, hurling a lightning-bolt. Also here is a stone head of Aphrodite, the famous marble statue of Aphrodite of Soloi dating from the 1st century AD (by this time under Turkish occupation), and an exquisite Sleeping Eros.

Room 6 features a larger-than-life bronze statue of the Emperor Septimius Severus (c.193-211), a masterpiece of Roman sculpture. The adjoining rooms contain a bronze statue of a Horned God from Enkomi at the eastern end of the island, as well as interesting collections of coins, jewellery, seals and other small artifacts. There are also sarcophagi, inscriptions, alabaster vases and the mosaic of Leda with the Swan found in Palea Pafos (**Room 7a**).

Further rooms contain reconstructed ancient tombs, as well as numerous items found during excavations in the Salamis area, including the marble statue of Apollo with a lyre. **Room 11** contains a reconstructed royal tomb from

Salamis with the famous bronze cauldron decorated with griffon and heads of sphinxes that was found inside. **Room 12** houses items found in the Royal Tombs, including a throne decorated with ivory and a silver-encrusted sword. Other interesting exhibits include a collection of silver and gold Byzantine vessels – part of the Lambousa Treasure.

The **Municipal Garden**, on the opposite side of the street, is a green oasis set in the town centre, providing welcome shade on hot days. It is the site of the **municipal theatre** built in 1967. With an auditorium for 1,200, it is used as a venue for drama performances, concerts, recitals and other cultural events. A short distance away, in Leoforos Nehrou, stands the **Cyprus Parliament** building.

Adjacent to the nearby Pafos Gate, right by the demarcation line that divides the city, stands the Roman Catholic **Church of the Holy Cross** and the **Apostolic Nunciature**. A short distance away, by the hotel, is a UN-controlled border crossing, linking the two parts of the town. The **Ledra Palace Hotel** is the headquarters of the UN Peacekeeping Forces in Cyprus.

Bronze statue of Septimius Severus, the Cyprus Museum

⑰ State Gallery of Contemporary Art

Corner of Gonia Leoforos Stasinou and Kritis. **Tel** 22 458 228. **Open** 10am–4:45pm Mon–Fri, 10am–12:45pm Sat.

This gallery occupies a splendid building situated beyond the wall, level with the Constanza Bastion. It displays a representative collection of the best works by Cypriot artists, dating from 1930–80.

When entering Nicosia from the south you will come across the **Cyprus Handicraft Centre**, situated in Athalassa Avenue, in a building adjacent to St Barnabas Church. Here you can see the production of traditional Cypriot handicrafts, including embroidery, lace, woodcarvings, ceramics, metalwork, mosaics, the making of leather and textile goods and traditional costumes. The centre was established in order to cultivate the tradition of artistic handicrafts in Cyprus, and give employment to refugees from the occupied territories. Visitors may watch artists at work and buy their products in the local shop.

Environs

In the suburban district of Strovolos, 2.5 km (1.5 miles) southwest of the Old Town, stands the **Presidential Palace**. It is located in an extensive park, with only its dome visible from the street. Built by the British, the palace was destroyed by fire during the riot of 1931. Rebuilt by the British Governor, Sir Ronald Storrs, it became his official residence. The first president of the independent Republic of Cyprus, Archbishop Makarios, had his office here and lived in the Archbishop's Palace in Old Nicosia.

Neo-Classical façade of the Cyprus Museum

NORTH CYPRUS

Inhabited and governed by the Turks, and isolated from the southern Greek side of the island for over 30 years, North Cyprus is probably the most beautiful region of the entire island. The sandy beaches along Famagusta Bay and the wild Karpasia (Karpas) peninsula attract thousands of tourists, although there are still far fewer here than in southern Cyprus. The heart of the region is North Nicosia, home to over one third of the population of North Cyprus.

Most hotels and facilities can be found on the northern side of the Pentadaktylos mountains, whose rugged peaks contrast with the azure of the sea. Kyrenia (Girne) has a charming yacht harbour, one of the most attractive in the Mediterranean, with a vast, old castle recalling the time the island was under Byzantine rule. Nearby, on the northern slopes of the Pentadaktylos range (Beşparmak), lies the most beautiful village in Cyprus – Bellapais, with the romantic ruins of a Gothic abbey. Nearby St Hilarion Castle is one of three fortresses in North Cyprus, alongside the castles of Buffavento and Kantara.

The western plains, in the vicinity of Morfou (Güzelyurt), are planted with citrus orchards. Wedged between the mountains and the blue sea are the archaeological excavation sites of Soli and ruins of the Persian Palace, located on top of Vouni Hill.

Numerous fascinating relics from the Lusignan, Venetian and Ottoman eras are enclosed by the Venetian walls of North Nicosia. Old Famagusta, full of Gothic remains, is equally interesting, with its Othello's Tower and several fascinating historic relics close by – including ancient Salamis (the island's first capital), as well as Enkomi, and St Barnabas monastery.

Nature lovers will be enchanted by the Karpasia peninsula, inhabited by tortoises and feral donkeys and boasting nearly 60 species of orchid.

A fruit and vegetable stall in Belediye Bazaar, in North Nicosia

◀ Popular beach in the Famagusta district, Protaras

Exploring North Cyprus

Previously, this region was fairly inaccessible, but is now visited by increasing numbers of tourists. The largest choice of hotels can be found in the regions of Kyrenia and Famagusta. North Nicosia (Lefkoşa) has only two hotels recommended by the local Ministry of Tourism. The area has good main roads, and is best explored by car. Nicosia, the world's only divided capital, is full of medieval churches, caravansarais and museums. The same can be said of Famagusta, whose old town, enclosed by a ring of Venetian walls, has a unique atmosphere. Nature lovers will be drawn to the wild Karpasia peninsula, while those interested in architecture should travel to the Kyrenia mountains, with its medieval castles and Bellapais Abbey.

Window from the Church of St Mary of Carmel Mountain, in Famagusta

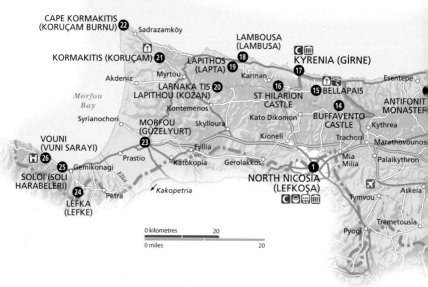

Apostolos Varnavas Monastery, built near the tomb of St Barnabas

Key

▬▬ Motorway

▬▬ Major road

▬▬ Secondary road

▭▭▭ Minor road

▬▬ Scenic route

– – Track

▬▬ Green Line

For hotels and restaurants in this region see pp162–5 and pp170–77

Getting There

There are no direct flights to Ercan (Tymbou) Airport from anywhere but Turkey, and ferries sail only from Turkish ports. These include a twice-daily service from Tasucu, a three-times-a-week sailing from Mersin and a catamaran ferry from Alanya (summer only). EU passport holders may cross from the south of the island to the north via the pedestrians-only Ledra Palace crossing point or via one of three vehicle crossing points (at Agios Dometios, Pergamos and Strovilia). North Cyprus is best explored by car but you will need to take out inexpensive special insurance if using a car rented in the South.

The picturesque harbour of Kyrenia

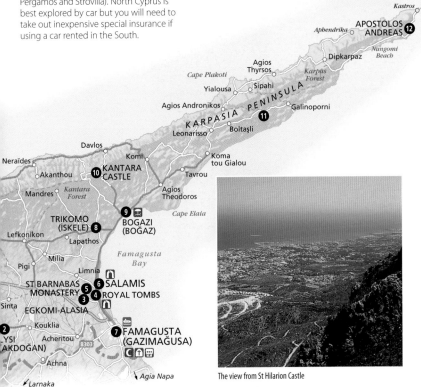

The view from St Hilarion Castle

Sights at a Glance

For additional map symbols *see back flap*

❶ North Nicosia (Lefkoşa)

Following the invasion by Turkish troops in 1974, the northern part of Nicosia became the capital of the Turkish part of the island. It is home to over half the population of North Cyprus, as well as the seat of government. It is also the administrative, business, banking and commercial centre of North Cyprus. The majority of local historic relics are found within the old Venetian walls – Gothic churches turned into mosques, bazaars, Ottoman fountains, baths and caravansarais stand among the often ugly residential buildings.

Exploring North Nicosia

The Old Town is best explored on foot. At the bus station you can board a free bus that will take you to the centre of old Lefkoşa. Do not take photographs in the vicinity of the "Green Line" that divides the city, guarded by UN and Turkish troops.

The roof terrace of the Saray Hotel in Atatürk Square (Atatürk Meydani) provides a great view. The best place for coffee and rest is the former caravanserai, Büyük Han.

🏛 Büyük Han

Asma Alti Sokagi. **Open** 8:30am–3:30pm daily.

The Big Inn, a former caravanserai, is one of the most interesting Ottoman buildings on Cyprus. The Turks built it shortly after the capture of Nicosia in 1572, as an inn for visiting merchants. Its architectural style is redolent of other inns of that period, seen in Anatolia. Under British administration, it became Nicosia's main prison. Following its restoration, the 68 former rooms spread around the inner courtyard now house souvenir shops, art galleries,

Colourful fruit and vegetable stalls in Belediy Ekpazari bazaar

cafés and a wine-bar. The courtyard itself features an octagonal building of a small Muslim shrine and prayer hall (*mescit*) with an ablution fountain. Büyük Han is used for theatrical performances, concerts and exhibitions.

The nearby Ottoman "Gamblers' Inn" (Kumarcilar Han), in Asma Alti Square, was built in the late 17th century. Its entrance hall features two Gothic arches, since the inn was built on the ruins of a former monastery. Now it houses the North Cyprus centre for the conservation of historic sites.

🏛 Belediye Ekpazari

Open 7am–5pm Mon–Fri, 7am–2pm Sat.

This covered bazaar, situated between the Bedesten and the "Green Line" that bisects old Nicosia, was the main shopping area in Ottoman times. It remains a market, where you can buy fresh meat and vegetables, as well as Turkish sweets and souvenirs. Hanging by the exit from the bazaar, on the wall of one of the houses, a plaque marks the centre of the Old Town.

🏛 Bedesten

By the Selima Mosque. **Closed** for restoration.

This 12th-century Byzantine Church of St George was remodelled in the 1300s in the Gothic style by the Lusignan kings. After the 16th-century occupation of Nicosia by the Turks, it was used as a warehouse, and subsequently as a market for selling jewellery and precious metal objects. The word *bedesten* means "lockable bazaar". The north wall has an original Gothic portal, a variety of carved stonework elements and the escutcheons of the Venetian nobility.

Gothic Selimiye Camii, the former Gothic Cathedral Church of St Sophia

❸ Gothic Selimiye Camii (Aya Sofya Cathedral)

At the centre of the old town, in Arasta Sokagi. **Open** 24 hours daily.

The former Cathedral Church of St Sophia (the Divine Wisdom), erected by the Lusignan kings from 1208 to 1326, is the oldest and finest example of Gothic architecture in Cyprus. It was once regarded as the most magnificent Christian sacred building in the Middle East. Its unique features include the entrance portal, stone-carved window and massive columns that support the criss-cross vaulting. It was in this church

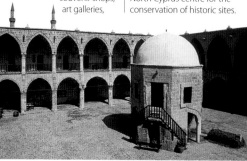
Büyük Han, a former caravanserai with a Muslim shrine in the courtyard

that the Frankish rulers were crown-ed kings of Cyprus. This ceremony preceded a second, purely nom-inal, coronation as Kings of Jerusalem, performed in St Nicholas's Cathedral, in Famagusta.

The cathedral was destroyed, in turn, by the Genoese, the Mamelukes and several major earthquakes. Following the capture of Nicosia by the Turks in 1570, the cathedral was transformed into Hagia Sophia mosque, which, in 1954, was renamed Gothic Selimiye Camii (Aya Sofya Cathedral).

All images of people and animals have been removed, and the Gothic stone sculptures in the main portal have been chipped away. The interior has been stripped of all ornamentation and painted white. Two 50-m (164-ft) tall minarets, entirely out of keeping with the rest of the building, have been added on the sides of the main façade.

Other adaptations made to the interior include the addition of three *mihrabs* indicating the direction of Mecca, and carpets.

🕮 Sultan Mahmut II Library
Kirilzade Sokagi.
Open 8am–3:30pm daily.

Shield above entrance to Lapidary Museum

This small domed, stone building is a classic example of Ottoman architecture. The library was erected in 1829 by Turkish governor, Al Ruchi. It holds a collection of 1,700 books and manuscripts, richly ornamented copies of the Koran and exquisite works of Turkish and Persian calligraphers.

🏛 Lapidary Museum
Kirilzade Sokagi.
Open 8am–3:30pm daily..

The 15th-century Venetian building at the rear of the Selima Mosque, near Sultam Mahmut II Library, houses a collection of stone sculptures removed from Gothic tombs, old houses and churches.

The garden includes a Lusignan royal sarcophagus, fragments of columns, stone rosettes and Venetian winged lions of St Mark.

🅒 Haydarpaşa Mosque
Haydarpasa Sokagi. **Open** 8am–1pm, 2:30–5pm Mon–Fri, 8am–1pm Sat.

This building was originally St Catherine's Church, erected by the Lusignans in the 14th century. Their coats of arms can be seen on the south portal in magnificently carved stone.

VISITORS' CHECKLIST

Practical Information
Road map D3. 🏠 50,000.
ℹ️ Kyrenia Gate, 0392 822 21 45.

Transport
🚌 Kemal Asik (next to Atatürk Cad). ✈️ Ercan, 20 km (12 miles) southeast of North Nicosia. The border crossing to South Nicosia is by the Ledra Palace Hotel.

Following the occupation of Nicosia, the Turks converted the beautiful church into Camii Haydarpaşa (Haydarpaşa Mosque), adding a dispropor-tionate minaret. Today it houses a modern art gallery.

Haydarpaşa Mosque, originally the Gothic church of St Catherine

North Nicosia City Centre

① Büyük Han
② Belediye Ekpazari (bazaar)
③ Gothic Selimiye Camii (Aya Sofya Cathedral)
④ Sultan Mahmut II Library
⑤ Lapidary Museum
⑥ Haydarpaşa Mosque
⑦ Kyrenia Gate
⑧ Mevlevi Tekke
⑨ Atatürk Square
⑩ Dervish Pasha Mansion
⑪ Arabahmet Mosque (Arabahmet Cami)

0 metres 400
0 yards 400

Key
▬ ▬ Green Line

Venetian Walls

Construction of the Venetian defence walls that encircle the Old Town of Nicosia was completed in 1567, three years before the Turkish invasion. Of the 11 bastions in the walls, five are now in the northern, Turkish sector. The **Quirini** (Cephane) bastion is now the official residence of the president of the Republic of North Cyprus. The **Barbaro** (Musalla) bastion houses the National Struggle Museum set up by the army. The **Roccas** (Kaytazağa) bastion is now a park. The other two in the Turkish sector are **Mula** (Zahra) and **Loredano** (Cevizli). A sixth bastion – **Flatro** – is split across the "Green Line" between the Greek and Turkish Cypriots.

Also on the north side is the **Kyrenia Gate**, one of the three original gates leading to the Venetian fortress.

At this point, the "no man's land" close to the Pafos Gate is at its narrowest; a mere few metres separate the Greeks strolling along the street from the Turks on the bastion.

Kyrenia Gate

Girne Caddesi, by Inönu Meydani.

The Kyrenia Gate between the Quirini and Barbaro bastions was once the main entrance to North Nicosia. It was originally named Porta del Proveditore, in honour of the Venetian engineer who supervised the fortification works. The gate walls bear inscriptions dating from the Venetian and Ottoman eras. The Turks erected the square, domed building above the gate in 1812. The street

Figures of Whirling Dervishes in Mevlevi Tekke

on either side of the gate was laid out in 1931 by the British, who took down part of the Venetian wall. Today, Kyrenia Gate houses a tourist information office.

Between the gate and the Atatürk monument are two huge iron cannons; several more have been placed along the walls. Although badly corroded, some of them still display British insignia. The cannons were cast in the late 18th century and used during the Napoleonic Wars.

Mevlevi Tekke

Girne Caddesi. **Open** 8am–3:30pm daily.

Less than 100 m (328 ft) south of Kyrenia Gate is the entrance to this small museum. It is housed in the former Muslim monastery (tekke) of the Mevlevi order (the Whirling Dervishes) that existed here until the middle of the 20th century. A kind of monastic brotherhood, it was founded in 13th century in Konya by the poet Celaleddin Rumi, later known as Mevlana and revered as one of Islam's greatest mystics. Dervishes whirl to the music of a reed flute, a Levantine lute and a drum. To them, the dance represents the spiritual search for Divine Love, and provides a means of inducing ecstasy that frees

A tombstone from Mevlevi Tekke

human beings from all suffering and fear.

The museum includes figures of Whirling Dervishes accompanied by an instrumental trio sitting in the gallery. The display cabinets contain musical instruments, traditional costumes, small metal objects (such as knives), embroidery, photographs, illuminated copies of the Koran and other Turkish mementoes. The adjacent hall features a replica of a dervish's living quarters. Next to this is a mausoleum with sarcophagi covered with green cloth, containing the bodies of 15 religious leaders, including the last leader of the order, Selim Dede, who died in 1953.

In the courtyard are several tombstones from a former cemetery that occupied this site.

Büyük Hamam

Irfanbey Sokagi 9. **Open** 8am–3:30pm daily. for a bath.

This 14th-century building was originally the Church of St George. After capturing the town, the Turks converted it into baths. Steep stairs lead down through a Gothic portal to the large hall, and from there to the bathing rooms.

The baths are open to the public; you can also treat yourself to a Turkish massage. Foreign visitors to the baths are charged higher prices than the locals.

The northernmost Kyrenia Gate

🚌 Atatürk Square (Saray Square)

Atatürk Meydani, also known as Sarajönü, was the political centre of Cyprus for many centuries. On the north side of the square stood a palace inhabited, in turn, by the Frankish, Venetian and Turkish rulers, or their commissioners. In 1904, the British dismantled the 700-year-old palace complex, with its splendid throne room, opulent staterooms and cloistered courtyard.

Atatürk Square is the main square of Turkish Nicosia. The grey granite column at its centre was brought here from Salamis by the Venetians. In Venetian times, the column bore the Lion of St Mark, while its base was decorated with the coats-of-arms of the Venetian nobility. The Turks overturned the column; the British raised it again in 1915 and added a globe in place of the lion.

The northern end of the square features a stone platform with the British national emblem, erected here in 1953 to commemorate the coronation of Queen Elizabeth II.

Nearby are the courts of law, police headquarters, numerous banks and a post office, which was built by the British.

Atatürk Meydani, the main square in the Turkish zone of Nicosia

The Dervish Pasha Mansion

🏛 Dervish Pasha Mansion

Belig Paşa Sokagi. **Open** 8am–3:30pm daily. 🚻

This two-storey building, typical of early 19th-century Turkish architecture, was owned by Dervish Pasha, the publisher of Cyprus's first Turkish newspaper, *Zaman* (meaning "Time"). Archival copies of the paper, published since 1891, can be seen among the other exhibits here.

Following its restoration, the building has been turned into an ethnographic museum, where you can see a panelled and carpet-lined drawing room, dining room, bedroom, and even a bridal room. The exhibits include embroidery, jewellery, hookahs, lamps, ceramics and copperware. The ground floor, intended as servants' quarters, is built of stone, while the upper floor, which was occupied by the owner, is built of brick.

🚌 Arabahmet District

Stretching southwest of Kyrenia Gate (Girne Caddesi), the Arabahmet district is full of imposing Ottoman houses, restored partly with funding from the European Union. At the junction of Zahra and Tanzimat, close to the Mula bastion, is an octagonal Ottoman fountain, somewhat neglected today.

Until 1963, this district was home to residents from a variety of countries, including Greece and Armenia. There was even an Armenian church dedicated to the Virgin Mary, which was originally a Benedictine monastery. Nowadays the church stands in the closed military zone.

The **Holy Cross Church**, straddling the border, has an entrance from the Greek side. Its tower, topped with a cross, dominates the entire Arabahmet district.

The **Roccas bastion** (Kaytazaga), which overlooks the "Green Line", was turned into a municipal garden in the 1990s.

This is the only place in Nicosia where the buffer zone vanishes and the inhabitants of both sides of divided Nicosia can see each other. Photography, as is to be expected, is prohibited.

🇨 Arabahmet Mosque (Arabahmet Cami)

Salahi Sevket Sokagi.

Standing at the centre of the Arabahmet district is the Arabahmet Cami, covered with a vast dome. Built in the early 17th century on the site of a former Lusignan church, it was remodelled in 1845. The mosque was named after the Turkish military commander, Arab Ahmet Pasha.

The floor is paved with medieval tombstones taken from the church that formerly stood on this site. In the courtyard is a fountain and several tombs, including that of Kemal Pasha, Grand Vizier of the Ottoman Empire. The mosque holds a relic – a hair believed to come from the beard of the Prophet Mohammed – that is shown to the faithful once a year.

The Arabahmet district with its traditional Ottoman houses

❷ Lysi (Akdoğan)

Road Map D3. 12 km (7.5 miles) southwest of Dörtyol (Prastio).

A small farming village in the southeastern part of the Mesaoria plain, Lysi lies close to the "Green Line". Its most interesting historic site is the unfinished Byzantine-style church decorated with Neo-Gothic architectural elements.

Environs

Along the road to Ercan airport are the remains of Ottoman aqueducts. The surrounding area is home to several neglected Orthodox churches, including Agios Themonianos, Agios Synesios, Agios Andronikos and Moni Agiou Spyridona monastery in Erdemli (Tremetousha). The latter is guarded, and visitors should not approach it.

The unfinished Neo-Byzantine church in Lysi

❸ Enkomi-Alasia

Road Map E3. **Open** summer: 8am–7pm daily; winter: 8am–3:30pm daily.

Remains of a Bronze Age town have been found near the village of Enkomi-Alasia. Archaeologists estimate that Alasia was founded in the 18th century BC. The town grew rich on trading in copper, which was excavated on the island and exported to Anatolia, Syria and Egypt.

Alasia was the capital of Cyprus and its main town – its name synonymous with the entire island. In the 12th century BC, when the Mycenaeans arrived here, the town's population numbered an

Ruins near the village of Enkomi, a few kilometres west of Salamis

impressive 15,000. Following an earthquake in the 11th century BC, the town was deserted and its inhabitants moved to Salamis.

Excavation works conducted since 1896 have unearthed the ruins of a Late Bronze Age settlement, with low houses lining narrow streets.

The Alasia ruins yielded a tablet with Cypriot-Minoan writing, not yet deciphered, and the famous bronze statue of the Horned God, dating from the 12th century BC, which is now kept in the Cyprus Museum in Nicosia. Strolling around the excavation site you will come across the Horned God's sanctuary and the "House of Bronzes", where many bronze objects were discovered.

Environs

Along the road to Famagusta is the village of Enkomi (Tuzla). Next to the shop is a white platform, known as the **cenotaph of Nikokreon**. It contains the remains of Nikokreon – the last King of Salamis. Refusing to surrender to the Hellenic king of Egypt, Ptolemy I, Nikokreon committed suicide by setting fire to the

royal palace. He perished, along with his entire family, in the flames that day.

❹ Royal Tombs

Road Map E3. **Open** summer: 8am–7pm daily; winter: 8am–3:30pm daily.

The royal necropolis by the side of the road leading to St Barnabas monastery has over 100 tombs from the 8th and 7th centuries BC. Some have been given names, and others designated numbers. Almost all of the tombs are opened to the east. Each one was approached by a slanting corridor known as a *dromos*, on which the most interesting artifacts were found.

Most of the tombs were looted in antiquity, but some, in particular numbers 47 and 49, contained a multitude of objects that could be useful to the royals in the next world. The most famous finds include the ivory inlaid royal bed and throne, showing clear Phoenician and Egyptian influences. The Kings of Salamis were buried with their servants and horses.

Tomb number 50, the so-called "St Catherine's prison", was built during Roman times on top of older tombs. According to legend, the Alexandrian saint, a native of Salamis, was imprisoned by her father, the Roman governor, for refusing to marry the man chosen by him. The tomb's walls bear the remnants of Christian decorations.

The site also features a small museum with plans and photographs of the tombs, and a reconstructed chariot used to carry the kings of Salamis on their final journey.

Royal Tombs from the 8th and 7th centuries BC, west of Salamis

St Barnabas Monastery, built near the tomb of the apostle Barnabas

❺ St Barnabas Monastery

Road Map E3. **Open** summer: 8am–7pm daily; winter: 8am–3:30pm daily. 🎫

The monastery of St Barnabas was erected in 477 on the western end of the Constantia (Salamis) necropolis, near the spot where the apostle's grave was discovered. The construction was financed by the Byzantine Emperor Zeno himself.

Two centuries later, it was demolished in one of the devastating Arab raids on Cyprus. All that remains of the original Byzantine edifice are the foundations. The present church and monastery were constructed in 1756 on the orders of Archbishop Philotheos, during Ottoman rule. The three-aisled church is covered with two flat domes resting on high drums. It now houses an **Icon Museum**.

Much more interesting, however, is the small **Archaeological Museum** occupying former monks' cells around the courtyard of the monastery. Displayed in a series of rooms are Neolithic tools and stone vessels, as well as a large number of ceramic items such as amphorae, jugs, vases and cups. Among the more curious items are a polished bronze mirror, swords,

hatchets and spearheads, made of the same metal. There are also terracotta figurines of people and animals, including an unusual horse with wheels instead of hooves, and clay baby rattles shaped like boars.

Other interesting exhibits are the black-glazed ceramics imported from Attica. These are decorated with intricate motifs of animal and human figures, including lions, wild boars and hares. There is also gold jewellery, a collection of Roman glass, and a stone figure of a woman holding a poppy – probably the goddess Demeter. The Classical period is further represented by sphinxes, showing the Egyptian influence, and carved lions. A short distance

A terracotta figurine, Archaeological Museum

east of the monastery stands a small **Byzantine-style church**. This rectangular, domed chapel was erected over the tomb of the apostle Barnabas. A stone staircase leads down to two chambers hewn into the rock where, according to legend, St Barnabas was buried. The saint was killed near Salamis for preaching Christianity, and his body was cast into the sea. His disciples fished the body out, and he was buried with St Matthew's gospel on his chest, under a lonely breadfruit tree to the west of Salamis.

From 1971 until the Turkish occupation of 1974, the St Barnabas Monastery was inhabited by the last three monks, the brothers Barnabas, Chariton and Stephen, who made a humble living by selling honey and painting icons.

St Barnabas

Born in Salamis, Barnabas accompanied St Paul on his missionary travels around Cyprus and Asia Minor. After parting from his master, Barnabas continued to promote Christianity on the island, for which he was killed in the year 57 AD. St Mark buried the body in secret.

St Barnabas acquired fame following a miracle that occurred after his death, when he revealed the site of his burial to Anthemios, the Bishop of Salamis. The discovery of the saint's relics, and the prestige they brought, helped preserve the autonomy of the Cypriot Church.

The tomb of St Barnabas

❻ Salamis

The former Roman Salamis, which later became Byzantine Constantia, was the island's main port and capital for a thousand years. Destroyed by the Arabs in 648, Salamis is still the largest and the most interesting archaeological excavation site on Cyprus. The unearthed relics date from the Roman and Byzantine periods. Allow a full day for a visit, including a relaxing break on the nearby beach.

Caldarium
The hot bath chamber, fitted with a central heating system, had walls decorated with abstract mosaics.

Sudatorium
The Greek-Roman baths complex included a steam bath, which was also decorated with mosaics. An underfloor heating system is in evidence.

Latrines
This semicircular colonnaded structure contained a latrine which could be used by 44 people simultaneously.

Gymnasium
A colonnade surrounded the rectangular *palaestra* of the gymnasium, which was devoted to the training of athletes.

KEY

① **Two pools** with cold water were located beyond the east portico.

② **The Backstage area,** housed dressing rooms for the actors.

Map of Salamis

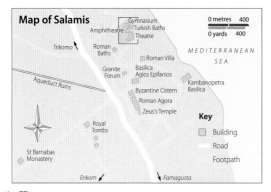

Trikomo

Amphitheatre

Gymnasium
Turkish Baths
Theatre

Roman
Baths

Roman Villa

Granite
Forum

Basilica
Agios Epifanios

Aqueduct Ruins

Byzantine Cistern

Kambanopetra
Basilica

Roman Agora

Zeus's Temple

Royal
Tombs

St Barnabas
Monastery

Enkom

Famagusta

MEDITERRANEAN
SEA

0 metres 400
0 yards 400

Key

Building

Road

Footpath

VISITORS' CHECKLIST

Practical Information
Road map E3. 8 km (5 miles)
N of Famagusta. 🚌 ℹ️ 0392
366 2864. Archaeological site:
Open summer: 8am–7pm daily;
winter: 8am–3:30pm daily. 🅿️
Necropolis: 1 km
(0.6 mile) W of Salamis.
Tel 0392 378 83 31. **Open**
summer: 9am–7pm; winter:
9am–1pm & 2–4:45pm. 🅿️

Aqueduct
To the east of the gymnasium are the
stone cisterns and other remains of
an aqueduct that used to supply the
baths and the pools with water.

★ **Roman Theatre**
Built 2,000 years ago, during the
reign of Emperor Augustus, this
auditorium could hold 15,000
spectators. Today the restored
theatre serves as a venue for
summer performances.

②

Amphitheatre
Built by the Romans in the early years of the
modern era, it was destroyed by an
earthquake in the 6th century.

❼ Famagusta (Ammochostos/ Gazimağusa)

Once the world's wealthiest city, present-day Famagusta (Ammochostos in Greek and Gazimağusa in Turkish) presents a somewhat depressing sight. Yet within the mighty fortifications that kept out the Turkish army for nearly a year, and amid the many derelict buildings, are true gems of Gothic architecture. Former magnificent churches have been destroyed or turned into mosques. South of the city lies deserted Varosha, once Cyprus's biggest resort.

Namik Kemal Square, once the site of the Venetian Palace

Exploring Famagusta
Virtually all of Famagusta's major historic sites are found within the Old Town, surrounded by the Venetian fortifications. The best way to enter the city is through the Land Gate, leaving your car behind. The tourist information office is located by the gate. The city is not large; it is possible to explore it on foot.

🅲 Lala Mustafa Pasha Mosque
Namik Kemal Meydoni.
Open 24 hours daily. 🖼
This former cathedral was built between 1298 and 1312 to a Gothic design modelled on the Reims cathedral in France. It was here that Lusignan royalty, after the coronation in Nicosia, received the symbolic title of "King of Jerusalem".
 Following the capture of the city in 1571, the victorious Turks converted the cathedral into a mosque and named it after the commander of the

Gothic portal of Lala Mustafa Pasha Mosque

besieging army – Lala Mustafa Pasha. They also added a minaret to the left tower. The building is still a functioning mosque; visitors are admitted only outside the hours of prayer.
 The white interior has 12 columns to support the Gothic vaulting. There is a modest *minbar* (pulpit) in the right aisle. The façade with its unusual window and enormous rosette, basking in the light of the setting sun, is one of the most beautiful sights in Cyprus.

🏠 Agia Zoni & Agios Nikolaos
Hisar Yolou Sokagi.
Open 24 hours daily.
This small, excellently preserved Byzantine-style church, decorated with wall paintings, dates from about the 15th century. It stands in an empty square, surrounded by a handful of palm trees. Close by is the larger Church of St Nicholas, which is now partly demolished.

🏛 Fountain and Jafar Pasha Baths
Naim Effendi Sokagi.
Located northwest of Namik Kemal Square, the fountain and baths were built in 1601 in the Ottoman style by the Commander of the Sultan's Navy and the Turkish Governor of Cyprus.
 Jafar Pasha ordered the building of the aqueduct in order to supply the city with water. Both the aqueduct and the original town fountain have been destroyed. The current fountain has been reconstructed using fragments salvaged from the original.

🅲 Sinan Pasha Mosque
Abdullah Paşa Sokagi.
Closed to visitors.
The former church of Saints Peter and Paul was turned into a mosque after the capture of the city by the Turks. This beautiful Gothic edifice, built of yellow stone and maintained in excellent condition, now houses the municipal library collection.

A former church turned into the Sinan Pasha Mosque

🏛 Venetian Palace
Namik Kemal Meydani.
Open 24 hours daily.
Not much remains of the former palace of the Lusignan kings and Venetian governors, built during Lusignan times. The area marked by its jutting stone walls is now a car park.
 On the side of Namik Kemal Square stands a triple-arched façade supported by four granite columns from Salamis. Above the central arch is the coat of arms of Giovanni Renier – the Venetian military commander of Cyprus. Between 1873 and 1876, the left section of the building was used as a prison in which Turkish poet and playwright, Namik Kemal, was locked up on the Sultan's order. Now it houses his museum.

Remains of the Venetian Palace

🏛 Nestorian Church

Somoundjouoglou Sokagi.
Closed to the public.

Syrian merchant Francis Lakhas built this church in 1338 for Famagusta's Syrian community. The façade is adorned with a lovely rose window. Inscriptions inside are in Syrian, the language of the Nestorian liturgy.

Later, the church was taken over by Greek Cypriots and renamed Agios Georgios Exorinos. The word *exorinos* means "exiler". Greeks believe that dust taken from the church floor and sprinkled in the house of an enemy will make him die or leave the island within a year.

🏛 Churches of the Knights Templar and Knights Hospitaller

Kişla Sokagi. **Closed** to the public.
These two adjacent medieval churches are known as the twins. On the north façade, above the entrance, you can still see the carved stone coats of arms of the Knights Hospitaller. In the early 14th century, following the dissolution of the Knights Templar order, their monastery

Romantic ruins of the Gothic Church of St John (Latin)

VISITORS' CHECKLIST

Practical Information
Road map E3. 🚗 42,000.
ℹ Land Gate, 0392 366 28 64.
🎭 Famagusta International Festival (Jun–Jul).

Transport
🚌 Gazi Mustafa Kemak Boulv.
🚌 east of the Sea Gate (for tickets, call 0392 366 45 57).

and the Chapel of St Anthony were handed over to the order of St John of Jerusalem (the Knights Hospitaller). The Hospitallers' chapel, featuring a lovely rose window in the façade, now houses a theatre and an art gallery.

🏛 Church of St John (Latin)

Cafer Paşa Sokagi.
Open 8am–3:30pm daily..

Built in the late 13th century, during the reign of the French king Louis IX, the Church of St John was one of Famagusta's ealiest churches, and a splendid example of Gothic architecture. Now largely in ruins, the original north wall with the presbytery and tall Gothic windows remains standing. The capital of the surviving column is decorated with floral motifs and winged dragons.

Famagusta City Centre

① Lala Mustafa Pasha Mosque
② Agia Zoni & Agios Nikolaos
③ Fountain & Jafar Pasha Baths
④ Sinan Pasha Mosque
⑤ Venetian Palace
⑥ Nestorian Church
⑦ Churches of the Knights Templar & Knights Hospitaller
⑧ Church of St John (Latin)

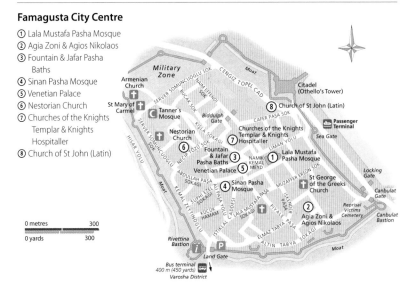

⬆ Agios Ioannis
Varosha (Maraş). Polat Pasa Bulvari.
Open 8am–3:30pm daily.

The Neo-Byzantine Church of St John stands in the Varosha (Maraş) district of Famagusta, where the Turkish army is currently stationed. The renovated church houses a museum of icons, mostly from the 18th century, that were gathered from many destroyed Greek Orthodox churches.

The Varosha area, controlled by Turkish and UN forces, has been uninhabited for more than 30 years, ever since the expulsion of the Greek Cypriots. It is forbidden to photograph the crumbling houses or dozens of decaying beachfront hotels, dating from the 1960s.

Iconostasis in Agios Ioannis Church

⬚ Canbulat Bastion
Open summer: 8am–7pm daily,
winter: 8am–3:30pm daily.
Tel 0392 366 28 64.

The bastion at the southeast corner of the Venetian defence walls was once called the Arsenal. Today it bears the name of the Turkish commander, Canbulat, who charged his horse at the Venetian war machine, which was studded with spinning knives, during the siege of Famagusta. Canbulat perished, cut to shreds, but his desperate attack put the machine out of action, and the Turks regard him as a hero. The bastion contains his tomb and a small museum with a collection of artifacts dating from antiquity and the Ottoman era.

⬚ Venetian City Walls
Famagusta's Old Town is encircled by huge defence walls erected by

Ruins of the Citadel (Othello's Tower)

the Venetians, who felt threatened by the Ottoman Empire's expansion into the eastern Mediterranean. The walls, 15 m (49 ft) high and up to 8 m (26 ft) thick, are reinforced with 15 bastions. The two gates leading to the town are the Land Gate and Sea Gate, which was constructed by the Venetian, Nicolo Prioli. His name, coat of arms, construction date (1496) and the Lion of St Mark have been carved in the marble brought from the ruins of Salamis.

To the right of the entrance are two marble statues of lions. Legend has it that one night the larger of the two will open its mouth, and the person who sticks his head in at that moment will win a fortune.

The entrance to the Old Town from the opposite side leads over a stone bridge that spans the moat. It is defended by the massive Rivettina (Ravelin) Bastion, which the Turks call Akkule ("White Tower"). It was here that the Venetians hoisted the white flag following the 10-month siege of Famagusta in

1571 by the Turkish army. From the Old Town side you can see wall paintings and the coats of arms of the Venetian commanders.

The passageway features a small shrine. The restored rooms beyond the gate now house the tourist information bureau. Under the Rivettina Bastion are subterranean casemates. In 1619, a small mosque was built for the Muslim guards.

⬚ Citadel (Othello's Tower)
Cengiz Topel Caddesi (adjacent to the Sea Gate). **Open** summer: 8am–7pm daily, winter: 8am–3:30pm daily.

The Citadel was erected in the 12th century by the Lusignan Kings, to defend Famagusta Harbour from attack. Carved in marble above the gate are the Lions of St Mark (symbolizing Venice) and the name of Nicolo Foscari, who supervised the rebuilding of the fortress in 1492. This was a vast structure for its time, and it included a system of fortifications and subterranean casemates.

The Citadel is popularly known as Othello's Tower, after Shakespeare's play *Othello*, which was set largely in Famagusta. The empty interiors, Gothic rooms and gloomy casemates are now inhabited by pigeons, and the floors littered with discarded bullets and fragments of broken sculptures.

The Citadel walls afford a magnificent view over old Famagusta and the harbour.

The massive Venetian defence walls

⛪ St George of the Greeks Church

Mustafa Ersu Sokagi.
Open 24 hours daily.

Erected in the 15th century, in Gothic-Byzantine style, just a shell remains of this church. The east apse still shows the fragments of wall paintings. The steps in the nave are typical of early Christian basilicas.

The roof was brought down by Turkish bombardment in the siege of Famagusta. To this day, the walls bear pockmarks of cannonballs. Legend says that a treasure belonging to St Epifanos (Archbishop of Salamis) lies under the floor.

Abutting the church to the south is the smaller church of Agios Symeon (St Simon's).

Ruins of St George of the Greeks Church

Biddulph Gate – a remnant of a Venetian merchant's home

🏛 Biddulph Gate

Naim Effendi Sokagi.
Open 24 hours daily.

This Renaissance gate standing in a side street is a remnant of a medieval merchant's house. It was named in honour of Sir Robert Biddulph, British High Commissioner, who saved it from being pulled down in 1879. Departing from the usual custom of demolishing old structures, Biddulph pioneered the protection of Famagusta's historic sites.

Another interesting relic found along Naim Effendi Sokagi is an old, intact merchant's house, an excellent example of secular Renaissance architecture.

⛪ Churches in North Famagusta

The area at the north end of old Famagusta, around the Martinengo, San Luca and Pulacazara bastions, was previously occupied by the Turkish army. Now some of its historic sites are open to visitors. Among them is the rectangular **Church of St Mary of Carmel**, built of a yellow stone. It may be viewed only from the outside. The adjacent **Armenian Church** was built in the 16th century, when the Armenians had their Bishops in Nicosia and Famagusta. The interior is covered with paintings and Armenian inscriptions. A short distance away, in the direction of the Moratto bastion and beyond the Tanner's mosque, stands the splendidly preserved medieval **Church of St Anna**, featuring an unusual belfry rising above the façade; unfortunately it is closed to visitors.

🏛 Medresa

Liman Yolu Sokagi.

The single-storey domed building to the north of the Lala Mustafa Pasa mosque was once a college of Islamic studies, attached to an Ottoman mosque. Nowadays it would be difficult to discern any particular style in it, although it is often cited as an example of classic Ottoman architecture. The two granite columns brought from Salamis, and placed in front of the

Coat of arms, Church of St Mary of Carmel

building, add to the overall impression of architectural chaos. The stone plinth opposite the entrance bears the bust of Namik Kemal, a 19th-century Turkish poet and playwright, who, on orders of the Sultan, was imprisoned in the Venetian Palace opposite. To the right are two domed Turkish tombs, one with an interesting wrought-iron gate.

After serving as a college, the former medresa was later used as offices, and then as bank premises. Today the building stands empty.

🏛 Tanner's Mosque

Somoundjouoglou Sokagi.

This small, yellow limestone building was erected in the late 16th century as a church. In 1571, following the capture of Famagusta by the Turks, it was converted into a mosque. Clay pots were built into its vaults, intended to improve the general acoustics of the building.

The mosque was later abandoned and left to decay. Since 1974 the building has been fenced-off in a compound used by the Turkish army; it now serves as a depot.

Ruins of St Mary of Carmel Church seen at sunset

❽ Trikomo (İskele)

Road Map E2.

This small town lies close to the base of the Karpas peninsula. At its centre, right by the roundabout, stands the tiny Dominican **Church of St James** (Agios Iakovos). Intricately carved in stone, it resembles an encrusted jewellery box. At the western end of the town stands the two-aisled, single domed **Church of Panagia Thetokos**, which was erected in the 12th century. The church was restored in 1804, when it was also given its marble-panelled belfry. Inside you can still see the original wall paintings dating from the 12th century.

The **Icon Museum**, opened here in 1991, houses a collection of icons removed from the local Greek churches. The images are modern and of little artistic merit, yet the museum is worth visiting for its lovely interior frescoes.

🏛 **Icon Museum**
Panagia Theotokos Church.
Open 8am–3:30pm daily. 📷

A mosque in Trikomo, a town at the base of the Karpas peninsula

❾ Bogazi (Boğaz)

Road Map E2. On the road leading to the Karpas peninsula.

At this little fishing port on Famagusta Bay you can watch the fishermen returning with their catch, and also buy fresh fish each morning. Fishing trips are available for visitors, as are lessons in scuba diving. There are beautiful long, sandy

The imposing walls of Kantara Castle, overlooking Famagusta Bay

beaches in this area. A half-dozen local restaurants specialize in fish and seafood. European cuisine is also on offer at Moon Over the Water, an English-run seaside restaurant 2 km (1 mile) south of Bogazi.

❿ Kantara Castle

Road Map E2. **Open** summer: 8am–5pm daily, winter: 8am–3.30pm daily. 📷

Kantara Castle is the easternmost medieval fortress of North Cyprus. It lies 630 m (2,068 ft) above sea level, at the base of the Karpasia peninsula, on a spot affording views of both Famagusta Bay and the shores of Asia Minor. This was already the site of a castle in Byzantine times. It was here that the English King Richard the Lionheart finally caught up with his adversary, Byzantine governor Isaac Komnenos, in 1191 and forced him to capitulate.

The castle rooms were mostly torn down by the Venetians, but the mighty walls survive in excellent condition. The route to the castle leads through a barbican with two towers; the vast southeastern tower has a water cistern at its base, also used as a dungeon. The two adjacent former army barracks are in good condition. The southwestern wing of the castle features

a secret passage that enabled the defenders to sneak out and launch a surprise attack on the besiegers. The north towers and the bastions afford magnificent views of the surrounding area.

Environs
A dozen or so kilometres (7.5 miles) west of the castle, close to the sea, is the lonely late Byzantine **Church of Panagia Pergaminiotissa.**

⓫ Karpasia Peninsula

Road Map E2, F1–2.
ℹ Yialoussa, 374 4984.

This long, rocky spit is the least developed part of the island, with sandy beaches on its north and south coast, and a scattering of historic Christian churches, including the monastery of Apostolos Andreas, which is awaiting restoration, to be funded by the UN and the EU. Known as Karpaz Yarimadasi (sometimes Karpas) to the Turks, this quiet

Picturesque Panagia Pergaminiotissa

peninsula has rolling hills, where wild donkeys roam, fringed by empty beaches, which provide nesting grounds for sea turtles. The eastern part of the peninsula is a nature reserve, home to birds and donkeys.

The best starting point for exploring the peninsula is the fishing village of **Bogazi**. A few kilometres to the left of the main road, near the village of **Komi** (Büyükkonuk), stands a small Byzantine church with beautiful 6th-century mosaics. The church is surrounded by the ruins of a Roman town. Only the apse remains of the 5th-century Church of Panagia Kanakaria, on the edge of **Boltaşli** (Lythrangkomi), east of Ziyamet (Leonarisso); the mosaics that used to decorate it can be seen in the Makarios Museum, in Nicosia. The rest of the church dates from the 11th century, except the tamboured dome which was added in the 18th century. The church is now closed.

The last petrol station is in **Yialousa** (Yenierenköy). Further south is the village of **Sipahi** (Agia Trias) with a three-aisled early Christian basilica. Dating from the 5th century, it was discovered by archaeologists in 1957, and is noted for its handsome floor mosaics. The marble-encrusted, cruciform font in the baptistry is the biggest in the island.

Beyond the small village of **Agios Thyrsos** stands Hotel Theresa, with the best accommodation on the peninsula.

Dipkarpaz (Rizokarpaso) is the peninsula's biggest, if somewhat neglected, village. It has a population of 3,000, comprised mainly of immigrants from Anatolia. Some 3 km (1.8 miles) to the north are the ruins of the 5th-century Church of **Agios Philon**, standing amid the ruins of the Phoenician town of Karpatia. The 10th-century basilica was later replaced by a chapel; just the south wall and the apse remain.

North of Agios Philon stands an ancient stone breakwater. A narrow road running along the coast leads to **Aphendrika**, with the ruins of an ancient harbour, a Hellenic necropolis and a fortress erected on bare rock. It also has three ruined churches: the Agios Georgios dating from the Byzantine period; the 12th-century Romanesque Panagia Chrysiotissa; and Panagia Assomatos, the best preserved of all three. On the opposite side of the peninsula is the beautiful Nangomi Beach.

Apostolos Andreas – the monastery of St Andrew

⑫ Apostolos Andreas

Road map F1. **Open** 24 hours daily.

Near the tip of the Karpasia peninsula stands the monastery of St Andrew (Apostolos Andreas), an irregular edifice of yellow stone with a white bell tower. According to legend, it was here that the Saint's invocation caused a miraculous spring to appear, whose water cures epilepsy and ailments of the eyes, and grants pilgrims their wishes. During the Byzantine period, a fortified monastery occupied the site; some historians believe that it was here, rather than in Kantara, that Richard the Lionheart caught up with Isaac Komnenos.

In the early 20th century the monastery gained a reputation for its miracles, and became the target of mass pilgrimages. After 1974, the site was taken over by the Turkish army. Today it is once again open to visitors.

The 19th-century church has been stripped of its icons, but on the Feast of the Assumption (15 August) and St Andrew's Day (30 November), services are held for the pilgrims arriving from southern Cyprus.

In the crypt beneath the church the holy well, famed for its healing properties, still gushes the "miraculous" water. The site is regarded as holy by Greeks and Turks alike.

Environs

Less than 5 km (3 miles) from Apostolos Andreas monastery is **Zafer Burnu**, the furthest point of the Karpasia peninsula. This cave-riddled rocky cape was a Neolithic settlement known as Kastros, one of the earliest places of known human habitation in Cyprus. In ancient times it became the site of a temple to the goddess Aphrodite.

The offshore **Klidhes islets** (the "Keys" islets) are a haven for a variety of sea birds.

Nangomi (Golden) Beach in the Karpasia peninsula

⓭ Antifonitis Monastery

Road Map D2. 29 km (18 miles)
E of Kyrenia via Esentepe (Agios
Amvrosios). **Open** summer:
8am–5pm; winter: 8am–3:30pm.

In a pine-covered valley on the
northern slopes of the Pentadaktylos mountains, some 8 km
(5 miles) south of Esentepe,
stands the disused 12th-century
monastery church of Antifonitis.
This was once the most
important Byzantine church in
the mountains of North Cyprus.
Its Greek name, meaning "He
who responds", is associated
with a legend about a pauper
who met a wealthy man and
requested a loan. When the rich
man asked who would vouchsafe
the loan, the pauper replied, "God
will". At this moment they both
heard a voice from heaven. The
monastery was built on the site
of this miracle.

The church was built in the
7th century; the narthex and
gallery date from the Lusignan
period and the loggia was
added by the Venetians. The
church was originally decorated
with magnificent frescoes, but
since 1974 these have been
defaced and damaged.

⓮ Buffavento Castle

Road Map D2. **Open** summer:
8am–7pm; winter: 8am–3:30pm.

Built on the site of a Byzantine
watchtower remodelled by the
Lusignans, this castle perches
950 m (3,117 ft) above sea level.
The date of its construction is
unknown, but this mountain
stronghold was captured in

Buffavento, the highest castle in Cyprus

1191 by the Frankish king
Guy de Lusignan. The castle
was used for years as an
observation post and political
prison. Under Venetian rule the
castle lost its importance and
was abandoned.

Steep stairs lead from the
gate to the top of the tallest
tower, where a magnificent
view awaits. In fine weather it is
possible to see Kyrenia, Nicosia
and Famagusta, as well as the
Troodos mountains and the
coast of Turkey.

Cold winter wind blowing
from Anatolia explains the
name of the castle, meaning
the "wind blast". In old days
bonfires lit on top of the tower
served as means of
communication with the
garrisons stationed at St
Hilarion and Kantara castles.

A marble monument by the
car park commemorates the
passengers and crew of a
Turkish aircraft that crashed in
fog in February 1988 on its
approach to Ercan airport.

Environs

West of the castle, on the
southern slopes of the juniper-
covered mountains, stands the
12th-century Byzantine
**Panagia Apsinthiotissa
monastery**. It was restored in
the 1960s, but after 1974 the
monks were forced to abandon
it. Its church is crowned with a
vast dome; on its north side is a
lovely original refectory.

The site is reached by turning
off the Kyrenia-Nicosia highway
and passing through Asagi
Dikmen (Kato Dikomo) and
Tasken (Vouno) villages.

Along the way is a giant stone
flag erected by Turkish Cypriot
refugees from Tochni (*see p78*)
where, in the 1960s, the Greek
EOKA organization murdered
all the Turkish men.

The breathtaking view from Buffavento castle

◀ View of the Old Harbour in Kyrenia

⓯ Bellapais

Road Map C2. 7 km (4.3 miles) SE of Kyrenia. **Tel** 0392 815 75 40. Abbey: **Open** summer: 8am–7pm; winter: 8am–3:30pm.

One of the most beautiful villages in Cyprus, Bellapais lies amid citrus groves on the northern slopes of the Pentadaktylos mountains. It features the splendidly preserved ruins of a Gothic abbey, to which the village owes its name. It is thought to be derived from the French *Abbaye de la Paix* (Peace Abbey).

The first monks to settle here were Augustinians from Jerusalem, forced to flee the city after its capture by Saladin. The first buildings were erected in the early 13th century, but the main section of the abbey was built during the reign of the Lusignan kings, Hugo III and Hugo IV. The abbey was destroyed by the Turks, following their conquest of the island.

Bellapais is one of the loveliest Gothic historic sites in the Middle East. The oldest part of the abbey is its well-preserved church, built in the French Gothic style.

A spiral staircase in the western end of the garth (the garden close) leads to the roof, affording a magnificent view of the sea and the mountains. The remaining parts include the living quarters, the kitchen, and the old refectory illuminated by the light entering through the vast windows facing the steep crag. The garth cloisters once contained a carved marble

Splendidly preserved ruins of Bellapais abbey

sarcophagus and a lavatory, where the monks washed their hands before entering the refectory. Now they are used for concerts during music festivals.

The English writer Lawrence Durrell lived in Bellapais from 1953–6, and described the struggles of the EOKA fighters in his novel *Bitter Lemons*. The house in which he lived bears a commemorative plaque.

Sign from Durrell's house in Bellapais

⓰ St Hilarion Castle

Road Map C2. 7 km (4.3 miles) SW of Kyrenia. **Open** summer: 9am–6:30pm; winter: 8am–3:30pm.

The best-preserved mountain-top stronghold in North Cyprus, this magnificent castle bristles with turrets from its walls built on sheer rock. It was named after the monastic saint from Palestine,

who came to Cyprus in search of solitude, dying here in 372. The Byzantines built the church and monastery in his memory.

The outer defence wall was erected by the Lusignans. The castle played an important role in the 1228–31 struggle for the domination of Cyprus between German Emperor Frederick II of Hohenstaufen and Jean d'Ibelin; and in the 1373 Genoese invasion. The lower section of the fortress held stables. A huge gate leads to the inner castle with a chapel and a refectory, which in the Lusignan period was converted into a banqueting hall. From here you can pass to the belvedere and the adjoining kitchen. An arched gate leads to the upper castle.

The south part of the castle has the Gothic "queen's window", with a spectacular view over Karmi village.

Ruins of St Hilarion Castle, on top of a steep rock

⓱ Kyrenia (Girne)

Enjoying a picturesque location flanked by a range of craggy hills and the sea, Kyrenia is built around a charming harbour – the most beautiful in Cyprus – guarded by a mighty medieval castle. Its compact Old Town is full of bars, tavernas and restaurants, yet remains a tranquil place. The nearby seashore is lined with the best hotels in North Cyprus. Home to a sizeable expatriate community until 1974, there is still a small number of expats living here today.

Town hall building with its forecourt fountain

View of the Lusignan Tower in the castle *(see pp152–3)*

Exploring Kyrenia

Once you arrive in Kyrenia, it is best to leave the car at the large car park near the town hall, and then continue exploring on foot. Most of Kyrenia's historic sites are clustered around the old harbour. The tourist information office is housed in the former customs house. The town's main attractions – the harbour, castle and small museums – can be explored in a day.

🏛 Byzantine Tower

Ziya Rizki Caddesi and Atilla Sokagi. **Open** daily. Summer: 8am–5pm; winter: 8am–3:30pm.

This massive stone defence structure, with walls several metres thick, once formed part of the town's defence walls. It now houses an art gallery selling local handicrafts, including rugs, paintings and other souvenirs. Strolling down Atilla Sokagi you will come across a similar, but more derelict tower; also a number of Greek and Roman tombs.

🏛 Market

Canbulat Sokagi. **Open** 8am–7pm. The covered town bazaar, was once a food market, but funding from the UN has allowed it to be renovated into a revitalised area housing trendy restaurants and a handicraft centre. The market stands along Canbulat street leading towards the shore.

🏛 Folk Art Museum

The old harbour. **Open** 8am–3:30pm daily. 🖼 Set in a centuries-old Venetian house midway along the harbour, the Folk Art Museum houses a small collection of traditional village costumes, household implements, furniture and tools. Also on display is a giant olive press made of olive wood.

Art gallery inside the Byzantine Tower

🏛 Town Hall

This modern building stands on a small square, just a stone's throw from the Old Town. Standing in the forecourt is a unique fountain featuring three huge birds carved in white stone.

The nearby Muslim cemetery is full of the distinctive tombs – *baldaken turbe*.

🕌 Djafer Pasha Mosque (Cafer Paşa Camii)

In the Old Town, close to the castle and the harbour. **Open** 24 hours daily.

This small mosque with a stocky minaret was erected in 1589 by Djafer Pasha, commander of the Sultan's army and navy, and three times the Turkish governor of Cyprus. The founder's body rests in the small stone tomb to the right of the entrance. The simple prayer hall is lined with carpets.

About a dozen metres (40 ft) west of the mosque is the small, abandoned Chysospiliotissa church which was erected by the Lusignans in the early 14th century.

⚓ Harbour

Kyrenia's once important harbour was the safest haven along the north coast of Cyprus, so heavily fortified was it. In ancient times the Romans built a defence castle here; later on the Lusignans and the Venetians rebuilt it, creating a vast fortress. In the Middle Ages the harbour entrance was protected by a strong iron chain. Evidence of its former importance are the medieval stone lugs that were used to fasten the mooring lines of large ships.

Now the old harbour is devoted exclusively to yachts

and pleasure boats, ready to take visitors on cruises along the coast. It is lined with an array of dining spots, particularly fish restaurants, with tables set close to the water's edge. The harbour looks particularly enchanting at night, when the calm waters reflect myriad sparkling lights.

Archangelos Church & Icon Museum

Near the harbour. **Open** 8am–3:30pm daily.

The former church of the Archangel Michael, standing on top of a hill close to the old harbour, now houses the Icon Museum.

This white edifice with its slender belfry was built in 1860. Some of its original furnishings remain, including the exquisite

The distinctive white silhouette and belfry of the Archangelos church

carved wooden iconostasis and pulpit. The walls are now hung with over 50 icons, dating from the 18th-20th centuries, that were removed from local churches. One of the oldest was painted in 1714. Other objects

on display are sacral books and a carved crosier. Outside are marble sarcophagi, dating from the Byzantine period.

During summer, Catholic mass is celebrated in the late-Gothic **Chapel of Terra Santa**, situated further west, in Ersin Aydin Sokagi. The only other Christian place of worship in Kyrenia is the Anglican **Church of St Andrew**, which was built in 1913 close to the castle and the Muslim cemetery.

Fine Arts Museum

Open 8am–3:30pm daily.

This fine arts museum is housed in a somewhat ostentatious villa that was built in 1938 in the western part of Kyrenia. Its eclectic collection of artwork comprises a variety of unrelated exhibits, ranging from anonymous paintings (both oil and watercolour) to European porcelain, to Oriental jewellery.

Kyrenia's natural horseshoe harbour, the most beautiful in Cyprus

Kyrenia Town Map

1. Town Hall
2. Byzantine Tower
3. Market
4. Djafer Pasha Mosque (Cafer Paşa Camii)
5. Folk Art Museum
6. Harbour
7. Archangelos Church & Icon Museum

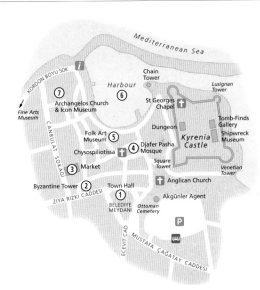

0 metres   150
0 yards   150

For keys to symbols *see back flap*

Kyrenia Castle and Shipwreck Museum

Kyrenia Castle was built by the Byzantines on the site of a Roman fort and later extended by the Lusignans. The Venetians turned it into a vast fortress occupied by the Turks in 1570. The castle was never taken by force.

Today it houses a Tomb-Finds Gallery and a Shipwreck Museum, with the wreck of an ancient vessel dating from the days of Alexander the Great. The magnificent view from the city walls encompasses the harbour and St Hilarion castle.

Shipwreck Museum
On display here is what remains of a merchant vessel that sank in a storm some 2,300 years ago.

Amphorae
Nearly 400 clay amphorae for storing wine were found in the wreck of a sailing vessel, probably bound for Anatolia from the Greek islands.

The Lusignan Tower
Arranged in the vaulted rooms of the two-storey tower are figures of medieval soldiers standing by the guns.

The Courtyard
Surrounded by stone walls, the large courtyard has a series of stone balls lying around and a quern (millstone) of volcanic rock.

KEY

① **The Tomb-Finds Gallery** comprises a reconstructed late Neolithic dwelling and tombs from both Kirini and Akdeniz (Agia Irini).

② **Square Tower**

③ **West Wall**

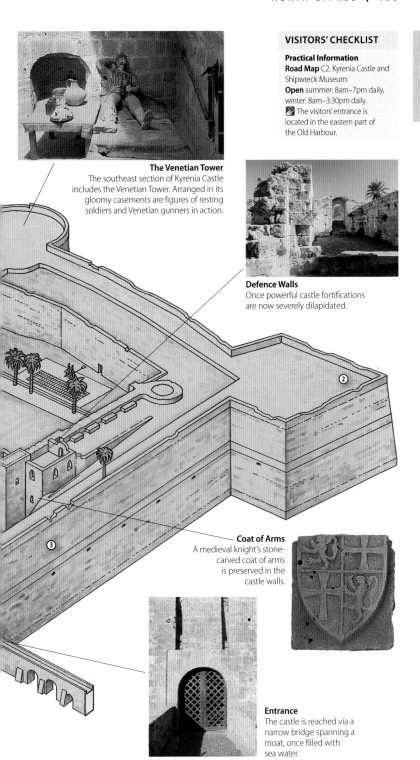

The Venetian Tower
The southeast section of Kyrenia Castle includes the Venetian Tower. Arranged in its gloomy casements are figures of resting soldiers and Venetian gunners in action.

VISITORS' CHECKLIST

Practical Information
Road Map C2. Kyrenia Castle and Shipwreck Museum:
Open summer: 8am–7pm daily, winter: 8am–3:30pm daily.
The visitors' entrance is located in the eastern part of the Old Harbour.

Defence Walls
Once powerful castle fortifications are now severely dilapidated.

Coat of Arms
A medieval knight's stone-carved coat of arms is preserved in the castle walls.

Entrance
The castle is reached via a narrow bridge spanning a moat, once filled with sea water.

Lapithos (Lapta) – a popular destination for daytrips from Kyrenia

⑱ Lambousa (Lambusa)

Road Map C2. Situated on the coast, 1.5 km (1 mile) from the village of Alsançak (Karavas).

On a small, rocky peninsula near Cape Acheiropitios, Lambousa was one of several ancient Cypriot kingdoms. This cosmopolitan city-state was inhabited by the Greeks, Phoenicians, Romans and Byzantines, as well as the Hittites and Franks. The earliest inhabitants arrived in the 13th century BC. In the 8th century BC Lambousa was conquered by the Phoenicians, but its most glorious times were in the Roman and Byzantine periods.

In the course of excavation works carried out in the early 20th century, archaeologists

Fragments of ruins from the ancient city-state of Lambousa

discovered on this site a 6th-century Byzantine treasure consisting of gold and silver artifacts. Some of these are now on display in the Cyprus Museum in Nicosia *(see p127)*, with the rest divided between the British Museum in London, the Metropolitan Museum in New York and the Dumbarton Oaks Collection in Washington, DC.

Only the eastern portion of ancient Lambousa is open to the public. It includes a dozen rock tombs and a series of vast tanks for keeping freshly caught fish alive.

⑲ Lapithos (Lapta)

Road Map C2. 18 km (11 miles) west of Kyrenia.

This picturesque village, with its isolated dwellings scattered around mountain slopes, is a popular day-trip destination from Kyrenia.

The abundant water supply made this a natural supply base for ancient Lambousa, until the threat of Arab raids in the 7th century caused the inhabitants to move to a safer site inland. The settlement was once famous for its silks and exquisite ceramics.

Lapithos was formerly inhabited by both Cypriot communities living in concord; they left behind seven churches and two mosques. In 1963–4 the local Turks were forced to

leave the village. After 1974 it was the Greeks' turn to leave.

Now, in addition to Turkish Cypriots, Lapithos' population includes settlers from Anatolia and a handful of foreigners.

Environs
Karman (Karmi) is one of the loveliest Cypriot villages, with whitewashed houses built on hillsides. The small church has a collection of icons removed from the abandoned Greek churches. Nearby is a necropolis dating from 2,300–1,625 BC. The village is now inhabited almost exclusively by British and German expatriates.

⑳ Larnaka tis Lapithou (Kozan)

Road Map C2.

This village enjoys a scenic location on the southern slopes of Selvii Dag (Kiparissovouno), the peak of the Kyrenian range at 1,024 m (3,360 ft). It makes an excellent base for hikes and bicycle trips around the neighbouring mountains. The local church was turned into a mosque, while the nearby monastery, Panagia ton Katharon, was sacked after 1974.

Kormakitis village, the capital of the Cypriot Maronites

㉑ Kormakitis (Koruçam)

Road Map B2. 9 km (6 miles) west of Camlibel (Myrton).

Kormakitis is the capital of the Cypriot Maronite Christian sect. In the 1960s this was a prosperous small town with a

Views from the Kormakitis peninsula

population of over 1,000. Now it has dwindled to about one tenth of that number. Although the Maronites tried to stay impartial in the Greek-Turkish conflict, after 1974 many were forced by Turkish persecution to leave their homes and emigrate. The current residents of the village are mostly elderly, and despite living through those difficult times, the people are unfailingly kind, cheerful and hospitable.

Daily mass is still celebrated in the local church, **Agios Gregorios**, which is now far too large for the needs of its current congregation. To visit the church you should contact the nearby convent or go to the next-door coffee-house to enquire about the church being opened. **Profitis Ilias**, standing close to the village, is the main Maronite monastery on the island.

Environs
Next to the village of Akdeniz (Agia Irini), which lies close to the Güzelyurt (Morfou) bay, is an interesting archaeological site believed to date from the late Bronze era to the Archaic era. A reconstruction of a tomb that was discovered here can now be seen in the Kyrenia Castle museum.

Just off the road leading to Nicosia stands a Bronze Age shrine – the Pigadhes sanctuary. Its stone altar is decorated with geometric reliefs and crowned by a pair of bull horns, indicating the Minoan influence.

22 Cape Kormakitis (Koruçam Burnu)
Road map B2.

Cape Kormakitis, called Koruçam Burnu by the Turks, is the northeasternmost part of Cyprus. In terms of landscape and wildlife, it is similar to the Karpasia and Akamas peninsulas; together they are the wildest and least accessible parts of the island. The few villages that existed in this areas have now been largely deserted. The North Cyprus authorities plan to turn this area into a nature reserve.

A rough track running among limestone hills covered with Mediterranean vegetation leads from the Maronite village of Kormakitis towards the small village of Sadrazamköy (Livera). From here, a 3.5-km (2.2-mile) unmade but serviceable road runs towards Cape Kormakitis. The cape lies in a desolate area

Waves breaking off Cape Kormakitis

of dreary rocks, a handful of deserted dwellings and an unmanned lighthouse at the very tip. The nearby rocky island of Nissi Kormakitis lies a mere 60 km (37 miles) from Cape Anamur on the Anatolian coast of Turkey.

For centuries, the cape has been inhabited by Maronites, a Christian sect that originated in Syria and Lebanon in the 7th century. This Eastern Christian sect, whose members proclaim themselves to be Catholic and to recognize the supremacy of the Pope, arose from a dispute between Monophysites (who postulated a single, divine nature of Jesus) and Christians (who believed Jesus to be both divine and human). The Maronites took their name from the 4th- or 5th-century Syrian hermit, St Maron. They arrived on Cyprus in the 12th century, with the Crusaders, whom they served during their campaigns in the Holy Land.

Endangered Sea Turtles

The legally protected green turtle (Chylonia mydas)

Both the loggerhead (Caretta caretta) and green (Chylonia mydas) species of sea turtle that nest on the beaches of Cyprus are endangered species subject to conservation programmes. Their nesting season lasts from mid-May to mid-October. The female digs a hole 30–60 cm (12–24 in) into the sand, in which she deposits her eggs. The hatchlings emerge after 55–60 days and head for the sea. Those that survive will return after 30 years to the same beach to breed. Only one in 40 turtles succeeds.

㉓ Morfou (Güzelyurt)

Road Map B3. 🎨 Orange Festival (May).

The Turkish name Güzelyurt means "beautiful place". And, indeed, the local citrus groves and picturesque bay add to the lovely scenery here.

It was close to the town that archaeologists discovered the earliest traces of human habitation in Cyprus, dating from the Neolithic and Early Bronze eras when copper was produced and exported.

The best historic site in Güzelyurt is the **church and monastery of Agios Mamas**, built during the Byzantine period on the site of a former pagan temple. In the 15th century it acquired Gothic embellishments, and in the 18th century a dome.

The interior features the throne of St Mamas, a Gothic window carved in stone, an iconostasis and a marble sarcophagus of the saint.

Until 1974 swarms of pilgrims streamed to Agios Mamas from all over Cyprus, but after the Turkish invasion it was shut and used to store icons brought here from the nearby Orthodox churches. It is now an **Icon Museum**.

Other than Agios Mamas, the town has few tourist attractions. Next to the church is the **Archaeology and Natural History Museum**. Besides several exhibits of stuffed animals and

Monastery buildings of Agios Mamas in Morfou

Atatürk's statue in Lefke

birds, and a collection of ancient ceramics, the museum also houses an exhibition of Late Bronze Age objects found in the course of excavations conducted in Töumba and Skourou.

🏛 **Icon Museum & Archaeology and Natural History Museum**
Agios Mamas. **Open** summer: 9am–6pm daily; winter: 8am–3:30pm daily. 🎨

㉔ Léfka (Lefke)

Road Map B3.

Inhabited for over 400 years by Turks, Lefke is a major centre of Islam on the island. The central square sports a huge equestrian statue of Atatürk. A few hundred metres further on stands the early 19th-century mosque of **Piri Osman Pasha**, built in the Cyprian style. The garden surrounding the mosque contains the tomb of Vizier Osman Pasha, who was supposedly killed by poison – a victim of a palace intrigue. His marble sarcophagus is one of the loveliest surviving works of its kind from the Ottoman period.

Lefke European University, one of five universities in North Cyprus, trains students from many countries of the Middle East and Central Asia. The pleasant **Lefke Gardens Hotel** occupies a renovated 19th-century inn (see p165). Lefke is also the seat of Kibrisli

Logo of the university in Lefke

Syke Nazim, the *murshid* or spiritual leader of the Naqshbandi order of Sufism, who decides on all spiritual aspects of life of the faithful.

Environs
In the nearby coastal town of Gemikonagi (Karavostasi) is the excellent **Mardinli** restaurant, standing on a beach surrounded by a garden and orchard that provide its kitchen with fruit and vegetables. On the other side of town, between the road and the sea, stands an imposing monument to a Turkish pilot killed during the 1974 invasion.

㉕ Soloi (Soli Harabeleri)

Road Map B3. 20 km (12.5 miles) W of Güzelyurt. **Open** summer: 9am–6pm daily; winter: 8am–3:30pm daily. 🎨

Soloi, a one-time city-state of Cyprus, was supposedly founded at the suggestion of the Athenian law-giver Solon, who persuaded King Philocyprus of Aepea to build a new capital close to the river Ksero. In his honour, the town was named Soloi. The reality, however, was probably quite different. As long ago as Assyrian times (c.700 BC) a town called Sillu stood on this site. It was a stronghold of Greek culture, and was the last town to fall to the Persians.

The town gave its name to the entire region of Solea, on the northern slopes of the Troodos mountains, where Cypriot copper was mined near the present-day town of Skouriotissa. The extraction and export of this metal spurred the growth of Soloi, particularly during Roman times. There was a good harbour, needed for the export of copper, and abundant water.

It was in Soloi that St Mark converted a Roman named Auxibius to Christianity; he later became bishop of Soloi. Stones taken from the ruins of the ancient town were used by the British and the French in the building of the Suez Canal and the coastal town of Port Said. It was only in the late 1920s that Swedish archaeologists unearthed a theatre, and in 1964 a Canadian team uncovered the basilica and part of the agora (market place).

The Roman theatre was built for an audience of 4,000 people, and had a lovely view over the sea. It has been restored and during summer is often used as a venue for shows and concerts.

Above the theatre the archaeologists uncovered remains of palaces and a temple to Athena. The famous 1st-century marble statuette of Aphrodite, found nearby, can now be seen in the Cyprus Museum in Nicosia (see p126). Lower down are the ruins of the 5th-century Byzantine basilica, which was destroyed in the course of the 632 Arab raid.

Displayed under a makeshift roof are some fairly well-preserved mosaics from the temple floor, featuring geometric and animal motifs. The most interesting mosaics depict water birds surrounded by dolphins. Another small medallion features a swan.

Unearthed to the north of the ruined basilica is a poorly preserved agora.

Soloi is surrounded by vast burial grounds, dating from various periods of antiquity.

Ruins of the ancient palace in Vouni

㉖ Vouni (Vuni Sarayi)

Road Map B3. 27 km (17 miles) west of Güzelyurt. **Open** summer: 9am–6pm daily; winter: 8am–3:30pm daily.

This magnificent, somewhat mysterious palace stands atop a coastal hill, 250 m (820 ft) above sea level. The site is extraordinarily beautiful, with panoramic views over the North Cyprus coast and the Troodos mountains to the south.

Mosaic from Soloi

The palace was likely built by a pro-Persian king of Marion (a city near present-day Polis), as evidenced by its Oriental architectural details.

Occupying a strategic spot, the residence was probably intended to intimidate the nearby pro-Athenian town of Soloi. Following an anti-Persian insurrection, Vouni (which means "mountain" in Greek) was taken over by the supporters of Greece. Having

occupied the palace, they rebuilt it, adding a temple to Athena, among other things. When the reversal of military fortunes resulted in the Persians returning to power, the palace was burned down in 380 BC.

Today the ruins are reached via a new, narrow and winding road. Above the car park are the scant remains of a temple to Athena, dating from the late 5th century BC. The stairs on the opposite side lead to the palace courtyard, which features a guitar-shape stone stele with a hole in it and an unfinished face of a woman, probably a goddess. The adjacent cistern was used to supply water to the luxurious baths in the northwestern portion of the palace, which reputedly had 137 rooms.

Environs

The small rocky island off the west coast, visible from Vouni palace, is **Petra tou Limniti**. This is the oldest inhabited part of Cyprus, colonized as early as the Neolithic era.

Remains of the ancient agora in Soloi

TRAVELLERS' NEEDS

WHERE TO STAY

Cyprus has a choice of places to stay that is every bit as wide as its portfolio of visitor attractions and holiday activities, with accommodation to suit all budgets. Its climate attracts holidaymakers all through the year, and most of the hotels and guesthouses are open year round. Accommodation ranges from simple, family-run guesthouses and small apartment complexes to large resort hotels with an array of facilities for families, luxury villas with private pools and stylishly restored village houses. Hotels in the three- and four-star categories are generally more luxurious than their equivalent in other Mediterranean countries, and Cyprus has a well-deserved reputation for affordable comfort.

Majestic exterior of the Roman Hotel in Pafos *(see p162)*

Package Deals

Some hotels in the popular resorts are fully booked by holiday companies, which can, at peak times, make it difficult for independent travellers to find good accommodation on arrival. Booking a holiday package (which includes flights and hotel) is often the best, and usually the cheapest, option. In low season, bargains may be found on the Internet. The **Cyprus Hotel Association** also has booking desks at Larnaka airport.

Hotels

Most of the island's hotels are clustered along the coast on either side of Larnaka and Limassol, and in the resorts of Pafos, Agia Napa and Protaras. There are few stretches of coastline that lack any accommodation options. In the Larnaka and Limassol areas most hotels are compact high-rise blocks, while many hotels in the Pafos and Agia Napa regions are low-rise resort complexes with swimming pools and play areas for children. There are also small hotels and apartment complexes in these resorts, though some are reserved by tour operators. Visitors looking for a tranquil stay can head to some of the lesser-known places inland.

All major hotels are modern and well equipped, almost always with air conditioning. The **Cyprus Tourism Organization (CTO)**, and the Turkish tourism ministry in the occupied North, grade hotels from one to five stars. Those rated one or two stars are likely to be slightly shabby with few facilities. Upper-end hotels may offer a wide range of activities, from watersports, spas, tennis and golf to cabaret, traditional music and dancing, and discos.

Rates

Rates vary depending on the season, with bargains available outside the peak spring and summer months. Rates are highest during Easter (both Greek Orthodox and non-Orthodox Easter), for the two weeks around Christmas, and from June to September.

The trend for most of the larger hotels is to offer all-inclusive options, with fewer bed and breakfast, half-board or full-board choices. Smaller hotels may not include breakfast in the rate. Make sure the quoted rate includes local taxes.

Private Accommodation

It is not always easy to find accommodation in private homes and, when found, they may not always offer a high standard of comfort or facilities. These are nonetheless graded by the **CTO** to ensure they meet their minimum standards. Avoid unofficial private accommodation. The **CTO** can provide a list of small bed-and-breakfast establishments.

Lodgings in monasteries were once a popular option, but today are available only to Orthodox pilgrims.

Agrotourism

Visitors who prefer the charm of a quiet, rural village to the hustle and bustle of a tourist resort can go for agrotourism options, which are increasingly popular among couples and independent travellers. Accommodation is usually in a restored traditional house, where guests have the opportunity to participate in some of the traditions of the

The vast Four Seasons hotel in Limassol *(see p163)*

◀ A picturesque restaurant with views over the Bellapis Village in North Cyprus

The mountains surround the Onar Holiday Village, Kyrenia *(see p165)*

village. This is especially common in the mountains.

Village houses usually feature modern kitchens and bathrooms, but be prepared for the occasional cut in the water and power supplies. These houses almost always have gardens with fruit trees. Basic home-made foodstuffs such as bread, fresh honey or jam can be bought from neighbours, while other supplies can be brought from the larger towns nearby.

The **Cyprus Agrotourism Company** can assist in finding village accommodation.

Hostels and Campsites

Youth hostels in South Cyprus that once belonged to the International Youth Hostel Association are no longer in operation. The **CTO** runs five officially designated camping sites at Governor's Beach (Limassol district), Geroskipou, Pegeia and Polis (Pafos district), and in the Troodos mountains. Facilities are basic, but include showers and toilets, and a simple bar-restaurant.

Reservations

While reserving a place to stay ahead of arrival is advisable, it is not always necessary, even in the more rugged North. Some hotels, especially those in Pafos, Agia Napa and Protaras are block-booked by package holiday companies. The **CTO** can supply hotel information for travellers to book directly with hotels or via websites.

Disabled Travellers

Most of the newer and larger hotels in the South of Cyprus are wheelchair-accessible (some even have ramp facilities leading to the beach) and hotels here are working to meet European accessibility norms. Cheaper, smaller hotels, village houses and villas are unlikely to offer wheelchair access. In the North, hotels are far less likely to be wheelchair-accessible. Contact the hotel, travel agent or tour operator well ahead of time to confirm accessibility details.

Recommended Hotels

The hotels listed on the following pages have been divided into several categories that are indicative of that hotel's most prominent feature, although it is fair to say that some establishments will

The bar area of the Hilton Resort *(see p164)*

fall into more than one category. Cyprus has a large number of luxury hotels and some of the best feature here. Similarly, many hotels offer family amenities like playgrounds, babysitting and children's clubs and for this reason have been judged ideal for families. The business hotels may have a full conference centre, or may have fewer facilities but be in locations that makes them ideal for meetings, for instance, closer to the airports or major towns. The rural and apartments/villa categories detail establishments in villages and for independent holidays respectively.

Many of the most interesting and remarkable options in Cyprus are not necessarily the most expensive ones, so look out for the hotels selected as a DK Choice. These establishments have been highlighted for their excellent service and come highly recommended. This may be due to them having a stunning location, notable history, an inviting atmosphere or, quite often, just being outstanding value. Whatever the reason, the accommodation selected should offer a memorable stay.

DIRECTORY

Information

Cyprus Hotel Association
Andreas Araouzos 12,
1303 Nicosia.
Tel 22 452 820.
🔘 cyprushotelassociation.org

Cyprus Tourism Organization (CTO)
Leoforos Lemesou 19,
2112 Nicosia.
Tel 22 691 100.
🔘 visitcyprus.com

Agrotourism

Cyprus Agrotourism Company
Leoforos Lemesou 19,
PO Box 24535, 1390 Nicosia.
Tel 22 340 071.
🔘 agrotourism.com.cy

Where to Stay

West Cyprus

CORAL BAY: Crown Resorts Horizon
Family   Map A4
Coral Bay Ave, Pafos, 8068
Tel *26 813 800*
W crownresortsgroup.com
All rooms in this complex have verandas. Children are well catered for with activities.

CORAL BAY: Coral Beach Hotel   €€€
Family   Map A4
Coral Bay Ave, Pafos, 8099
Tel *26 881 000*
W coral.com.cy
Sprawling resort offering a crafts workshop, kids' facilities, an Olympic-sized pool and a spa.

DK Choice

LATSI: Anassa   €€€
Luxury   Map A3
Baths of Aphrodite Rd, Neo Chorio, 8830
Tel *26 888 000*
W anassa.com.cy
Luxuriously stylish with a thalassotherapy spa, tennis courts and five sea-view restaurants, the five-star Anassa overlooks the picturesque Chrysochou Bay. Offers good facilities for kids, including special menus.

PAFOS: Lasa Heights   €
Rural   Map A4
Lasa village, 8021
Tel *26 732 777*
W lasaheights.com
Agrotourism hotel housed in an 18th-century former coffee shop. Stone walls and a pretty courtyard.

The sleek inerior of Anassa, in Latsi

PAFOS: Mayfair Hotel   €
Family   Map A4
Pari St, Kato, 8064
Tel *26 948 000*
W mayfair.com.cy
Range of amenities and facilities for families, including babysitting. Good international restaurant.

PAFOS: Kissos Hotel   €€
Modern   Map A4
Queen Verenikis St, 8045
Tel *26 936 111*
W kissoshotel.com
Attractive low-rise hotel near the Tombs of the Kings. With a mini golf course and lagoon-style pool.

PAFOS: Queen's Bay Hotel   €€
Family   Map A4
Coral Bay Rd, 8102
Tel *26 946 600*
W queensbay.com.cy
Set in lavish gardens, this hotel has modern rooms and excellent sports facilities.

PAFOS: Roman Hotel   €€
Family   Map A4
Tombs of the Kings Ave, 8040
Tel *26 945 411*
W romanhotel.com.cy
Built to resemble an ancient temple, with rooms decorated in an elaborate style.

PAFOS: St George   €€
Modern   Map A4
Coral Bay Rd, 8063
Tel *26 845 000*
W stgeorge-hotel.com
Luxurious yet informal hotel with minimalist rooms and stylish restaurants and bars.

PAFOS: Amathus Beach   €€€
Modern   Map A4
Poseidon Ave, 8098
Tel *26 883 300*
W amathus-hotels.com
Luxury hotel with impressive views. Sleek design.

PAFOS: Annabelle   €€€
Luxury   Map A4
Poseidon Ave, 8102
Tel *26 885 000*
W thanoshotels.com
Located on the seafront, Annabelle is a sumptuous hotel with relaxation at its heart.

PAFOS: Azia Beach   €€€
Luxury   Map A4
Akamas Rd, Chlorakas, 8061
Tel *26 845 100*
W aziaresort.com
Elegantly decorated hotel nestled among palm trees. Good health complex and spa.

PAFOS: Elysium Beach Resort   €€€
Luxury   Map A4
Queen Verenikis St, 8107
Tel *26 844 444*
W elysium.com.cy
A beach resort with a Byzantine chapel, a spa and children's park.

POLIS: Bougainvillea Apartments   €€
Apartments/Villas   Map A3
Verginas St, 8820
Tel *26 322 203*
W bougainvillea.com.cy
Villas set around a pool and covered in bright bougainvillea.

POLIS: Natura Beach   €€
Family   Map A3
Papanikopoulos Ave, 8831
Tel *26 323 111*
W natura.com.cy
Eco-friendly, family-run hotel near the beach. Good restaurant.

Southern Cyprus

AGIA NAPA: Limanaki Beach Hotel   €€
Family   Map E3
1st October St, 5330
Tel *23 721 600*
W ayianapahotels.net
Small seafront hotel with terraces, a health suite and a restaurant.

AGIA NAPA: Grecian Bay Hotel   €€€
Luxury   Map E3
Kriou Nerou 32, 5330
Tel *23 842 000*
W grecianbay.com
Fantastic beachside hotel. Spa, lagoon pool and à la carte dining.

AGIA NAPA: Nissi Beach   €€€
Family   Map E3
Nissi Ave, Nissi Beach, 5343
Tel *23 721 021*
W nissi-beach.com
Centrally located popular hotel with great sports amenities.

LARNAKA: Boronia Hotel Apartments   €
Apartments/Villas   Map D3
Dhekelia Rd, 7040
Tel *24 646 200*
A cosy complex of apartments centered on a pool. Close to the

beach. The restaurant serves international cuisine.

LARNAKA: Flamingo Beach €€
Modern   **Map** D3
Piale Pasha Ave, 6028
Tel *24 828 208*
w flamingobeachhotel.com
Business and leisure hotel where most rooms have beach views.

LARNAKA: Lordos Beach
Hotel   €€
Family   **Map** D3
Dhekelia Rd, Pyla, 7080
Tel *24 647 444*
w lordosbeach.com.cy
Next to a long sandy beach. Offers pools, watersports and a spa.

LARNAKA: Princess Beach
Hotel   €€
Family   **Map** D3
Dhekelia Rd, Oroklini, 7041
Tel *24 645 500*
w princessbeachhotel.com
Attractive hotel among palm trees, with on-site health suite, pools and eateries.

LARNAKA: Hotel-E €€€
Modern   **Map** D3
Farou 70, Pervolia, Larnaka, 7560
Tel *24 747 000*
w hotel-e.com
Contemporary and eco-friendly. Business suite and rooftop bar.

LARNAKA: Palm Beach Hotel €€€
Luxury   **Map** D3
Dhekelia Rd, Oroklini, 6303
Tel *24 846 600*
w palmbeachhotel.com
Seafront five-star hotel with all the amenities. Beautiful gardens.

LARNAKA: The Golden Bay
Beach Hotel   €€€
Family   **Map** D3
Dhekelia Rd, Pyla, 7080
Tel *24 645 444*
w goldenbay.com.cy
A five-star hotel complex with luxury rooms and modern decor. Fantastic Greek-style taverna.

LEFKARA: Lefkarama €
Rural   **Map** C4
Pano Lefkara, 7700
Tel *24 342 154*
w lefkarahotels.com
Housed in a traditional Cypriot stone inn, this pretty hotel has 10 guestrooms and a restaurant.

LIMASSOL: Pefkos Hotel €
Modern   **Map** C4
Kavazoglou & Mishiaouli St, 3608
Tel *25 577 083*
w pefkoshotel.com
Family-run hotel with comfortable rooms, a pool, restaurant and attractive lounge area.

The popular Four Seasons resort in Limassol

LIMASSOL: Chrielka Hotel
Apartments   €€
Apartments/Villas   **Map** C4
Olympion St, 3720
Tel *25 358 366*
w chrielka.com
Family-run apartment complex near the beach. Whirlpool and bar.

LIMASSOL: Episkopiana Hotel €€
Modern   **Map** C4
Kremmastis Rd, 3505
Tel *25 935 098*
w episkopianahotel.com
Popular with business and sports travellers, with its conference suite, huge pool and football grounds.

LIMASSOL: Four Seasons €€€
Luxury   **Map** C4
Amathous Ave, 3313
Tel *25 858 000*
w fourseasons.com.cy
One of the island's best hotels, with six gourmet restaurants, luxurious rooms and the renowned Shiseido spa.

LIMASSOL: Grand Resort €€€
Luxury   **Map** C4
Amathous Ave, 3724
Tel *25 634 333*
w grandresort.com.cy
A seafront hotel with fine dining options, a health suite and poolside gardens to relax in.

LIMASSOL: Le Méridien Limassol
Spa and Resort   €€€
Luxury   **Map** C4
Amathous Ave, 3308
Tel *25 862 000*
w lemeridienlimassol.com
Luxury at its best, with children's play areas, a bowling alley and a large thalassotherapy centre.

LIMASSOL: Londa €€€
Luxury   **Map** C4
George I Ave, Potamos Yermasoyias, 4048
Tel *25 865 555*
w londahotel.com
For business and leisure travellers. Ultra-stylish decor and upmarket restaurant, spa and patisserie.

LIMASSOL: Mediterranean €€€
Luxury   **Map** C4
Amathous Ave, 3310
Tel *25 311 777*
w medbeach.com
Five-star beachside complex with decadent rooms. Swimming pool on a separate connected island.

LIMASSOL: St Raphael Resort €€€
Family   **Map** C4
Amathous Ave, 3594
Tel *25 634 100*
w raphael.com.cy
Well-equipped rooms, excellent restaurants and many sports and health amenities.

PISSOURI: The Bunch of
Grapes Inn   €
Rural   **Map** B4
Loannou Erotokritou 9, 4607
Tel *25 221 275*
w thebunchofgrapesinn.com
Quaint family-run inn offering apartments and a courtyard fine-dining restaurant.

PISSOURI: Hill View €€
Apartments/Villas   **Map** B4
Stadiou 30, 4697
Tel *25 221 972*
w hillview.com.cy
This superb apartment complex enjoys fantastic views. Top-class accommodation and dining.

DK Choice

PISSOURI: Columbia Beach
Hotel & Resort   €€€
Luxury   **Map** B4
Coastal Rd, Pissouri Bay, 3779
Tel *25 833 333*
w columbia-beach.com
This complex comprises a resort and a five-star beach hotel with luxurious rooms. Looking out over the bay, it is designed to resemble a traditional Cypriot village. There are a range of amenities: an upmarket spa, lagoon-style swimming pools, gourmet restaurants and a chapel.

For more information on types of hotels *see p161*

The relaxed lounge area of the Hilton Cyprus

Troodos Mountains

KAKOPETRIA: The Mill Hotel €
Family   **Map** B3
Mylou 8, 2800
Tel *22 922 536*
🅦 cymillhotel.com
This picturesque 17th-century former mill boasts a fantastic restaurant specializing in trout.

KAKOPETRIA: Makris Hotel €€
Rural   **Map** B3
Kakopetria village, 2810
Tel *22 922 419*
Traditional hotel in a pine forest with a swimming pool, tennis courts and organized excursions.

KAKOPETRIA: Maritsa Lodge €€
Rural   **Map** B3
Paleas Kakopetria 70, 2800
Tel *22 754 727*
Cosy stone-house lodge. Well located for cycling and hiking in the Troodos mountains.

PEDOULAS: Mountain Rose €
Rural   **Map** B3
Filoxenias 35, 2850
Tel *22 952 727*
🅦 mountainrosehotel.com
Experience quaint village life at Mountain Rose. Well-equipped rooms, a restaurant and a shop.

PLATRES: Minerva Hotel €
Rural   **Map** B3
Spyrou Kyprianou 36, 4820
Tel *25 421 731*
Warm and welcoming place set in lush gardens. Great for wildlife enthusiasts, offering access to the owner's botanical library.

PLATRES: Petit Palais Hotel €
Rural   **Map** B3
Pano Platres village, 4825
Tel *25 421 723*
🅦 petitpalaishotel.com
Lodge-style rooms with amazing views of the Troodos. The two restaurants serve local cuisine.

PLATRES: New Helvetia Hotel €€
Family   **Map** B3
6 Helvetia St, 4820
Tel *25 421 348*
🅦 newhelvetiahotel.com
Charming Colonial-style hotel with classic decor. Good base for exploring nearby trails.

PLATRES: The Pendeli Hotel €€
Rural   **Map** B3
Pano Platres village, 4825
Tel *25 421 736*
🅦 aquasolhotels.com
Centrally located yet peaceful, with a pool, sun terrace and fitness suite.

DK Choice

TROODOS: Jubilee Hotel €€
Rural   **Map** B3
Troodos Cillage, 1504
Tel *25 420 107*
🅙 jubileehotel.com
Cyprus's highest hotel close to the runs for winter skiing, and to hiking and cycling trails. A perfect antidote for the beach resorts. Offers a games room, restaurant and playground for the kids.

Central Cyprus

DK Choice

AGROS: Rodon Hotel €
Rural   **Map** C3
Rodou 1, 4860
Tel *25 521 201*
🅦 rodonhotel.com
The Rodon is a beautifully renovated country house with stylish rooms and lounge areas. It retains a rustic charm while offering modern amenities including two swimming pools, a tennis court and a gymnasium.

AGROS: Vlachos Hotel €
Family   **Map** C3
Agros village, 4860
Tel *25 521 330*
A cosy hotel with babysitting services and a good restaurant serving international cuisine.

ASKAS: Evghenia's House €
Rural   **Map** C3
Gregori Afxentiou 77, 2752
Tel *22 642 344*
🅦 agrotourism.com.cy
Housed in a charming 17th-century cottage, part of the country's agrotourism project. An ideal base to explore the area.

LYTHRODONTAS: Avli Georgallidi €
Rural   **Map** C3
Georgallidi Courtyard, 2565
🅦 agrotourism.com.cy
Rustic self-catering cottages from the 19th century. The focus is on the natural environment.

South Nicosia

Asty Hotel €€
Modern   **Map** C3
12 Prince Charles, Agios Dometios, 1300
Tel *22 773 030*
🅦 astyhotel.com
Close to the business district, with a gymnasium and restaurant.

Classic Hotel €€
Modern   **Map** C3
Regeana 94, 1513
Tel *22 664 006*
🅦 classic.com.cy
Stylish rooms, plus restaurants and bars. Within the city walls.

Castelli €€€
Luxury   **Map** C3
Ouzounian 38, 1504
Tel *22 712 812*
🅦 castellihotel.com.cy
Housed in a 19th-century mansion. Elegant rooms and many leisure amenities on offer.

Cleopatra Hotel €€€
Luxury   **Map** C3
Florinis 8, 1065
Tel *22 844 000*
🅦 cleopatra.com.cy
Located close to attractions with comfortable rooms, upmarket restaurants and a health suite.

Hilton Cyprus €€€
Luxury   **Map** C3
Archbishop Makarious III, 1516
Tel *22 377 777*
🅦 hilton.com
The five-star Hilton is the finest hotel in the capital, with a health

spa, gourmet dining restaurants and stylish bars. Luxurious guest-rooms and communal areas.

DK Choice

Holiday Inn
Family €€€
Map C3
Regeana 70, 1504
Tel 22 712 712
W holidayinn.com
One of the few hotels located within the city walls, the Holiday Inn is ideal for exploring the historic heart of Nicosia. The hotel offers luxurious rooms, an indoor swimming pool and spa complex, and restaurants where children eat for free.

North Cyprus

BELLAPAIS: Ambelia Village Hotel
Apartments/Villas €€
Map C2
Bellapais village
Tel 0392 815 36 55
W cyprus-ambelia.com
Self-catering villas and studios near the village's famous abbey and tavernas. Good restaurant.

FAMAGUSTA: Portofino Hotel €
Family **Map** E3
Fevzi Çakmak Blvd, Ammochostos
Tel 0392 366 43 92
A small traditional hotel with panoramic views from its rooftop restaurant and bar. Comfortable rooms with balconies.

FAMAGUSTA: Arkin Palm Beach Hotel
Family €€
Map E3
Nadir Yolu, Deve Limani
Tel 0392 366 20 00
W arkinpalmbeach.com
Contemporary seafront hotel great for families, with gardens, a spa and babysitting facilities.

FAMAGUSTA: Salamis Bay Conti Resort Hotel €€
Family **Map** E3
Coast Rd
Tel 0392 378 82 00
W salamisbay-conti.com
One of Famagusta's best, with restaurants, a fitness centre, kid's club and nightly entertainment.

KYRENIA: Acapulco Resort & Convention & Spa €€
Family **Map** C2
Catalkoy
Tel 0392 824 44 49
W acapulco.com.tr
Offers many daily activities from tennis and football to aerobics.

KYRENIA: Club Lapethos €€
Family **Map** C2
Maresai Febri Cakmak Cad, Lapta
Tel 0392 821 86 69
W lapethosresort.com
Resort with an aqua park of pools and slides. Fantastic multi-cuisine restaurant.

KYRENIA: Dome Hotel €€
Family **Map** C2
Kordonboyu Cad
Tel 0392 815 24 53
W hoteldome.com
A constant near the harbour since 1937 its rooms feature classic decor. Good fine-dining restaurant.

KYRENIA: Merit Crystal Cove €€
Family **Map** C2
Karavas
Tel 0392 821 23 45
On a hill overlooking the beach, this hotel has beautiful rooms, a health suite and a casino.

KYRENIA: Onar Holiday Village €€
Apartments/Villas **Map** C2
Coast Rd
Tel 0392 815 58 50
W onarvillage.com
This sprawling complex of villas is designed to resemble a village.

Includes a swimming pool, play areas, Turkish bath and spa.

KYRENIA: Cratos Premium Hotel €€€
Luxury **Map** C2
Catalkoy
Tel 0392 444 42 42
W cratospremium.com
Luxurious vacation spot with a gourmet French restaurant, terrace bar and casino.

KYRENIA: Savoy Ottoman Palace Hotel €€€
Luxury **Map** C2
Sehit Fehmi Ercan 5
Tel 0392 444 30 00
W savoyhotel.com.tr
One of Kyrenia's finest hotels, with deluxe rooms featuring classic Ottoman decor.

DK Choice

KYRENIA: The Colony Hotel €€€
Luxury **Map** C2
Ecevit Ave
Tel 0392 815 15 18
W parkheritage.com
This Colonial-style hotel is Kyrenia's most famous. Set between the North Cyprus mountains and the Mediterranean sea, the luxurious guestrooms and fine-dining restaurant ooze style. Relax in the spa and health centre or in the cocktail lounge. Located on the approach to Kyrenia harbour.

LAPITHOS: Manolya Hotel €
Rural **Map** C2
Fevri Cakmak Cad
Tel 0392 821 84 98
W manolyahotel.com
Modern hotel hugging the rocky shoreline. Rooms and the restaurant offer panoramic views. Snorkelling equipment available.

LÉFKA: Lefke Gardens Hotel €
Rural **Map** B3
Guzelyurt
Tel 0392 728 82 23
Housed in a period property in the centre of the village. Good base to explore the area. Rooms have traditional Cypriot decor.

NORTH NICOSIA (LEFKOŞA): Merit Hotel €€€
Modern **Map** C3
Bedrettin Demirel Cad
Tel 0392 600 55 00
W meritlefkosa.com
A five-star business hotel with contemporary rooms, conference facilities, upmarket restaurants and a health suite.

View towards the sea from the Onar Holiday Village

For more information on types of hotels *see p161*

WHERE TO EAT AND DRINK

The range of restaurants in Cyprus is wide enough to satisfy even the most discerning gastronome. For those looking for options beyond their hotel, there are many tavernas and restaurants to choose from. Many hotels now offer an all-inclusive option. The true atmosphere of a Cypriot banquet can be experienced in a traditional taverna, while smart restaurants are more likely to serve European cuisine. Greek-style tavernas and Turkish-style restaurants (*meyhane*) guarantee an evening with a great Cypriot atmosphere, often featuring folk performances and music. In general, the further one goes from the popular resorts, the more authentic the cuisine.

A traditional Cypriot taverna in Nicosia

Choosing a Restaurant

A vast selection of eating establishments exists in Cyprus. This is particularly evident in the popular resorts, where there are tavernas and restaurants on every street, serving a range of local and international cuisine. In addition to the traditional tavernas serving Greek and Turkish-influenced dishes, there are French, Italian, Mexican, Thai, Chinese, Indian, Middle Eastern, Russian and even Japanese restaurants. There are also cafés and snack bars, along with international fast-food eateries.

Most restaurants are casual, without a dress code. In terms of value, restaurants in town are usually cheaper than those found in hotels. Look out for establishments frequented by locals – these tend to serve good-value, tasty food.

On the whole, eating out in Cyprus is reasonable. Do bear in mind, however, that imported wines are much more expensive than locally produced wines.

When to Eat

Breakfast is usually eaten between 7:30am and 10am.

Most budget and inexpensive hotels serve a Continental breakfast comprising tea or coffee, fruit juice, toast, white bread, jam, honey and butter. Upscale hotels usually provide guests with a self-service bar stocked with light salads, a selection of cheeses, scrambled eggs and sausages. In North Cyprus it is customary to serve the traditional Turkish breakfast of bread, jam, white cheese and olives.

Lunch is usually eaten between noon and 2:30pm and may consist of *souvlaki* and doner kebabs, as well as sandwiches. Dinner, is the main

Menu boards outside a fish restaurant

meal of the day eaten between 8pm and late into the night by Cypriots, although earlier by other European countries or in hotels or international restaurants. Traditionally, an evening around the table in a Cypriot home is a social event, and can last several hours. The meal usually starts with a selection of *mezédhes* (appetizers), followed by a meat or fish main course accompanied by wine.

What to Eat

The exquisite cuisine of Cyprus is famous for the simplicity of its ingredients and ease of preparation. Traditional local recipes tend to be influenced by modern European trends, and British cuisine plays a major role.

The most important items on a Cypriot menu are the starters – called *mezédhes* – a vital element of a meal in any Mediterranean country, accompanied by traditional Cypriot bread baked on a hotplate. A decent restaurant will always include grilled *halloumi* (a cheese made from goat and sheep's milk), roast courgettes, and the real delicacy, *koupepia* – stuffed vine leaves. Other specialities include hummus (chickpea dip), *tahini* (sesame sauce) and *kleftiko* (lamb roasted in a clay stove).

For main courses, the Cypriot menu is dominated by lamb and seafood, and an array of vegetables, usually served with rice or roast potatoes. Lamb dishes are complemented by strong Cypriot wines.

Fish can be the most expensive item on the menu, although at coastal locations it is generally very fresh and tasty, so well worth the cost. Chicken is usually the cheapest meat dish available.

Happily for visitors, there should be no problem choosing from the menu, as the names of dishes are usually translated.

Vegetarians

Cypriot cuisine is based on essentially healthy Mediterranean produce and includes many vegetarian dishes traditionally eaten in Cypriot homes during the Lenten period and other Orthodox fasts, when meat is shunned. As well as huge "village salads" (*choriatiki*) of tomatoes, cucumber, onions, peppers, olives and feta cheese, there is plentiful fresh fruit and a good array of grilled and fried vegetable dishes, based on aubergines (eggplant), courgettes (zucchini), artichokes, peppers and tomatoes, and lots of tasty dips based on chickpeas, fava beans and other pulses. Cypriot cheeses are also worth recommending, especially the traditional fried *halloumi* cheese.

An increasing number of restaurants and hotels now also prepare vegetarian meals.

Alcohol

As far back as ancient times, Cyprus has produced good local wines, helped by the fertile soil and mild climate. The quality has been maintained to this day, using traditional methods of wine production. Wine-tasting sessions are held in wineries all over the island. Together these wineries produce nearly 40 varieties of wine, sherry and brandy. In the villages at the foot of the mountains visitors can sample home-made liqueurs which, in terms of quality and flavour, are often as good as branded products.

Cyprus' best-known product is the sweet dessert wine Commandaria. Nicknamed "Cypriot sun", this fortified wine with a raisin-like flavour makes an excellent digestive to round off a traditional Cypriot dinner and a good souvenir to take home. The strong, dry *zivania* apéritif is classified by the European Union as *eau-de-vie*.

The locally produced beers have a good flavour and are also inexpensive. When in North Cyprus try cold Efes; in the south, try KEO or the island-bottled Carlsberg.

Prices

The highest prices are charged by restaurants in fashionable resorts. Here the best-value meals are generally the chef's recommended dishes of the day. Set menus may be substantially cheaper than a selection of à la carte items. Seafood dishes tend to be particularly expensive.

One can eat at a more reasonable cost at restaurants

Enjoy cocktails in a stylish setting at Domus Lounge Bar *(see p176)*

in town – especially those frequented by the locals. The total bill always includes VAT and usually a service charge of around 10 per cent. Most restaurants accept credit cards.

Recommended Restaurants

The restaurants recommended on the following pages have been chosen to provide a insight into the island's diverse cuisine. Cyprus has a large number of traditional tavernas and those selected offer the most authentic Cypriot dining experience. Many can be found in the Troodos region. The island also has a wide choice of restaurants serving international cuisine, especially in the coastal resorts, although it many of these may also include classic Cypriot dishes on their menu.

Cyprus is a multicultural destination and our restaurant selection also includes suggestions for those who might want something different, for example Italian, French, Chinese, Japanese, Arabic or Indian cuisine. Cyprus also has a large number of fish restaurants, and restaurants that offer good vegetarian menus. Places marked DK Choice are considered to have outstanding quality and come highly recommended. They may have historical charm, exceptional cooking or an oustanding location. Be sure to book ahead.

Elegant table setting at Oliveto in Pafos *(see p170)*

The Flavours of Cyprus

Cypriot food is a mixture of Greek and Turkish cooking, along with some British influences, and features all the rich flavours typical of Mediterranean produce. Fruit such as oranges, lemons, cherries and figs are all grown locally, and the island's grapes are made into delicious wines. Vegetables, herbs and olives (to eat and for oil) grow in abundance. Meat is predominently lamb, pork and chicken, and fresh seafood is plentiful along the coast. A good way to try a selection of local food is with a platter of *mezedhes* (*meze* for short), which may comprise of up to 20 dishes.

Oregano and thyme

Cypriot fisherman preparing his catch for sale

Southern Cyprus

The cuisine of the south is inspired by the flavours of the Mediterranean area. Popular ingredients include olives and fresh herbs from the rich soils of the foothills of the Troodos mountains, and lemons from the groves found largely in the western region near Pafos. Locally made cheeses such as feta and halloumi give a distinctive taste to many dishes. Most meals start with a selection of dips made using recipes that have been handed down from generation to generation for centuries. These recipes have their roots in Greek cuisine, and are generally served with a freshly baked "village" loaf. Bread plays an important part in the diet of southern Cypriots. A flattish-domed loaf, village bread, is usually plain white but may also be flavoured with cheese or olives. Main courses tend to be meat-based rather than fish, although swordfish, in particular, is caught fresh everyday and almost always is served grilled with lemon. Chickens, pigs and goats are reared in most rural areas and provide meat that is usually cooked with herbs and served with potatoes grown in the red soil found in the Larnaka area. A "village salad"

Pita breads
Grilled halloumi
Dolmades (kupepia)
Taramosalata
Roasted red peppers
Olives
Tzatziki
Selection of typical Cypriot *mezedhes*

Regional Dishes and Specialities

Dishes of the south include *afelia* (pork simmered in red wine with coriander) and *kleftiko*. Moussaka and *dolmades* (stuffed vine leaves) are among the dishes drawn from Greek cuisine. Dips include *taramosalata* (puréed salted mullet roe) and *tzatziki* (yoghurt, cucumber, garlic and mint). The cuisine of northern Cyprus includes dishes such as *imam bayildi* (tomato-and onion-stuffed aubergines), *borek* (cheese-filled pastries) and *bamya bastisi*, a tomato and okra stew. Meat dishes include *doner* kebabs of sliced, spiced roast lamb, *iskender* or *bursa* (kebabs in a thick, spicy tomato sauce) and *adana*, a length of minced lamb bound together with red pepper flakes and cooked on a skewer.

Sweet pastries

Souvlakia are small chunks of pork, marinated in lemon juice, herbs and olive oil, grilled on skewers.

Local grocer offering a wide range of fresh and dried produce

(choriatiki salata), made of lettuce, cabbage, tomatoes, olives and feta cheese is a typical accompaniment to the main course. Bananas, oranges and cherries are among the many fruits grown in this part of the island and, along with sweet cakes, generally complete a meal.

Northern Cyprus

Cuisine in north Cyprus takes its influences from the island itself and the Turkish mainland, where many of the staple dishes were inspired by Middle-Eastern and central Asian cooking. Spices such as saffron and paprika, along with garlic, chillies and peppers, are used extensively; these ingredients give a colourful hue and a spicy kick to traditional northern dishes.

Most meals are based around meat, usually chicken or lamb, and vegetables grown on the flat plains south of the Pentadaktylos mountain range and along the coast. Many recipes come from the days of the Ottoman Empire and are characterized by their spicy

Cypriot coffee, served strong and black with pastries

tomato, yoghurt and cream based sauces. Meze-style meals, usually for large groups of friends or family, are a staple on the menu too, but differ slightly from those found in the south in that they are more often inspired by Turkish cuisine. Main courses are generally served with rice, boiled potatoes and salad accompaniments, and are usually followed by sweet pastries, such as sticky baklává, or milk puddings and fresh fruit, especially citrus fruits, which grow prolifically in the north of the island.

What to Drink

Cyprus offers the ideal climate and geography for growing grapes for winemaking, and production can be traced back to around 2000 BC. Of the over 40 varieties, the most famous is Commandaria, a sweet wine dating from the time of Richard the Lionheart. Zivania vodka and ouzo (along with Cyprus brandy used to make the island's signature cocktail, the Brandy Sour) are popular drinks too, as is sherry. Freshly squeezed fruit juices are also very good, and inexpensive. Cyprus, however, is above all the land of the coffee shop and villagers, mostly men, will spend hours over a strong Cypriot coffee, which is always served with a glass of cold water.

Scharas means "from the grill". Here, swordfish has first been marinated in lemon juice, olive oil and herbs.

Kleftiko is usually goat meat wrapped in paper and cooked so that the juices and flavours are sealed in.

Giaourti kai meli (yoghurt with honey) is served in speciality "milk shops", to be eaten there or taken home.

Where to Eat and Drink

West Cyprus

KATHIKAS: Yiannis
Tavern €
Cypriot **Map** A3
Georgiou Kleanthous 11, 8573
Tel *26 633 353* **Closed** *Thu*
A welcoming restaurant, with
amiable hosts. Its lengthy menu
offers classic Cypriot dishes such
as *kleftiko* (slow-cooked lamb)
and *moussaka* (lamb and
eggplant casserole).

KATHIKAS: Petradaki
Tavern €€
Cypriot **Map** A3
Kato Vrisi 45, 8573
Tel *99 596 528*
This taverna is popular with both
locals and tourists. A good choice
of Cypriot dishes – try the pork
in blue cheese sauce – and
delicious desserts. Good wines.

PAFOS: Koh-i-Noor €
Indian **Map** A4
110 Tombs of The Kings Rd, 8042
Tel *26 964 083* **Closed** *Mon*
Fantastic curries and tandoori
dishes on offer at this elegant,
family-run Indian restaurant in
the heart of Kato Pafos. Good
selection of wines to complement
the delicious food.

PAFOS: Petra Tou
Romiou €
International **Map** A4
*Pafos-Limassol Coastal Rd,
Petra Tou Romiou, 4607*
Tel *26 999 005*
Occupying an elevated position
overlooking the sea near
Aphrodite's birthplace, this large
taverna specializes in grills and
local dishes such as *souvlaki*
(Greek kebab).

PAFOS: Politia €
International **Map** A4
25th March St, 8047
Tel *26 222 288*
Housed in a period mansion with
a modern dining space, Politia
has generous portions of Cypriot
and international food. Serves
breakfasts, lunch, snacks and
evening meals.

PAFOS: Cavallini €€
Italian **Map** A4
Poseidon Ave, 8098
Tel *26 964 164*
Enjoy expertly prepared pasta
and gourmet pizzas, compli-
mented by a long list of regional
wines. The garden terrace at
Cavallini has great sea views.

PAFOS: Demokritos €€
Cypriot **Map** A4
Dionysos 1, 8041
Tel *26 933 371*
Live folk music and dancing
accompany meals at Demokritos,
one of Pafos' oldest restaurants.
Savour Cypriot cuisine with an
international flavour.

PAFOS: Kouyiouka
Watermill Restaurant €€
Cypriot **Map** A4
Pafos–Polis Rd, Giolou village, 8720
Tel *26 632 847*
Housed in a lovely 19th-century
restored watermill, complete
with wooden beams and stone
walls, this village restaurant
specializes in Cypriot *mezédhes*
(meze) and grills.

PAFOS: La Spaghetteria €€
Italian **Map** A4
Iasonos 15–16, 8041
Tel *26 952 544*
From the colourful decor to its
extensive and imaginative menu
of antipasti, home-made pasta
dishes and wines, this trattoria is
a taste of Italy in Cyprus.

DK Choice

PAFOS: Laona €€
Cypriot **Map** A4
Votsi 6, 8010
Tel *26 937 121*
A traditional taverna housed
in a beautiful period mansion,
hidden away down one of the
old town's side streets. The
chefs are experts in authentic
local cuisine such as *kleftiko*
(slow-cooked lamb with
herbs) and *afelia* (pork in red
wine). Delicious Cypriot wines
on the menu as well.

PAFOS: Muse €€
International **Map** A4
Mousalla, 8027
Tel *26 941 951*
An informal alfresco-style eatery
located in the centre of the old
town, with panoramic views over
the coast. Grills, pasta dishes and
salads make up the menu.

PAFOS: Ocean Basket €€
Seafood **Map** A4
Avanti Holiday Village Piazza, 8042
Tel *26 961 379* **Closed** *Sat*
Delicious selection of fish and
shellfish dishes, along with sushi.
The seafood platter with chips is
excellent value.

PAFOS: Oliveto €€
International **Map** A4
96 Tombs of the Kings Rd, 8102
Tel *26 220 099*
Elegant restaurant with crisp
white linens, specializing in
stone-grilled steaks cooked by
the chefs or the guests
themselves. Delicious desserts
and excellent wines.

PAFOS: O'Neills Irish Bar
and Grill €€
International **Map** A4
Tombs of the Kings Rd, 8022
Tel *26 935 888*
You'll find a good selection of
hearty meals at O'Neills. The
extensive drinks list includes
speciality Irish beers amongst
others. A large flatscreen TV
shows the latest sports.

The exterior of grill restaurant Oliveto in Pafos

Outdoor seating and sea views at Vassos Fish Harbour Restaurant, Agia Napa

PAFOS: Phuket Chinese €€
Chinese/Thai Map A4
44 Tombs of the Kings Rd, 8102
Tel *26 936 738*
Upmarket yet good-value restaurant with Oriental decor. Serves Chinese and Thai à la carte dishes with fine wines.

PAFOS: Sense €€
International Map A4
Coral Bay Rd, 8575
Tel *26 621 200*
This stylish venue is an informal eatery by day that transforms into a glamorous bar-restaurant at night. Try a delicious steak with all the trimmings, or one of the fish and pasta dishes.

PAFOS: Theo's Seafood Restaurant €€
Seafood Map A4
Apostolou Pavlou Ave, 8046
Tel *26 932 829*
Located in the harbour, this is one of the area's long-established favourites. The specials focus on fresh fish, although other Cypriot and international dishes also feature on the menu.

PAFOS: Chloe's €€€
Chinese Map A4
Tombs of the Kings Rd, 8102
Tel *26 934 676*
Beautifully decorated in an Oriental style, with soft background music, Chloe's serves some of the finest Chinese food in Cyprus. Attentive staff.

PAFOS: Gold Sakura €€€
Japanese Map A4
Agiou Antoniou St, 8041
Tel *26 947 492*
Popular Japanese restaurant just minutes from the beach. The extensive menu includes a delectable range of sushi to choose from. Beautiful contemporary decor.

PAFOS: Psari Seafood Grill €€€
Seafood Map A4
Coral Bay, 8099
Tel *26 881 500* **Closed** *Mon*
Housed within the upmarket Thalassa Hotel, Psari serves sumptuous fresh fish, with great attention to detail and presentation. Panoramic views.

POLIS: Archontariki Tavern €€
Cypriot Map A3
Makarios Ave, 8830
Tel *26 321 328*
Informal restaurant located in a traditional town house. A wide choice of Cypriot fish and seafood dishes to choose from. Alfresco dining in a quiet courtyard hidden from the road.

POMOS: Kanalli Restaurant €€
Cypriot Map A3
Pomos Harbour, 8870
Tel *26 342 191*
Pleasant location in the harbour overlooking the dramatic coastline of Pomos. The dishes on offer are classic Cypriot. Especially popular with families.

Southern Cyprus

AGIA NAPA: Odyssos €
International Map E3
Nissi Ave, 5343
Tel *23 816 231*
Popular option next to Nissi Beach, this family-friendly place serves excellent burgers, fish and chips, grilled meat and vegetarian dishes. Open all day.

AGIA NAPA: Captain Andreas €€
Seafood Map E3
Evagorou 33, 5340
Tel *25 724 065*
Family-owned restaurant located right on the harbour. Sample the fresh fish caught by Captain Andreas himself and cooked using locally grown lemons and herbs. Prices are calculated by weight.

AGIA NAPA: Limanaki Fish and Grill €€
International Map E3
1 October St, 3322
Tel *23 721 600*
Right on the seafront with alfresco dining on the terrace. Cypriot and international dishes on the menu, with a focus on fish *mezédhes*.

AGIA NAPA: Sage Restaurant and Wine Bar €€
International Map E3
Kryou Nerou 10, 5342
Tel *23 819 276*
Choose from gourmet-style steaks, burgers, pasta and salads. Excellent speciality whiskies and coffees. Cosy atmosphere with live music at weekends.

AGIA NAPA: Vassos Fish Harbour Restaurant €€
Seafood Map E3
Makariou 51, 5342
Tel *23 721 884*
Lively taverna renowned for its seemingly endless fish *mezédhes* selection, along with dishes that include lobster straight from the tank.

LARNAKA: Art Café 1900 €€
International Map D3
Stasinou 6, 6305
Tel *24 653 027*
Housed in a building dating to 1900, hence its name, with frescoes and wooden floors. The bistro-style menu features vegetarian dishes as well as meat and fish.

LARNAKA: Captain's Table Fish Tavern €€
Seafood Map D3
Grigoris Afxentiou 48, Zygi, 7739
Tel *24 333 737*
Upmarket seafood restaurant located next to the old harbour. Dishes include lobster and seafood soufflé. Good wine list. Reservations recommended on weekends.

LARNAKA: Loizos Koubaris Fish Tavern €€
Seafood Map D3
Grigoris Afxentiou 34, Zygi, 7739
Tel *24 332 450*
Located in a former fisherman's home right next to the sea, this comfortable taverna specializes in fresh fish. Try the various combinations of the *mezédhes*. Popular with local families, especially on weekends.

For more information on types of restaurants *see p167*

The elegant dining area at Cleopatra Lebanese restaurant, Limassol

LARNAKA: Meze Meze €€
Cypriot   Map D3
Athinon 102, 6022
Tel *96 798 718*
A stylish bar-cum-taverna overlooking the Phinikoudes promenade, great for people-watching. Choose from an excellent selection of traditional Cypriot and Greek dishes.

LARNAKA: Nippon Bistro €€
Japanese   Map D3
Grigoris Afxentiou 57, 6023
Tel *24 657 555*
The award-winning Nippon Bistro combines trendy minimalist decor with a maki mono bar, teppanyaki tables and a vast selection of sushi and sashimi dishes.

LARNAKA: The Coral Inn €€
International   Map D3
Dhekelia Rd, 7040
Tel *24 646 200*
Modern eatery with wood-panel decor reminiscent of Native American styling. Serves delicious steaks and pasta dishes, and unusual desserts.

LIMASSOL: Incontro Café €
International   Map C4
Agios Nikolaos Makariou, 6017
Tel *25 377 519*
Stylish venue with art on the walls and comfortable sofas. The menu has salads, burgers and bistro-style sandwiches, plus there's a good wine list.

LIMASSOL: Oleastro Restaurant €
Cypriot   Map B3
Oleastro Olive Park, Anogyra, 4603
Tel *99 525 093*
The restaurant at the Oleastro Olive Park prides itself on using organic ingredients in the preparation of home-made à la carte meat, fish and vegetarian meals, and snacks. There is also a good Sunday buffet.

LIMASSOL: St Ermogenis Valley €
Cypriot   Map B4
Episkopi village, 4620
Tel *25 933 939*
Sit inside or on the outside terrace shaded by trees at this wonderful eatery. Enjoy scrumptious Cypriot and international cuisine.

LIMASSOL: Caballeros Restaurant €€
International   Map C4
Old Town, 3036
Tel *25 878 982*
Elegant restaurant located opposite Limassol's medieval castle. Serves Cypriot and international favourites including *souvlaki*.

LIMASSOL: Chesters €€
International   Map C4
194 Amathous Ave, 4044
Tel *25 635 155*
Chesters is an intimate bar-cum-restaurant serving bistro-style cuisine. There are several speciality platters available, including one with Lebanese flavours. Good cocktail menu.

The outdoor seating area at Oleastro Restaurant, Limassol

LIMASSOL: Cleopatra Lebanese Restaurant €€
Lebanese   Map C4
John Kennedy St, 3106
Tel *25 586 711*
One of the best Lebanese restaurants on the island. Prides itself on using authentic age-old recipes to provide a great culinary experience. For dessert, try the delectable small pastries.

LIMASSOL: Dino Art Café €€
International   Map C4
Eirinis 62, 3042
Tel *25 762 030*
Trendy café with quirky cream-and-lime minimalist decor and paintings on the walls. Choose from an extensive menu of pastries, main course grills and desserts.

LIMASSOL: Il Sapore €€
Italian   Map C4
Amathous Ave, 3606
Tel *25 313 184*
This traditional trattoria-style restaurant serves authentic Italian cuisine. Delicious antipasti, fish and meat dishes and home-made pasta. Be sure to try the mouthwatering ravioli.

LIMASSOL: Longmen Restaurant €€
Chinese   Map C4
Academias 60, Potamos Yermasoyias, 3076
Tel *25 318 844*
A landmark Chinese restaurant in Limassol for nearly two decades and one of its most popular. With Oriental decor and a menu of Chinese classics.

LIMASSOL: Mairkon Sikaminia €€
Cypriot   Map C4
Eleftherias 26, 3042
Tel *25 365 280*
A traditional taverna in the heart of the old town, Mairkon Sikaminia serves light Cypriot

delicacies such as *souvlaki* and salad for lunch, and seemingly endless *mezédhes* dishes nightly.

LIMASSOL: Polycarpou Restaurant €€
Cypriot   Map C4
Saripolou 45, 3036
Tel *25 352 135*
Lively little eatery that opens early for breakfast and serves informal meals all day. Enjoy omelettes and burgers, or Cypriot classics such as stuffed vine leaves and *souvlaki*.

LIMASSOL: Salamina €€
International   Map C4
Amathous Ave, 3724
Tel *25 634 333*
Spacious, stylish restaurant inside the Grand Resort, decorated in terracotta with crisp white linens. Offers an eclectic mix of Greek, Asian, Italian and French cuisine.

LIMASSOL: The Noodle House €€
Chinese   Map C4
Agiou Andreou, 3036
Tel *25 820 282*
Bright and airy restaurant in the heart of Limassol, with a kid's menu and a play area. Try the tempura fish and spring rolls.

LIMASSOL: To Mairkon tis Lysis €€
Cypriot   Map C4
Franklin Roosevelt, 3012
Tel *25 560 555*
Family-run with friendly staff, this is a welcoming traditional taverna that serving Cypriot classics. Be sure to try its speciality *afelia* (pork cooked in wine with coriander).

LIMASSOL: Zen Room €€
Japanese   Map C4
194 Amathous Ave, 4533
Tel *25 812 659*
With a relaxed dining ambience, the award-winning Zen Room features an open kitchen, a teppanyaki bar and exquisite Japanese food.

LIMASSOL: Caprice €€€
Italian   Map C4
72 George 1st St, 4048
Tel *25 865 555*
Located inside the Londa Hotel, the luxurious Caprice has panoramic views of the coastline. Its gourmet menu of antipasti, pasta, meat, fish and vegetarian dishes promises the best of Italian cuisine. The Sunday BBQ platters are great value, and the desserts are fantastic.

LIMASSOL: Hadjiantonas Winery €€€
Cypriot   Map A3
Parekklissia, 4520
Tel *25 991 199*   **Closed** *Sun–Tue*
This luxurious restaurant is in the Hadjiantonas Winery on the edge of Parekklisia village. Expect artfully presented à la carte cuisine and an reliably superb list of wines. Cooking with wine is the speciality here; try the *boeuf bourgignon* made with Cabernet Sauvignon, and the fish drizzled with Chardonnay.

LIMASSOL: La Maison Fleurie €€€
French   Map C4
Christaki Kranou 18, 4041
Tel *25 320 680*   **Closed** *Sun*
Popular, award-winning restaurant where the menu is classic French with a modern twist. Try the succulent steak Béarnaise, *foie gras* and oysters. Good French wine list.

PISSOURI: Dionysos €€
Cypriot   Map B4
Coastal Rd, Pissouri Bay, 3779
Tel *25 833 791*
Bright taverna-style spot with views over picturesque Pissouri Bay. Specializes in Cypriot dishes such as *sheftalia* (a sausage dish) and *afelia*. Live music.

PROTARAS: Polyxenia Isaak €€
Cypriot   Map E3
Coastal Rd, 5310
Tel *23 829 29*
A sprawling complex on the Protaras seafront, Polyxenia Isaak offers great views. The menu is Cypriot with international influences. Try the speciality lobster served with local lemons.

PROTARAS: Sfinx €€
International   Map E3
Cavogreko 381, 5310
Tel *23 831 277*
Designed to resemble an Egyptian temple, except with TV screens inside showing live sports. Sample hearty food such as *moussaka* and *souvlaki* with fries.

Troodos Mountains

KAKOPETRIA: Pine Hill Lodge €
Cypriot   Map B3
Nicosia–Troodos Rd, 2800
Tel *25 923 142*
A popular stop for tour groups, this eatery serves mainly Cypriot

dishes such as *moussaka* and *kleftiko*. Lovely views of the mountains.

KAKOPETRIA: Mylos Restaurant €€
Cypriot   Map B3
The Mill Hotel, Mylou 8, 2800
Tel *22 922 536*
Spacious restaurant with a wooden vaulted ceiling and fabulous mountain views. Enjoy *tahini* and *tzatziki* dips, and traditional Cypriot ravioli and *moussakas*, made using time-honoured recipes.

LANEIA: Lania Tavern €€
Cypriot   Map B3
Laneia village, 4744
Tel *25 432 398*   **Closed** *dinner Sun–Thu*
Traditional eatery in the centre of a pretty artists' village. Excellent Cypriot cuisine served daily for lunch and on Friday and Saturday evenings. Dine inside or on the terrace.

LANEIA: Platanos Tavern €€
Cypriot   Map B4
Laneia village, 4744
Tel *25 434 273*
Local favourite named after the mighty plane tree outside. Delicious Cypriot classics with specialities including home-made *loukanika* (small smoked sausages) and *moussaka*.

LOFOU: Lofou Traditional Tavern €€
Cypriot   Map B4
Tsindouri, Lofou village, 4716
Tel *25 470 202*   **Closed** *Mon*
For a real Cypriot experience head to this lovely tavern housed in an old stone cottage. Enjoy home-made local dishes and fine wines and listen to the jovial owner Costas playing traditional folk music in the background.

The historical stone exterior of Lofou Traditional Tavern, Lofou

For more information on types of restaurants *see p167*

MONIATIS: Paraskeuas Restaurant €
Cypriot   Map B3
Moniatis village, 4747
Tel *25 433 626*
Famous for its *kleftiko* (lamb), cooked for hours with a special mix of herbs in the restaurant's outdoor domed oven. Eat inside or alfresco on its vine-covered terrace. Great views.

MONIATIS: Andreas Makris Restaurant €€
Cypriot   Map B3
Moniatis village, 4747
Tel *25 433 626*
A family-run restaurant, Andreas Makris is always lively with music and occasional dancers. The menu is traditional Cypriot grills and barbecues.

OMODOS: Ambelothea Taverna €€
Cypriot   Map B4
Omodos village, 4760
Tel *25 421 366*
Housed in a large, beautifully renovated stone property, this taverna serves delicious traditional dishes such as *loukanika* (sausages) cooked in local wine.

DK Choice

PANAGIA: Vouni Panagias €€
Cypriot   Map A3
Archiepiskopou Markariou III 60, 8640
Tel *26 722 770*
Enjoy gorgeous panoramic views from the large restaurant and dining terrace of this winery. The menu is classic Cypriot with an emphasis on organic produce and healthy eating options, accompanied by the winery's own labels.

PLATRES: Belvetere Restaurant €€
Cypriot   Map B3
Spyrou Kyparianou 62, 4820
Tel *25 421 751*
Fine-dining restaurant housed within the Forest Park Hotel. Serves Cypriot dishes with a contemporary twist as well as international cuisine, including kosher food. Regular theme nights and live music.

PLATRES: Psilo Dendro €€
Cypriot   Map B3
13 Aidonion, 4820
Tel *25 813 131*
Busy restaurant with a great location near the waterfalls. Try the legendary freshly caught trout cooked with herbs and lemon, sourced from the owner's own trout farm.

PRODOMOS: Louis Restaurant Coffee Bar €
Cypriot   Map B3
Prodomos village, 4840
Tel *25 462 049*
Popular with tour groups, this Cypriot restaurant serves excellent *souvlaki*, salads, cakes and pastries. Breathtaking views.

STATOS-AGIOS FOTIOS: Kolios Restaurant €€
Cypriot   Map A3
Kolios Winery, 2651
Tel *26 724 090*
This large, modern restaurant is part of the Kolios Winery complex. Fantastic *mezédhes* served on Sundays. Dining at other times is by appointment only, so book well ahead.

TROODOS: Fereos Park Restaurant €
Cypriot   Map B3
Troodos village, 1504
Tel *25 420 114*
Fereos Park is an attractive little eatery that serves local

dishes. Try the excellent *souvlaki* and barbecued *sheftalia* (sausages).

TROODOS: Dolfin Taverna €€
Cypriot   Map B3
Troodos village, 1504
Tel *25 420 215*
A popular stop for visitors on Troodos mountain tours, Dolfin is a typical taverna serving up delicious *souvla* (chargrilled pork) and *sheftalia*.

VASA: Arisdne Restaurant €€
Cypriot   Map B4
Vasa village, 4505
Tel *25 942 185*
Sample from an extensive selection of *mezédhes* dishes, including *tahini* and *skordalia* dips, grilled halloumi and herb sausages with fresh bread. Lovely courtyard seating.

VRETSIA: Vretsia Village Tavern €
Cypriot   Map B3
Vretsia village, 8644
Tel *25 821 833*
A quaint stopover in a quiet hamlet close to the Venetian bridges, this village tavern dishes up basic and delicious Cypriot cuisine.

Central Cyprus

DK Choice

AGROS: Agros Tavern €
Cypriot   Map C3
Agros village, 4860
Tel *25 521 558*
Agros Tavern usually caters only to the locals, and perhaps the passing tourist, but the classic Cypriot dishes on its menu warrant a visit. Try the excellent home-made moussaka and *kleftiko* cooked with herbs for hours in a special outdoor oven. Call ahead for opening times.

AGROS: Rodon Hotel Restaurant €€
International   Map C3
Rodon Hotel, Rodou 1, 4860
Tel *25 521 201*
Cypriot and international cuisine served in this bright and spacious fine-dining restaurant located in a renovated country house. Imaginative home-made desserts.

AGROS: Vlachos Restaurant €€
Cypriot   Map C3
Agros village, 4860
Tel *25 521 330*
Vlachos Hotel's excellent restaurant serves up classic Cypriot dishes

Enjoy scenic views whilst you dine al fresco at Vouni Panagias, Panagia

The rustic dining area at Brasserie Au Bon Plaisir, South Nicosia

such as *afelia* (pork in wine) and *kleftiko* (lamb) complemented by local wines.

DALI: Daliou Mills €
Cypriot **Map** D3
Archbishop Makarios III 41, 2540
Tel *22 521 308*
One of Dali's few eateries, and believed to be its oldest taverna, the Daliou Mills is best known for its *mezédhes* platters. Call ahead.

FIKARDOU: O Yiannakos €€
Cypriot **Map** C3
Fikardo village, 2623
Tel *22 633 311*
Popular restaurant in a renovated centuries-old stonehouse. Good Cypriot menu with stuffed vine leaves and *sheftalia* sausages highly recommended. Call ahead for opening times.

LAZANIA: Estiatorio Mageia €
Cypriot **Map** C3
Lazania village, 2618
Tel *22 781 083*
Estiatorio Mageia is one of a handful of small eateries in this traditional cobbled village. Known for its delicious *kleftiko*, which is cooked in its outside domed oven, and *souvlaki* that sizzles on the barbecue.

PANO LAKATAMIA: Tsantali €
Cypriot **Map** C3
Kallitheas 8, 2313
Tel *22 382 782* **Closed** *Mon*
Popular taverna specializing in *mezédhes*. Sample from over 15 dishes starting with dips and culminating in spare ribs, pork *souvlaki* and *loukanika* sausages.

TSERI: Gonia tou Anastasi €€
Cypriot **Map** C3
Archbishop Makarios III 4, 2480
Tel *22 384 884*
Intimate, family-run taverna with outside seating and traditional Cypriot cuisine on the menu. Specialities include quail and

delicious marinated chicken kebabs. Vegetarian menu as well.

South Nicosia

Da Capo €
International **Map** C3
Archbishop Makarios III 30, 1065
Tel *22 757 427*
With eclectic decor and a menu of inventive dishes, this café-bar is popular with trendy locals. Serves steaks, burgers, salads and pasta dishes. Great buffet.

Rocket Diner €
International **Map** C3
Diagorou 2, 1097
Tel *22 818 333*
Bright and airy informal eatery decorated in a 1940s style. Serves mouthwatering steaks, grills and burgers. As fresh accompaniments, the salad cart has a host of international and local produce.

Aigaio €€
Cypriot/Greek **Map** C3
Ektoros 40, 1087
Tel *22 433 297* **Closed** *Sun*
Favoured by loyal diners for over 25 years, Aigaio dishes up the best of Cypriot and Greek cuisines. Superb selection of wines. Reservations are advised.

Café La Mode €€
International **Map** C3
Archbishop Makarios III 12A, 1065
Tel *22 510 788*
One of four branches in the city, this lovely café serves everything from salads and light lunches to steaks, along with delicious coffees and desserts.

Loukoulios €€
Cypriot/Greek **Map** C3
Florinis 8, 1065
Tel *22 844 000* **Closed** *Sun*
Located inside the Cleopatra

Hotel, Loukoulios specializes in Greek and Cypriot cuisine. Go for the *afelia* or *souvlaki* or sample the *mezédhes*.

Mediterranean Restaurant €€
Seafood **Map** C3
Klimentos 43, 1061
Tel *22 766 727*
With decor reminiscent of the Mediterranean, this busy eatery specializes in fish and seafood. Try the oven-baked salmon. Meat and vegetarian options available. Good wine list.

1900 Oinou Melathron
Bistrot €€€
International **Map** C3
Pasikratous 11, Eleftherios Sq, 1011
Tel *22 667 668* **Closed** *Sun*
Award-winning trendy restaurant with an imaginative bistro-style menu influenced by French cuisine. More than a thousand vintage and new wines to choose from.

Bagatelle Gardens €€€
International **Map** C3
Kyriakou Matsi 16, 1082
Tel *22 317 587*
With steaks and seafood, vegetarian dishes and platters of sushi, Bagatelle Gardens has something for everyone. Wide selection of wines and cocktails. Dine alfresco in the garden.

DK Choice

Brasserie Au Bon Plaisir €€€
French **Map** C3
Alasias 15E, 1075
Tel *96 755 111*
One of Nicosia's best French restaurants, this fine-dining establishment serves delectable dishes such as *foie gras* in a Madeira sauce, oysters, *Charolaise* steak and veal with a Béarnaise sauce. Excellent list of French and Cypriot wines. Reservations recommended.

For more information on types of restaurants *see p167*

Cayena Latin Fusion €€€
Mexican Map C3
Metochiou 38, 1101
Tel *22 777 787*
Busy Mexican restaurant
beautifully decorated in shades
of terracotta. Excellent chicken
quesadilla, gourmet tortas, platters
and superb desserts on the menu.

**Domus Lounge Bar and
Restaurant** €€€
International Map C3
Adamantiou Korai 5, 1016
Tel *22 433 722*
Lavishly decorated fine-dining
spot serving international à la
carte cuisine. After dinner, the
restaurant transforms into a
swanky bar and lounge.

Fanous Lebanese Restaurant €€€
Lebanese Map C3
Solonos 7C, 1011
Tel *22 666 663*
Choose from a menu of
traditional and contemporary
Lebanese dishes, including their
speciality tabbouleh. There is
belly dancing on Saturdays and
regular theme nights.

Pagoda Montparnasse €€€
Chinese Map C3
Acropolis 1, Engomi, 2413
Tel *22 444 740*
Upmarket restaurant ideal for
dinner dates with its breathtaking
views of Nicosia every table. The
extensive menu features
Chinese classics along with
Japanese sushi.

Paragadi Restaurant €€€
International Map C3
Niovis 3, 1086
Tel *22 491 310*
Luxury restaurant specializing in
seafood. Try the octopus and
squid dishes served with Cypriot
starters and accompaniments,
followed by home-made sweets.

DK Choice

Peninsula Sushi Bar
Seafood €€€
Map C3
Holiday Inn, Regeana 70, 1504
Tel *22 712 712*
This minimalist restaurant's
decor features subtle lighting
and mirrors around the sushi
conveyor belt. Choose from a
tempting range of sashimi,
sushi and teppanyaki dishes as
they pass by. The place gets
extremely busy during peak
lunch and dinner hours, so be
sure to book ahead.

North Cyprus

**BELLAPAIS: Altinkaya Fish
Restaurant** €€
International Map C2
Bellapais village
Tel *0392 081 55 001*
Popular eatery specializing in fish
dishes, each well-cooked and
beautifully presented. Excellent
service. Good value for money.

BELLAPAIS: Bella Moon €€
Cypriot Map C2
Bellapais village
Tel *0392 815 43 11*
Located near the abbey ruins,
this alfresco eatery serves Cypriot
dishes on its airy terrace. Great
local desserts.

**BELLAPAIS: Bellapais
Gardens** €€
International Map C2
Crusader Rd
Tel *0392 815 60 66*
Good restaurant in the Bellapais
Gardens hotel complex.
Gourmet-style dishes on the
menu include *carpaccio* of beef
and steak in brandy cream sauce.
Champagne menu available.

**BELLAPAIS: The Abbey Bell
Tower** €€
International Map C2
Bellapais village
Tel *0392 815 75 07*
With a first-floor terrace
commanding breathtaking
panoramic views, the Abbey
Bell Tower offers Turkish and
Cypriot cuisine along with lots
of international dishes.

**DIPKARPAZ: Big Sand Beach
Restaurant** €€
International Map F1
Dipkarpaz village
Tel *0533 865 34 88*
One of the few good restaurants
on the Karpaz peninsula, the Big
Sand Beach serves excellent
international cuisine. Terrace
seating overlooks the sea.

**FAMAGUSTA: Bedis Bar and
Restaurant** €€
International Map E3
Near Salamis Ruins
Tel *0392 378 82 25*
Eat outside on the terrace or in
the cosy interior dining hall at
this popular spot servicing
visitors to the Salamis ruins.
Turkish and international cuisine.

FAMAGUSTA: DB Café €€
International Map E3
Namik Kemal Meydani 14
Tel *0392 366 66 10*
Lively eatery specializing in pizzas
with an array of toppings to
choose from. Also on the menu
are burgers, sandwiches and
kebabs. Great option for lunch
or an informal dinner.

FAMAGUSTA: Petek Patisserie €€
International Map E3
Yeavil Deniz 1
Tel *0392 366 71 04*
Extremely popular spot serving
international and Turkish dishes,
including delicious pastries. Fun
decor with indoor fountains and
ornaments on display. The
outside terrace has sweeping
views of the Famagusta harbour.

KYRENIA: Buffavento €€
International Map C2
Mağusa Dağ Yolu Beşparmak Zirvesi
Mountainside restaurant with
panoramic views of the Kyrenia
coastline and a lengthy menu
featuring Cypriot and Turkish
cuisine. Try their grills and
delicious *borek* cheese pastries.

KYRENIA: Canli Balik €€
International Map C2
Kyrenia Harbour
Tel *0392 815 21 82*
Housed in a lovely period
building on the harbour.

The elegant fine-dining Domus Lounge Bar and Resataurant, South Nicosia

Choose from grills and vegetarian dishes, or try the daily specials of fresh, locally caught fish.

KYRENIA: Carpenters €€
Turkish/Cypriot **Map** C2
Karaoglanoglou
Tel *0392 822 22 51*
Welcoming, family-run restaurant close to the harbour. Sample local Turkish dishes such as *borek*, kebabs and honey-drenched dessert pastries.

KYRENIA: Chinese House €€
Chinese **Map** C2
Karaoglanoglou
Tel *0392 815 21 30*
Dine inside or on a pretty terrace surrounded by flowers. Authentic Chinese delicacies are on offer along with a good choice of wines.

KYRENIA: Dolca Vita Café €€
International **Map** C2
Off Ugur Mumcu Bulvari, Coast Rd between Ozankoy and Catalkoy
Tel *0392 844 68 41*
Seafood features prominently on Dolca Vita's menu, with salmon, lobster, prawns and calamari dishes. Pretty garden setting.

KYRENIA: Green Valley Bar €€
International **Map** C2
Alsancak Rd
Tel *0392 821 88 49*
A menu of local and European dishes, including *mezes* with a dozen or more small plates per person. Lively entertainment during dinner.

KYRENIA: Guler's Fish Restaurant €€
Cypriot **Map** C2
Coast Rd
Tel *0392 851 14 10*
Come to Guler's for some of Kyrenia's best seafood, with a Cypriot twist. Memorable dining experience in a beautiful beachside setting.

KYRENIA: Jashan's €€
Indian **Map** C2
Karaoglanoglou
Tel *0392 822 20 27*
Long-established eatery popular with locals for its superb Indian cuisine. Try the speciality curry and *tandoori* dishes. Also serves some international dishes and has an excellent wine list.

KYRENIA: Lemon Tree Fish Restaurant €€
International **Map** C2
Catalkoy
Tel *0392 815 24 96*
With coastline views and a setting amid lemon groves,

Indian cuisine in an outdoor setting at Jashan's, Kyrenia

this popular restaurant offers artfully presented fish and meat dishes plus vegetarian options.

KYRENIA: Mirabelle €€
Turkish/Indian **Map** C2
Uger Mumen 2
Tel *0392 815 73 90*
Having served classic Turkish cuisine for many years, Mirabelle now also features Indian cuisine on its menu. Outside dining is on a wonderful terrace surrounded by palm trees.

KYRENIA: Missina Fish and A La Carte Restaurant €€
International **Map** C2
Omer Faydeh 12, Karaoglanoglou
Tel *0392 822 38 44*
An à la carte and fish restaurant in the heart of Kyrenia, Missina has a lengthy menu and excellent wine selection. Eat outdoors on its large terrace or inside in the elegantly decorated dining hall.

KYRENIA: Niazi Restaurant €€
International **Map** C2
Kordonboyn
Tel *0392 815 21 60*
Well-established restaurant near the town centre. Order their speciality meze and enjoy the small dishes of Turkish Cypriot classics brought to the table.

DK Choice

KYRENIA: Patina A La Carte Restaurant €€
Cypriot **Map** C2
13 Sinir Sok Ozankoy
Tel *0392 824 54 00*
Artfully presented gourmet-style dishes are served at this atmospheric restaurant featuring lovely red decor and crisp white linens. Try the steak meals or the speciality *oska buka olla marina* (beef medallions in a watercress cream sauce). Reservations recommended.

KYRENIA: Sez-I Fish Restaurant €€
Seafood **Map** C2
Kervansaray Karaoglanoglou
Tel *0392 822 30 60*
Located in the heart of Kyrenia's tourist area, this popular fish restaurant has a colourful nautical-themed decor and breathtaking views.

KYRENIA: No14 €€€
International **Map** C2
14 Yazicade Sokak
Tel *0392 859 20 72*
An elegant bistro-style eatery in the heart of the town's old quarter. Serves international cuisine, including Turkish dishes such as *bamya basrisi* (vegetarian stew). Lovely seating around a pool.

LAPITHOS: Ali Pasha Taverna €
International **Map** C2
Coast Rd
Tel *0392 821 83 29*
This popular taverna has an extensive menu of Cypriot and Turkish favourites. Specialities include *imam bayildi* (stuffed aubergines). Live entertainment including belly dancing, some evenings.

NORTH NICOSIA (LEFKOŞA): Boghtalian Konak €€
Cypriot **Map** C3
Selhi Sevket Sok, Arabahment
Tel *0392 228 07 00*
Housed in a grand building with an Ottoman-style banqueting hall and a courtyard. Go for the speciality meze.

NORTH NICOSIA (LEFKOŞA): Californian Bar and Grill €€
International **Map** C3
Mehmet Akif Cad 74
Tel *0392 227 07 00*
While the decor downstairs is reminiscent of an American diner, there is also an elegant dining area upstairs. Choose from sizzling steaks, grilled chicken, burgers and kebabs.

For more information on types of restaurants *see pp167*

SHOPPING IN CYPRUS

Cyprus is famous for its handicrafts, especially the intricate laces and beautifully embroidered fabrics created by Cypriot women. Artisan food and drink, such as honey and jam as well as fruit- and herb-flavoured alcohol, are widely available. A variety of rose products, including oils, soap and perfume, are also gaining popularity. Other popular gifts are silver and copper jewellery based on traditional designs, and inexpensive leather goods. One of the pleasures of a trip to Cyprus is sampling the local food, whether in a market (where fresh fruit and spices abound) or bakery. Halloumi cheese, washed down with an inexpensive but enjoyable Cypriot wine, such as Othello, tastes delicious.

Where to Shop

Souvenirs can be bought anywhere on the island. Shops, boutiques and street stalls are found in abundance in the larger towns and along the promenades of the famous resorts. In the mountain villages, small family-run shops sell basic commodities, while home-made foodstuffs, such as orange marmalade, jam and excellent honeys, can be bought directly from their producers at tree-shaded roadside stalls.

Near every major historic site you will find a stall that sells typical local souvenirs, postcards and handicrafts. The most common items for sale are clay amphorae and jugs, baskets and traditional lace and embroidery.

Supermarkets and small local shops, which are usually open late, have the best prices for foodstuffs, but you can also buy a variety of cold drinks and snacks at the beach. The larger hotels have their own shops.

Opening Hours

The peak holiday season is June to mid-September, when shops have the longest hours.

A shop selling handicrafts in the centre of Larnaka

They open between 7am and 9am until 8pm (7:30pm in winter), some with a 3-hour lunch break (1–4pm). On Wednesdays and Saturdays most shops close between 1pm and 3pm.

Many larger shops now open on Sundays in the summer months, usually from around 7am or 8am until 4pm. Supermarkets generally have longer opening hours.

Markets are best seen early in the morning, when the choice of produce is largest.

How to Pay

In small boutiques, beach shops and markets it is customary to pay by cash. Credit cards are widely accepted in larger establishments, including supermarkets, and souvenir and jewellery shops.

A stall with a variety of home-canned fruits and jams

Markets

An inherent feature of the Mediterranean scenery, markets are found in all larger towns of Cyprus. The most picturesque are the fruit and vegetable markets in Nicosia, Pafos and Larnaka. They are held mainly for the benefit of the local community, so even in high season few articles intended for visitors are available; nevertheless, their local colour and character make them a great tourist attraction. Haggling is a common practice. Most markets sell fresh fruit, vegetables and spices. Those in seaside resorts may also have interesting costume jewellery, flip-flops and beach bags. Printed T-shirts are another popular tourist item.

Markets that specialize in fresh local produce are best visited early in the morning. At that time of day, the air is cool and you can take a leisurely stroll

A typical Cypriot market, brimming with fresh produce

stroll between the rows of stalls, savouring the flavours and scents. Here you will find readily available fresh produce, including exotic fruit and vegetable varieties little known in mainland Europe. You can also buy traditional cheeses, sausages, many types of fish, and a variety of nuts and sweets. Sacks full of fragrant, colourful spices stand next to the stalls.

Every now and then you can also find antiques offered at reasonable prices.

A well-stocked wine shop in Omodos, in the Troodos mountains

Food

One of the island's specialist foods is *halloumi* – the traditional goat's cheese, which is excellent in salads and delicious when fried or grilled. Another tasty delicacy is *soujoukkos* – a sweet almond filling covered with thickened grape juice.

The best souvenir from Cyprus is the sweet "Cyprus sun" – the local full-bodied Commandaria wine with its rich, warm and truly sunny bouquet. Other noteworthy beverages include *ouzo*, also known in Greece and Turkey, and the very strong *zivania* (virtually pure grape alcohol) that will knock you off your feet, even in small quantities. Other good food purchases include delicious dried fruit, and rose petal jam. The sweet fruit jellies – *loukoumia* – are the Cypriot version of Turkish delight. The highlanders produce exquisite herb-scented honey. The most popular spices on the island are small, hot peppers.

Souvenirs

A wide range of souvenirs is available for sale to tourists in Cyprus, but by far the most popular take-home items are

The owner of a jewellery studio at work on a new piece

ceramics and wickerwork. The Cyprus Handicraft Service has shops and workshops that sell such handicrafts in many towns and cities around the islands.

Traditional Cypriot lace is produced in the villages of Lefkara and Omodos, and makes a beautiful souvenir or gift. In North Cyprus you can buy embroidery based on traditional Turkish designs.

Exquisite icons are sold in the mountain monasteries, sometimes hand-crafted and painted by the monks themselves.

Traditional copper pots and bowls, and attractive and inexpensive leather goods, are available throughout Cyprus and make good gifts.

DIRECTORY

Markets

Larnaka
Raphael Santi Str, Oroklini. **Open** 9am–5pm Mon–Sat. Dromolaxia Rd. **Open** 5am–2pm Sat.

Limassol
Central market. **Open** 6am–2pm Mon–Sun. Town market, Makarios III Ave. **Open** 6am–1pm Sat. Linopetra. **Open** 7am–5pm Sat. Kolossi. **Open** 8am–1pm.

Nicosia
Market square. **Open** 6am–5pm Sat. Strovolos, Dimitri Vikellou Str. **Open** 6am–6pm Fri. Ochi Square. **Open** 6am–6pm Wed.

Pafos
Agora Str. **Open** 6am–1pm Mon–Sat. Duckpond. **Open** 8am–3pm Wed & Sun. Timi. **Open** 8am–2pm.

Cyprus Handicraft Service

Larnaka
Cosma Lysioti 6. **Tel** 24 304 327.

Limassol
Themidos 25. **Tel** 25 305 118.

Nicosia
Leoforos Athalassas 186. **Tel** 22 305 024.

Pafos
Leoforos Apostolou Pavlou 64. **Tel** 26 306 243.

Beautifully embroidered, colourful shawls from Lefkara

What to Buy in Cyprus

Thanks to the centuries-long influence of a variety of cultures, Cyprus offers its visitors a wealth of souvenirs of every description, from beautiful icons in the south, to typical Turkish water pipes in the north. Some towns are famous for their unique lace designs, ceramics and exquisite jewellery. Leather goods are particularly attractive in the northern part of the island. The choice of souvenirs is truly astounding, and searching for that original item to take home with you is half the fun.

Icons

Icons, painted by Greek Orthodox monks, are very popular with tourists. They vary from simple to elaborate designs, some with robes depicted in silver or with golden floral motifs.

Madonna and Child icon

Republic of Cyprus

Textiles

Colourful stripes form the traditional pattern seen on tablecloths and rugs. The hand-woven fabric used in these articles is called lefkonika. Its name comes from the town of Lefkonikon (now in North Cyprus) where the fabric was first produced.

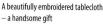
A beautifully embroidered tablecloth – a handsome gift

Lace

The most famous Cypriot lace – lefkaritika – comes from Lefkara. The best-known motif is the Da Vinci pattern, which, according to legend, was passed on to local lace-makers by the famous Italian artist.

Exquisite lace

Woven rug with the distinctive striped pattern

Tin and Copperware

Tin-plated kettles decorated with fine patterns are a practical, as well as a decorative present. Copper ornaments are also popular. The most beautiful of these include bracelets with traditional Greek designs.

An original tin kettle

A beautifully decorated silver trinket

Tray decorated with a map of Cyprus

Tourist Souvenirs

The most common souvenirs from Cyprus are plates, ashtrays, mugs and T-shirts decorated with the image of Aphrodite or a map of the island. But the inventiveness of the souvenir producers knows no bounds, and stalls are loaded with fancy knick-knacks.

Silver

In addition to lace, Lefkara prides itself on its silver creations. Here, you can find the finest jewellery made to unusual designs, and intricately decorated trinkets.

Statuette of Aphrodite – the patron goddess of Cyprus

Alcoholic Beverages

One of the best souvenirs from the island is "Cyprus sun" – sweet local Commandaria wine, full-bodied, with a rich bouquet reminiscent of the famous Madeira wine. Other noteworthy beverages include ouzo and the strong zivania (grape spirit).

Wicker basket

"Cyprus sun" – the sweet Commandaria

Bottle of white wine

Wickerwork

Inexpensive wicker baskets can be bought in the markets of Nicosia, Limassol and Larnaka, or directly from their makers in the villages of Liopetri or Sotira, near Agia Napa.

Cypriot Music

Traditional Cypriot music is based on Greek motifs. The famous "Zorba's Dance" is a favourite with tourists.

CD of traditional Cypriot music

Local Delicacies

The outstanding local delicacy is halloumi – a goat's cheese. People with a sweet tooth should try soujoukkos – made of almonds and grape juice, or loukoumi (Cyprus delight).

Pottery

Cypriot markets are full of clay jugs, bowls and other vessels, of all shapes and sizes, often richly ornamented.

Clay water jug

Cypriot sweets

North Cyprus

Ceramics

A wide variety of ceramic products is on offer. Available in all shapes and sizes, they are decorated in traditional patterns. The loveliest and most popular with tourists are the traditional bowls and jugs.

A jug – a popular form of earthenware

Hookah (or narghile)

The hookah is a typical souvenir from the north. Tourists buy these water pipes, tempted by the fruity aroma of tobacco. The full set also includes charcoal and tobacco.

A hookah – a typical souvenir from North Cyprus

Tourist Souvenirs

The most popular souvenirs are hand-woven rugs and tablecloths, and plates decorated with pictures of popular historical sites, with commemorative inscriptions. The selection of souvenirs is not great, but prices are reasonable. Stalls selling souvenirs can be found at the main tourist sites.

A colourful souvenir plate

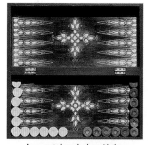

An encrusted wooden box with the popular game backgammon

Traditional knife with a beautifully decorated handle

ENTERTAINMENT IN CYPRUS

Every visitor to Cyprus, whether young or old, will find plenty of entertainment to enjoy. Hotels stage folk evenings, with traditional music and dancing. Guests can dance to the tune from *Zorba the Greek*, watch an unusual display in which a dancer places a tower of glasses on his head, or join in games of skill based on traditional Greek entertainment.

In addition to this, every major resort has modern bars, pubs and clubs playing music mostly from the 1970s and '80s. Festivals, casinos and amusement parks provide even more diversions.

In Cyprus, European-style fun and games combine with traditional local entertainment, which is very popular with the tourists.

CTO office in Pafos

Cultural life in Cyprus is not limited to bars, cafés, nightclubs or folk shows staged on hotel terraces. Larger towns also have theatres performing a classical repertory as well as modern plays in historic settings. It is worth dropping into one of the stylish cafés in the pedestrianised Laiki Geitonia area of Nicosia, to taste Cypriot coffee. Served in small glasses, this strong and sweet coffee will revive you in no time at all.

Children dressed up during the Flower Festival in Larnaka

Information

Information on current cultural events can be obtained from tourist offices and hotel reception desks. Even before leaving for your trip, it's worth checking out Cyprus on the Internet, so that you can time your arrival to coincide with local festivals, such as the wonderful wine festivals, which are accompanied by free tastings. Leaflets handed out on the streets may contain interesting information on local events, as do posters displayed in public places.

Clubs and Cafés

The island has a thriving nightlife. The major resorts, full of noisy clubs, modern bars and crowded pubs, are the most popular places to enjoy a lively night out. People looking for all-night parties and dancing should stay in Limassol – the centre of entertainment on the island. In the resort of Agia Napa it is customary to take a refreshing morning swim in the Mediterranean Sea after a night on the town. Tickets to the largest clubs can be booked in advance over the telephone or via the Internet.

Hotel Entertainment

Many hotel concierges and travel agents will arrange activities for visitors, including equipment hire for anything from tennis rackets or bicycles to a luxury yacht. They can also organize lessons for you. Their offers are displayed in hotels, where you can also book a boat cruise, an excursion or a diving course. Most hotels also sell tickets to concerts, dance shows and other performances by local artists. In some venues, Cypriot orchestras entertain dinner guests nightly. Other traditional Cypriot evenings are popular and easy to book.

Feasts and Festivals

Traditional religious festivals in Cyprus coincide with those celebrated in Europe. On New Year's Day, Cypriots exchange presents and eat the traditional New Year cake – *vasiloptta*. Epiphany is celebrated in the seaside towns with a swimming competition: the winner is the person who recovers the crucifix hurled out over the water. During Holy Week, an effigy of Judas is burned, and icons are covered with a pall.

Elegant alfresco dining at Oliveto, Pafos *(see p170)*

Anthestiria – the flower festival held in May, heralds the arrival of spring. In September the annual arts festival is held in Nicosia. The same month sees the Limassol wine festival.

The North celebrates mainly Muslim festivals. The most important widely celebrated of these is Eid-al-Fitr.

Casinos

Gambling is not particularly popular in Cyprus, but there are some who enjoy casino games. Roulette and blackjack attract mainly tourists from Turkey. Casinos are found only in North Cyprus. Inhabitants of South Cyprus often cross the border to try their luck in one of the gambling dens. The best casinos are found in the larger, more upmarket hotels of Kyrenia and Famagusta.

A casino in the Colony hotel *(see p165)*, located in Kyrenia

Excursions

Information about organized excursions and sightseeing bus tours can be obtained from hotel reception desks or tourist information centres. The most popular excursions are daytrips to major tourist attractions and historic sites, visits to traditional villages, and Cypriot evenings with traditional food, drink and dancing. Boat cruises along the coast are also available.

Amusement Parks

Unlike most rival Mediterran-ean resorts, Cyprus has lots of purpose-built attractions for

The colourful waterpark in Agia Napa

younger visitors. A visit to a waterpark or a mini-zoo is a must when on holiday with children. The vast waterparks, usually occupying several hectares, offer numerous amusements. In addition to swimming pool complexes, they have scenic routes that can be travelled by small boat, while admiring Greek ruins scattered along the shores. Large swimming pools have secret coves, artificial waves, thickets and diving sites. They vie with one another to provide the most unusual attractions, such as the Zenith Zeus slide with its 370 bends. The waterpark in Agia Napa, styled after ancient Greek designs, combines entertainment with a history lesson. Waterparks, being outdoor attractions, are open only during high season.

Educational parks and their collections of island fauna and flora are also sources of unforgettable delight and knowledge for youngsters.

In the summer the most popular parks are crowded. Every amusement park is virtually a small town in itself, with shops, restaurants and numerous attractions.

Those who fail to get their fill of fun during the daytime can take a stroll along the seaside promenades during the evening, and drop into a funfair for a ride on a carousel sparkling with flashing lights. Limassol *(see pp72–7)* and other large resorts have such funfairs.

DIRECTORY

Excursions

CitySightseeing Pafos
Harbour Coach Park, Pafos.
Tel 99 393 766.
Open 10am–4pm daily.
W cypruscitysightseeing.com

Salamis Tours Excursions
Salamis House, 28 Oktovriou,
Limassol.
Tel 25 860 000.
W salamisinternational.com

Waterparks

Aphrodite Waterpark
Geroskipou-Pafos,
Poseidonos Ave.
Tel 26 913 638.
Open daily. May & Jun: 10:30am–
5:30pm; Jul & Aug: 10am–6pm;
Sep & Oct: 10am–5pm.
W aphroditewaterpark.com

**Fasouri Water
Mania Waterpark**
Near Trahoni village, Limassol.
Tel 25 714 235.
Open daily. May, Sep & Oct:
10am–5pm; Jun–Aug: 10am–6pm.
W fasouri-watermania.com

Waterworld Waterpark
Agia Napa.
Tel 23 724 444.
Open daily. Apr & Oct:
10am–5pm; May–Sep:
10am–6pm.
W waterworldwaterpark.com

OUTDOOR ACTIVITIES

Contrary to popular belief, Cyprus offers much more in the way of recreation than splashing in the sea and sunbathing on the beaches. Certainly many visitors are drawn by the prospect of sunshine, peace and tranquillity. But the island's mild, warm climate, combined with its unique topography, attracts all types of outdoor enthusiasts. Visitors seeking an active holiday will find numerous facilities for sport, as well as excellent and professional coaching and instruction. You can enjoy a wide array of watersports, including snorkelling, diving and wind-surfing. On land there is excellent hiking, horse riding and cycling. In winter, you can even learn to ski or snowboard on the slopes of Mount Olympus.

Hiking in the Troodos mountains

Hiking

The island's best hiking areas are in the mountain regions. Clearly signposted walking trails and scenic nature trails, found mainly in the Troodos mountains and on the Akamas peninsula, help hikers to discover the most fascinating corners of Cyprus. The most enjoyable island hikes lead through nature reserves.

When hiking, you should always carry a detailed map of the region. And before setting off, it is important to pack appropriate warm clothing; even when it is hot on the coast, it can be quite chilly high up in the mountains. Also be sure to bring plenty of drinking water and sunblock.

Cycling Trips

Virtually all tourist resorts on Cyprus have bicycles available for hire. The island's cycling routes are magnificent, particularly in the mountains, and this is a great way to enjoy the scenery. Maps showing the routes are available from tourist information centres, in every resort and larger town.

It is a good idea to carry a pump with the correct tip, and self-adhesive patches for inner-tubes in case of punctures. For more complicated repairs, you can ask for help from a specialist bicycle shop.

Horse Riding

Cyprus's beaches and gentle hills provide the ideal terrain for horse riding. Horse-lovers will appreciate a beautiful ride along the paths that wind their way gently through the pine-clad hills. An

A leisurely family cycling trip

unhurried walk through a cypress grove, or a wild gallop over wooded hills, will be a memorable part of your holiday in Cyprus.

Virtually all you need to enjoy horse riding is a well-trained, docile animal. But for those who are nervous of horses, donkey rides are also widely available.

Snowboarder on the slopes of Mount Olympus

Skiing and Snowboarding

Depending on the weather, it is possible to ski and snowboard on the northeast slopes of Mount Olympus between December and mid-March. The island's highest mountain provides good snow conditions, with four ski lifts and an equipment hire centre for visitors. Individual and group tuition is available for both skiers and snow boarders to help novices negotiate the complexities of a downhill run. If you are planning to engage in snow sports during your holiday in Cyprus, you can keep an eye on the weather forecast and snow conditions by checking on the Internet or teletext information service, or asking your tour operator.

Tennis

Most top hotels have their own hard courts and tennis schools, and floodlit, all-weather public tennis courts can be found in most major towns. Aficionados will enjoy a game played at high altitude (above 1,500 m/ 4,921 ft), amid the pine and cedar woods. This is made possible by the location of one of the most scenic courts, near Troodos.

Golf

Cyprus has perfect golfing weather for much of the year, though some may find July and August uncomfortably hot. There are several 18-hole courses, all offering golf clubs for hire. Particularly noteworthy is the Tsada Golf Club, situated near Pafos on the picturesque grounds of a 12th-century monastery. There are many other high-quality, scenically located golf courses of varying degrees of difficulty for golfers of every ability.

The north of the country has no public golf courses, but visitors may use the golf

Tourists relaxing and bathing at Fig Tree beach, Protaras

course in Pentayia, which is located to the southwest of Morfou (Güzelyurt).

Other Activities

Increasingly popular excursions in four-wheel-drive vehicles give visitors the chance to discover the lesser-known parts of the island and to admire its beauty away from the tourist centres.

Rock-climbers may head for the crags of Troodos, Droushia or Cape Greco, around Agia Napa. Novice climbers should always be assisted by an experienced instructor.

Cyprus is full of ancient relics, and among its main attractions are the archaeological sites. The ruins at Amathous, near Limassol, are partially flooded, so they can be viewed while swimming in the sea. Other important sights are Kato Pafos and Salamis, in the north.

DIRECTORY

Cyprus Airsports Federation
PO Box 28940, 2084 Nicosia.
Tel 22 339 771.
W caf.org.cy

Cyprus Cycling Federation
Amphipoleos 21, Strovolos, Nicosia.
Tel 22 449 870.
W cypruscycling.com

Cyprus Equestrian Federation
Deligiorgi 1, 1066 Nicosia.
Tel 22 872 172.
W cyef.org.cy

Cyprus Golf Resorts Ltd.
PO Box 62085, 8062 Pafos.
Tel 26 642 774.
W cyprusgolf.com

Cyprus Ski Federation
Amfipoleos 21, Strovolos, Nicosia.
Tel 22 449 837.
W cyprusski.com

Cyprus Tennis Federation
Ionos 20, Engomi, 2406 Nicosia.
Tel 22 666 822.
W cyprustennis.com

Nicosia Race Club (horse riding)
Grigoriou Afxentiou, Nicosia.
Tel 22 782 727.
W nicosiaraceclub.com.cy

Car Rallies

Drivers travelling around Cyprus will get enough excitement from driving the narrow streets of Nicosia or steep roads of the Troodos mountains. But if you want even more driving thrills, you can attend one of Cyprus' several car rallies, sprints or hill

climbs. These are held at various locations including Limassol, Larnaka, Nicosia and Pafos. Further details, including the routes and the results of recent years, can be obtained from the website of the Cyprus Motor Sports Federation (www.cmf.org.cy) or from any of the individual towns' automobile clubs.

Churning out clouds of dust at the popular International Rally of Cyprus

Watersports

The beaches of Cyprus are fun places for the whole family. Sunbathing, volleyball and all kinds of watersports are available to keep you entertained. The numerous attractions include snorkelling, diving, windsurfing, waterskiing and sailing. Sea breezes moderate the high temperatures, and the clear water is ideal for swimming. There is no shortage of places to hire equipment, allowing you to practise even the most ambitious watersports or take a scuba-diving course.

Snorkelling in the clear blue waters near rock formations

Diving

The clear, clean coastal waters of Cyprus simply beckon underwater exploration. Diving is extremely popular in Cyprus, and there are diving schools and centres in virtually every seaside resort in the island.

The greatest thrills can be experienced from underwater explorations in the regions of Larnaka and Agia Napa, famous for the island's loveliest beaches. Experienced divers may look for the local wrecks of cargo boats and naval vessels. This is quite a unique attraction since, unlike many countries, the Cyprus Tourism Organization does allow the exploration of vessels that have sunk off its coast.

Visitors will be flooded with offers from hundreds of diving clubs and schools. These organizations offer not only diving lessons for novices and children, but also sea cruises combined with diving. The initial lessons can often be taken in the hotel, since many of them run their own diving schools.

Snorkelling

There is plenty to see underwater, even within a few metres of the shore if you are a beginner at this sport. The shallows teem with tiny fish, sea anemones and urchins clinging to the rocks. If you're lucky, you may even see an octopus slither past.

It's well worth heading out to the more rocky shores where there is more to see than on the sandy bottom. One of the best places for snorkelling is the north coast of the Akamas peninsula, where rocky coves and tiny offshore islands abound in a variety of sealife.

Many hotels hire out snorkelling equipment. You can also buy masks with snorkels and flippers at local sports shops; these do not cost much.

It is prohibited to collect sponges or any archaeological items found on the seabed.

Windsurfing and Kiteboarding

Almost all the beaches run courses for windsurfing. The gentle afternoon breezes may not meet the expectations of the more competitive windsurfers. The best winds blow around the capes, between Agia Napa and Protaras, and in the region of Pafos. Kiteboarding, which involves being towed at high speeds by a giant parachute-like kite, is starting to catch on in Agia Napa.

Dozens of yachts moored in Larnaka marina

Sailing

Sailing is very popular in Cyprus, and the island's marinas play host to vessels from practically every European country. Skippered yachts can be chartered from island marinas (Larnaka and Limassol are the main centres) by the day or for longer cruises, and smaller dinghies and catamarans are available by the day or half-day from beaches around Agia Napa, Protaras, Limassol and Latsi. The many boat charter companies have their offices in coastal resorts, where you will also find sailing schools.

The waters around Cyprus offer magnificent sailing conditions, and the island is often referred to as a "sailor's paradise". Southwesterly winds prevail in the summer. The delicate westerly breeze blowing in the morning

A diver exploring the sights under water

The Cypriot coast – an ideal destination for an active holiday

changes gently around noon to a westerly wind of 15–20 knots. In the winter, the temperatures are milder and the sun less scorching. In December and January the winds are mainly 10–20 knots from the southeast. There can be occasional rain at this time, but the prevailing clear weather makes sailing conditions close to ideal.

From Cyprus you can sail to nearby Israel, Lebanon, Egypt, the Greek islands and Turkey.

Beach Sports

For the most part, beaches are found close to hotels, and are watched over by lifeguards in the summer, making them peaceful and comfortable recreation grounds. The beautiful sandy beaches in small sheltered coves are particularly welcoming to those who are lured by the charm and appeal of Aphrodite's island.

The delightful small rocky coves and beaches provide a quiet and charming spot for a refreshing dip. The best known of these scenic beaches is the rocky coast by Petra tou Romiou – the Rock of Aphrodite.

Private hotel beaches as well as public beaches become very crowded during peak season. One of the most famous beaches in Cyprus – Agia Napa's Nissi Beach – buzzes with activity from morning until night. Tourists remain in beach bars and nearby clubs until the small hours

Colourful inflatable rings for children

and, after a night of partying, head straight for the beach to enjoy a refreshing swim. Named after the nearby island (the word *nissi* means "island"), Nissi Beach has consequently been nicknamed the "Cypriot Ibiza". The beach lures visitors with its clear water and sand, not seen in other parts of south Cyprus. According to legend, the sand was brought here from the Sahara.

Less famous but equally beautiful beaches can be found in the northern part of the island, in the region of Famagusta (Gazimağusa).

Deckchairs, umbrellas and towels are available for hire, but watch out because in some places the owners charge exorbitant prices. Many beaches are set up with volleyball courts; you can also have a game of beach ball or frisbee. Numerous sport centres hire out diving or snorkelling equipment, as well as boats and canoes.

Since there is no shortage of daredevils, Cyprus's beaches also offer bungee jumping, water skiing, water scooters, paragliding and "banana" rides behind a motorboat.

The very popular water scooter

DIRECTORY

Watersports

Cyprus Federation of Underwater Activities
PO Box 21503,
1510 Nicosia.
Tel 22 754 647.
w cfua.org

Diving

Blue Dolphin Scuba Diving
Jasmine Court Hotel,
Kyrenia (Girne).
Tel 0542 851 5113.
w bluedolphin.4mg.com

Cydive Diving Centre
1 Poseidonos Ave,
MYRRA Complex, Pafos.
Tel 26 964 271.
w cydive.com

Scuba Cyprus
Kazim Ozalp Sok. 1a,
Alsancak,
Kyrenia (Girne).
Tel 0533 865 2317.
w scubacyprus.com

Boat & Yacht Charter

Armata
Agiou Neophytou 4,
Larnaka.
Tel 24 665 408.

Interyachting Ltd.
PO Box 54292,
Limassol.
Tel 25 811 900.
w interyachting.com.cy

Navimed Ltd.
Nicosia.
Tel 22 430 101.

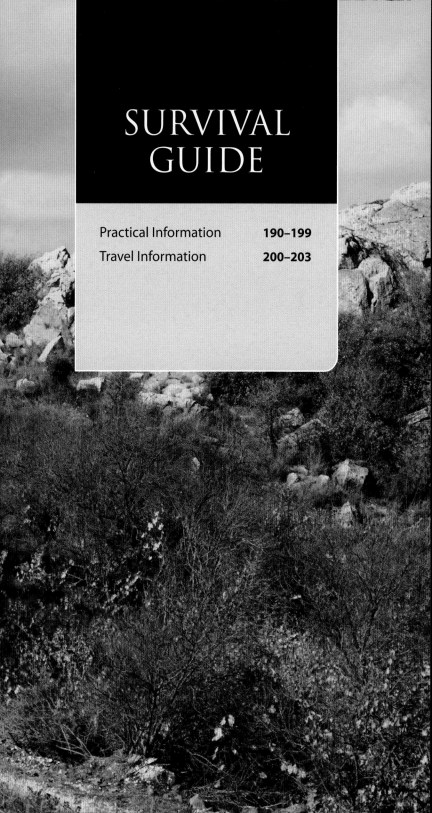

SURVIVAL
GUIDE

PRACTICAL INFORMATION

Cyprus is a popular year-round destination, due to its Mediterranean climate. It is easily accessible from mainland Europe and the Middle East, yet being an island is a true getaway. The Cypriots are extremely friendly and well inclined towards tourists.

The Greek South and Turkish North have very different characters. Entry requirements are straightforward for visitors who travel solely to either the South or the North. But due to the island's partition, visitors wanting to see both parts of the island should follow the latest advice. The Cyprus Tourism Organization (CTO), representing Southern Cyprus, has offices overseas and throughout the South. The Turkish Republic of Northern Cyprus Ministry of Economy and Tourism represents the North.

When to Go

Cyprus is a year-round destination, so any time of year is suitable for a visit. The main tourist season runs from April until October, and peaks during July and August, when the air and water temperatures are at their highest. At this time the late-night bars, taverns and restaurants fill up to capacity, and the beaches are packed with sun worshippers. The hotel swimming pools, pubs and discos are equally crowded. During peak season you can hear an international mix of languages in the streets, dominated by English, German and Russian.

Those who enjoy the mild, warm climate but prefer to avoid the crowds should visit Cyprus outside the peak season. In April, May and October it is warm enough to swim in the sea, but the beaches are not crowded. In winter (December–February), it is cool for swimming, but good for beach walks, while in the Troodos mountains you can even ski. In spring, Cyprus is an ideal place for hiking, cycling and horse riding.

The pretty harbour of Kyrenia, North Cyprus

Passports & Visas (The South)

Most visitors, including citizens of the EU, the USA, Canada, Australia and New Zealand do not require a visa to visit the Republic of Cyprus, and can stay there for up to three months. However, entry to the South may be refused if visitors' passports show they have previously entered North Cyprus.

Tourists may be asked to show that they have adequate means to support themselves for the duration of their stay. No vaccinations or health certificates are required.

Passports & Visas (The North)

To visit North Cyprus, most visitors (including citizens of the EU, USA, Canada, Australia and New Zealand) require only a valid passport. But to avoid being refused entry on later visits to the South, passports should be stamped on a separate loose sheet of paper.

There are no currency restrictions in the North, which has no currency of its own and uses the Turkish lira.

Crossing the Border

Until 2003, the only entry route to North Cyprus was via plane or ferry from Turkey. Nowadays visitors can fly directly to the Republic of Cyprus and from there travel to the buffer zone. Most visitors do not require a visa to visit North Cyprus, but you will be issued a document free of charge when crossing the border between the two parts of the island. There are seven border crossings (two for pedestrians and one for cars in Nicosia; a further four for cars outside the capital).

Cycling is a popular mode of transport

◀ Mountain biking along the rural roads of Cyprus

Apart from the largest cities, such as North Nicosia, Kyrenia and Famagusta, North Cyprus is less crowded than the South of the island. The climate is the same, so in spring it is pleasant to stroll among the orange groves, and in the summer to enjoy the beaches and the sea.

Customs

Customs regulations allow visitors to bring in, duty free, 200 cigarettes, one litre of spirits and two litres of wine. The import of perishable food items is strictly prohibited. Visitors may import any amount of banknotes, which should be declared to customs on arrival.

Embassies & Consulates

Many countries have embassies or consulates in southern Nicosia, the capital of the Republic of Cyprus. There are no embassies or consulates north of the Green Line because North Cyprus is not recognized as an independent country.

What to Take

For the most part, Cyprus is a relaxed, casual holiday destination. Visitors should pack beachwear, sunglasses, hats and smart casual wear for the resorts. If you're staying in an upmarket hotel, or dining in a fancy restaurant, you will fit in better if you dress up more, as the Cypriots themselves do.

In summer you will seldom need a sweater, but in late autumn, winter and early spring temperatures are cooler and you will need to bring some warm clothing for the evenings.

If you plan to visit the mountains, at any time of year, it is advisable to bring warm clothes and rain gear. Visitors taking medication should travel with an adequate supply. It's also a good idea to bring high-factor sun lotion and insect repellent.

Some hotels don't supply bath or sink plugs, so you may consider bringing your own.

Etiquette

When visiting religious buildings, modest attire is expected. For churches, monasteries and mosques this means long trousers or skirts, and a shirt that covers your back and shoulders. Shoes must be removed before entering a mosque.

Tourist Organizations

Tourist information bureaux can be found easily in all major tourist centres, such as Nicosia, Larnaka, Limassol, Pafos and Agia Napa. They distribute free information packs and maps, as well as providing useful advice on sightseeing. The **Cyprus Tourism Organization (CTO)**, with offices in many European cities, has a website with lots of information on the Republic of Cyprus. Visit their website at: www.visitcyprus.com.

The **Turkish Republic of Northern Cyprus Ministry of Economy & Tourism** has overseas offices, too. You can learn more about the North at www.welcometonorthcyprus.co.uk. Nowadays travel agents, hotels, car hire companies, and organizations that offer special activities have their

Automatic tourist information kiosk

own websites. These websites are often in several languages, with pictures to illustrate the services offered. It's a good idea to browse through their websites to look for good offers before travelling; many arrangements can be made before you leave home, allowing you to start enjoying your visit from the moment you arrive in Cyprus. Just be sure to check when the website was last updated, as some of the information, particularly for the North, may be out of date and quote the last season's prices.

A range of brochures and illustrated booklets covering individual tourist sights is usually available for sale at the sights themselves.

Languages

Two languages – Greek and Turkish – have co-existed in Cyprus in the centuries between the Turkish conquest of 1571 and the partition of the island in 1974. Due to the current political situation, however, you will find that Southern Cyprus uses only Greek and Northern Cyprus uses only Turkish. In the main holiday resorts in the Southern part of the island, English (as well as German and Russian) is commonly understood and spoken widely. Restaurant menus and shop signs are in several languages.

In the North it is more difficult to communicate in English and other European languages, although there is usually no problem in hotels. Road signs throughout the island carry the names of towns written in the Latin alphabet. In the North, however, only the Turkish names are given, so check your map to ensure that you know where you are going.

A tourist information centre

Religion

The Cypriot Orthodox Church, which is dominant in the south of the island, is independent from the Greek Orthodox Church. It is also the oldest national church in Christendom, its history tracing back to the times of St Paul.

In the towns you often encounter Orthodox priests dressed in long black robes. The main Orthodox services, lasting two to three hours, are held on Saturday evenings and Sunday mornings.

Monasteries have served as Cypriot pilgrimage sites for centuries. Today, they are visited by tourists in such vast numbers that access to some of them has been restricted.

In the North the dominant religion is Islam, though, like Turkey, the North is a secular state. All larger towns and cities have mosques, from which the muezzin's voice calls the faithful to prayer five times a day. Services are held on Friday afternoons.

Cypriot monastery

Travelling with Children

Major brands of baby food, medicines and toiletries, including nappies (diapers) are sold in all supermarkets and pharmacies. Both parts of the island are family-friendly, with children welcomed everywhere and plenty of kids' facilities. However, risks for smaller children include sunburn, occasional rough waters and pests such as jellyfish, sea urchins and stinging insects.

Worshipper inside an Orthodox church in southern Cyprus

Young Visitors

Cyprus is an ideal holiday destination for young people. Its sunny beaches, clean waters, watersports facilities, and rich and varied nightlife attract young people in their thousands. Hundreds of nightclubs, discos, pubs and bars await the revellers.

Holders of ISIC or Euro<26 cards qualify for discounts on public transport and reduced admission to museums and some other tourist sights.

Women Travellers

Women travelling alone or together should exercise normal caution. Cyprus is generally safe, but there have been reports of sexual assaults against women travellers so avoid walking alone at night.

Disabled Visitors

Facilities for the disabled have improved somewhat, but even so, few public buildings, shops or visitor attractions have wheelchair ramps so access can be very difficult for wheelchair users. Many museums are in older buildings without lifts. Access to archaeological sites is

also difficult. Pavements in towns and villages (if there are any) are often uneven. A leaflet with information on facilities for wheelchair users is available from the CTO.

Only a few museums and archaeological sites in the south (and none in the North) offer Braille or audio guides for visually impaired people or induction loop devices for those with hearing difficulties. The British charity RADAR (for people with hearing and visual impairment) can supply information on facilities in Cyprus (www.radar.org.uk).

Gay and Lesbian Visitors

Homosexuality is no longer illegal in southern Cyprus, and gay visitors are generally welcomed; there are gay clubs and bars in Agia Napa, Larnaka, Limassol and Pafos.

In North Cyprus, homosexuality is still illegal.

Single Travellers

Most visitors to Cyprus come as couples, families or groups of singles, and most hotels offer only double or twin rooms and charge a "single supplement" for those travelling alone. Individuals travelling independently may be able to negotiate a better deal out of season. Several companies specialize in tours for singles: lists are available from the CTO or the Association of Independent Tour Operators in the UK.

Senior Citizens

Both Cypriot communities are notably respectful to older people, but hazards include urban traffic (Cypriot drivers sometimes ignore pedestrian

Sign prohibiting photography

crossings) and noise – Agia Napa, especially, is geared to younger visitors.

Photography

Be aware that taking photographs of military bases or facilities, and the border between southern Cyprus and the North is strictly prohibited. United Nations soldiers guarding the Green Line are used to groups of tourists, but taking photographs at any point is strictly forbidden.

Archaeological sites can be photographed and filmed free of charge; however, the state museums generally charge a fee for taking photographs.

In places of worship, ask in advance whether photography is permitted. Most churches will not allow you to use flash photography.

Electrical Equipment

The mains supply on the island is 220/240V, with standard British triple rectangular-pin plugs. Most hotel reception desks will provide you with a suitable adaptor. Some hotel rooms are equipped with hairdryers, and irons are usually available to borrow. Most hotels have adapted their supply sockets to suit European plugs, so in theory there should be no problem using your own electrical equipment (but in practice this isn't always true).

Time

Cyprus lies within the Eastern-European time zone, and local time is two hours ahead of GMT. Like the UK, Cyprus puts its clocks forward by one hour from late March to late September. "Morning" in South Cyprus is *proí*; "afternoon" – *mesiméri*; "evening" – *vrádhi*; and "night" – *níchta*.

Weddings

Cyprus is one of the world's most popular wedding destinations and some hotels have their own wedding chapel. The bride and groom are required to have all the correct documentation.

Discussing Politics

The events of 1974, when the island was divided between the Turkish and the Greek Cypriots, are still remembered with bitterness. In both the south and the North, local people vehemently argue the justice of their cause. Politics and recent history are subjects that are best avoided.

Military Zones

Britain's sovereign bases in the south, at Akrotiri (Episkopi) and Dhekelia, are also used by US forces and are likely to be on heightened alert in these security-conscious times. Do not intrude on military installations. The same applies to Turkish Army personnel, equipment and installations in the occupied North.

DIRECTORY

Embassies & Consulates

Australia
Pindarou 27, Nicosia.
Tel 22 753 001.
W cyprus.embassy.gov.au

Germany
Nikitaras 10, Nicosia.
Tel 22 451 145.
W nikosia.diplo.de

Ireland
Aiantos 7, 1082 Nicosia.
Tel 22 818 183.
W embassyofireland.com.cy

Representation of the European Commission
Byron 30, 1096 Nicosia.
Tel 22 817 770.
W ec.europa.eu/cyprus

Russia
Arch. Makarou III, 2406 Egkomi, Nicosia.
Tel 222 774 622.
W cyprus.mid.ru

UK
Alexandrou Palli 1, 1106 Nicosia.
Tel 22 861 100.
W ukincyprus.fco.gov.uk/en

USA
Ploutarchou, Nicosia.
Tel 22 393 939.
W american embassy.org.cy

Tourism Organizations

Association of Cyprus Tourism Organization (CTO)
Leoforos Lemesou 19, Nicosia.
Tel 22 691 100.
W visitcyprus.com

Association of Independent Tour Operators
W aito.co.uk

Cyprus Hotel Association
Andreas Araouzos 12, 1303 Nicosia.
Tel 22 452 820.
W cyprushotel.association.org

Cyprus Tourist Guides Association
Spyrou Kyprianou 14, 1640 Nicosia. **Tel** 22 765 755.
W cytouristguides. com

Cyprus Travel Agents
Tel 22 666 435.
W acta.org.cy

Turkish Republic of Northern Cyprus Ministry of Economy & Tourism
Tel 0392 228 96 29.

Weddings

Union of Cyprus Municipalities
Regainiou 78, Nicosia.
Tel 22 445 170.
W ucm.org.cy

Useful Websites in the Republic of Cyprus

W cyprus-mail.com
W visitcyprus.com
W kypros.org
W pio.gov.cy
W windowoncyprus.com

Useful Websites in North Cyprus

W cypnet.com
W northcyprus.net

Personal Security and Health

Cyprus has a low crime rate, but even here crimes do occur; these can be minimized by taking simple precautions. The risk of mugging and theft is greatest in crowded places. Take extra care on crowded promenades or streets and in markets to protect your belongings. Keep documents, money and credit cards hidden from view, and leave what you don't need in the hotel safe. Never leave anything visible in your car when you park it. When in need, you can always ask a policeman for help. Basic medical advice is available at pharmacies. All medical treatment must be paid for; insurance is strongly advised.

Entrance to a police station in the North

Any case of theft should be reported immediately to the police. Passport theft should also be reported to your embassy in Nicosia.

Personal Belongings

Before travelling abroad, it is wise to ensure that you have adequate insurance to protect yourself financially from the loss or theft of your property. Even so, it is advisable to take precautions against loss or theft in the first place. Be vigilant when you are out and about but especially in crowded places, where the risk of theft or mugging is greatest.

Make photocopies of your important documents and keep these with you, leaving the originals behind in the hotel safe (where you can also deposit money and jewellery).

Make a note of your credit card numbers and the phone number of the issuing bank, in the event of loss or theft.

Cameras and camcorders should be carried on a strap or inside the case. Your car should always be locked, with any valuables kept well out of sight.

Cyprus Police

The police in Cyprus are friendly towards tourists and ready to offer advice. The majority of them also speak English. But in the event that you are caught breaking the law, they can be stern and unwilling to accept excuses.

Heavy fines are levied for failing to wear a seat belt and for using a mobile telephone when driving a vehicle.

Personal Security in the North

In terms of personal safety, North Cyprus is no different from the south. Special care should be taken when visiting the buffer zone and when passing by military facilities, of which there is no shortage. In particular, resist the temptation to photograph any military installations, vehicles or soldiers. The latter are visible in great

Typical southern Cyprus police car

numbers, but if you follow the rules of normal behaviour, they will not interfere with your visit.

Roads in North Cyprus are comfortable, wide and of very high quality, including the mountain roads.

Manned lifeguard post at one of the beaches

Beaches

During the holiday season, most beaches employ lifeguards. The areas allocated for swimming are marked with coloured buoys. While swimming outside the marked areas is not prohibited, it is inadvisable, particularly for weaker swimmers. Some beaches have first-aid stations, with lifeguards trained to help casualties.

Beach facilities, such as showers, are standard almost everywhere. Hotels with direct access to the sea have stretches of beach allocated to them.

Smaller beaches have no lifeguards; they are generally found in coves sheltered from the open sea, so their waters are calm and safe. The most beautiful beaches are found in the regions of Agia Napa in the south, and Famagusta in North Cyprus. The south coast beaches are generally rocky and pebbly.

In summer, Cyprus has some of the highest temperatures in Europe, and it's easy to get sunburnt anytime from early April to late October. Young children are especially vulnerable to the hot sun. Avoid being directly in the sun during the middle of the day, when the rays are strongest. Sunhats, sunglasses, a high factor sunscreen and sunblock are vital to protect your skin. During the day, carry bottled water with you, and drink lots of it, to avoid dehydration.

Medical Care

Cyprus is free from most dangerous infectious diseases (although AIDS is present), and no immunizations are required. Drinking tap water is safe. However, all medical treatment must be paid for, and comprehensive insurance to cover hospital and medical charges, as well as emergency repatriation, is advisable. Before travelling to the North, double check that your insurance policy will cover you there.

Some medical procedures (such as dental treatment) are not covered by insurance.

Emergency medical care in the Republic of Cyprus is free for all European Union citizens. The European Health Insurance Card (EHIC), available from the UK Department of Health or from a main post office, covers emergencies only. The card comes with a booklet that contains general health advice and information about how to claim free medical treatment when travelling abroad. You may find that you have to pay and reclaim the money later.

Hotels can usually recommend a local doctor or dentist, many of whom speak English. All bills must be settled at the time of treatment, but these practitioners will provide a receipt for you

ΦΑΡΜΑΚΕΙΟ

ΠΑΝΑΓΙΩΤΑ ΚΑΛΑΪΤΖΗ

Pharmacy sign with the easily recognisable green cross

to claim a refund from your insurance company.

Visitors on package holidays to Cyprus should check with their tour operator if medical insurance is included.

Pharmacies

Most pharmacies keep normal shop opening hours *(see p178)*. They display the green cross sign and the word *farmakeio* or *eczane*. A list of pharmacies open at night and on holidays can be found in the English-language *Cyprus Mail*. In an emergency, an all-night pharmacy can offer medical help and advice.

In tourist resorts and large cities pharmacists speak English. They can usually advise and provide remedies for minor ailments and injuries, but if you need specialist prescription drugs it is best to bring an adequate supply with you.

A uniformed fireman

Fire Service

Winters are dry and mild, and summers are hot, creating prime conditions for fires, which can spread with alarming speed and present a particular danger to forests. Mountain fires, especially, are difficult to put out.

Cyprus has two types of fire brigade; one that responds to general emergency calls, the other specifically dedicated to forest fires.

During excursions to the island's drier inland areas, or when camping, you must take particular care not to start a fire, or keep one under control. Be especially careful to extinguish cigarettes thoroughly and dispose of them safely. When leaving a picnic area or campsite, ensure that any bonfires are completely extinguished when you are leaving, and take all glass bottles with you to prevent accidental fires.

DIRECTORY

Emergency Services

Police
Tel 112 (South), 155 (North).

Fire Brigade
Tel 112 (South), 199 (North).

Forest Fire Teams
Tel 1407 (South), 177 (North).

Ambulance
Tel 112.

Hospitals

General Hospitals
Agia Napa/Paralimni.
Tel 23 816 512.
Kyrenia.
Tel 815 2266.
Larnaka.
Tel 24 800 500.
Limassol.
Tel 25 801 100.
Nicosia.
Tel 22 603 000.
North Nicosia.
Tel 228 5441.
Pafos.
Tel 26 803 100.

Pharmacies

Information in English
Famagusta.
Tel 90 901 413.
Larnaka.
Tel 90 901 414.
Limassol.
Tel 90 901 415.
Nicosia.
Tel 90 901 412.
Pafos.
Tel 90 901 416.

Standard fire engine of the Cyprus Fire Brigade

Communications

The quality of telecommunications services in Cyprus is very good, especially in the south. Public telephone booths are widespread. In larger towns and cities, you will have no trouble finding an Internet café, if your hotel doesn't have access. Postal services are decent. A good selection of newspapers is available, and there's no shortage of TV or radio stations.

Telephone booth

Using the Telephone

Cyprus has a well-developed telephone network. Public phones accept coins, as well as phonecards, which can be purchased from newsagent kiosks, post offices and banks in various denominations. Instructions for using the phone are provided in both Greek and English. Calls to the police, fire brigade or ambulance service are free.

Hotel rooms are equipped with telephones, but calls made from them are usually very expensive; make sure you check the rates before using them. The country code for Cyprus is 357 except for North Cyprus, where it is 90 (for Turkey) followed by (0)392. Local area codes in Cyprus include: Nicosia 22; Limassol 25; Larnaka 24; Pafos and Polis 26; Agia Napa and Protaras 23.

When making an international call from Cyprus, first dial 00, followed by the country

Public phone booths

code, and then the area code (omitting the zero that precedes some area codes). Useful country codes are: UK (44), USA and Canada (1), Ireland (353), Australia (61), New Zealand (64) and South Africa (27). All public telephones in the south can be used to make international calls. Calls are cheaper at night (after 6pm) and at weekends.

Every hotel and many public buildings have Yellow Pages directories where, in addition to local phone numbers, you can find information on hotels, restaurants, and many outfits offering activities and entertainment.

Telephones in North Cyprus

There are fewer public telephones in the North than in the South and the quality of connections can be poor. In the North, phones don't accept coins; instead you insert a pre-paid phone card (*telekart*). These are available from *Telekomünikasyon* offices, post offices and newsagents. There are also metred counter phones (*kontürlü telefon*) – where you speak first, and pay after completing the call. These calls are more expensive than card-operated phones. Metered phones can be found in branches of the *Telekomunikasyon*.

Hotel room telephones are the most expensive. To avoid unpleasant surprises, check the rates first.

The area codes for Northern Cyprus are as follows:
228 for Nicosia (Lefkoşa);
822 for Kyrenia (Girne);
366 for Famagusta (Gazimağuza);
723 for Morfou (Güzelyurt);

and 660 for Lefke. The remaining area codes are the same as for southern Cyprus.

Mobile Phones

The Cyprus mobile telephone (cellphone) network covers most of the island, although reception may be patchy, especially in the mountainous regions. Mobile phone usage is widespread in Cyprus, and international visitors who bring their own mobile phone are likely to experience few problems, although individual calls will invariably cost more than at home.

Making and receiving calls requires an active roaming facility on the phone. While abroad, mobile telephone users are charged for both outgoing and incoming calls, as well as text messages. Information on the cost of calls and how to activate international roaming can be obtained from individual network providers.

A cheaper alternative may be to buy a prepaid SIM card upon arrival in Cyprus to use with your mobile. Handsets must be GSM-compatible, and users will need to check with their local service provider that the handset is unlocked to allow for a new SIM card.

Prepaid SIM cards and top-up vouchers are available from newspaper stands, petrol stations and convenience stores. The SIM card gives the user a local Cyprus mobile number, allowing for standard local rates, very reasonable international rates and free incoming calls. Prepaid data packages are also available for smartphones.

Useful Numbers
- Directory enquiries 11892 (South), 192 (North)
- International directory enquiries 11894 (South), 192 (North)
- International calls via the operator 80000198
- Speaking clock 1895
- Infoline 132
- International access code 00

Internet

The Internet provides a great way to research your trip before heading off. Many hotels have their own websites where you can view the facilities, and make reservations. The same is true of car hire companies and various organized activities. A particularly informative site is the CTO's own website www.visitcyprus.com.

Once you're in Cyprus, the Internet provides a great way to stay in touch with people back home, and to learn more about Cyprus. Internet cafés can be found in all the island's major towns, and most hotels provide Internet access for a fee. Fees for this service are usually reasonable.

Postal Services

Most post offices in the south are open from 7:30am to 1:30pm and 3 to 6pm Monday to Friday (except in July and August, when they close daily at noon). They are closed from noon on Wednesdays. On Saturdays, main post offices are open only in the mornings. Letters and postcards sent to European countries arrive

Postage stamp vending machine

quite quickly, taking about four days to reach their destination.

In the North, post offices are open from 8am until 5pm on weekdays, with a lunch break from 1 to 2pm; and on Saturdays from 9am until noon.

Post offices accept letters and parcels. Postage stamps can be bought at post offices and almost any shop that sells postcards. You can also post your letter at the reception desk in most hotels.

Beware posting mail in the North – it will invariably take longer to reach its destination; due to the international non-recogition of North Cyprus, all mail sent from here has to travel via Turkey.

Radio and Television

Cyprus has an extraordinary number of TV channels for a country of its size.

In the south there are five free-to-air islandwide channels plus several local stations in each town. Many Cypriots also subscribe to one or more Pay-TV channels. Greek national TV is relayed to the south and Turkish TV to the North. Most large hotels have satellite TV tuned to

CNN, BBC World and other foreign-language channels.

The most popular of the English-language radio stations in Cyprus is BFBS (www.bfbs. com), which is primarily aimed at the British Forces stationed on Cyprus, but is listened to by English-speakers throughout the island. Its two channels resemble BBC Radio 1 and BBC Radio 2, though the latter also transmits programmes from BBC Radio 4 and Radio Five Live.

Cyprus's has its own national broadcaster, CyBC (www.cybc. com.cy), which provides a limited English-language service on Channel 2, and there are also several independent English-language stations to tune in to, including Radio Napa (106.3 FM broadcast in Agia Napa) and Coast FM (91.4 FM broadcast in Limassol).

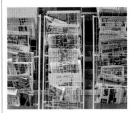

Range of English-language newspapers available at Larnaka airport

Press

The English-language newspapers published in southern Cyprus include the daily *Cyprus Mail* and the weekly *Cyprus Weekly*, as well as the *Cyprus Lion* – the British Forces newspaper. In the North, you can find the English-language *Cyprus Times*. Many popular British newspapers (*Daily Mail*, *Daily Express* and *Mirror*) are on sale on the day of publication.

These newspapers are sold at newsagent kiosks, airports and hotels. There are also a dozen or so local papers published in the island. The cultural bulletins, published in several languages, contain information on current events and activities, and may prove of interest to visitors.

Post office in Pafos, with the bright-yellow letterbox outside

Banking and Local Currency

Banks in Cyprus operate efficiently. There is a wide bank network on the island, and many foreign banks also have branches here. Cash machines can be found along the main streets and in hotel lobbies, making debit and credit cards a convenient way to withdraw cash. Most larger shops and boutiques, as well as hotels and restaurants, accept credit cards.

Tourists drawing money from a cash machine

Banks and Cash Machines

Bank opening hours are from 8:15am–1:30pm (Monday to Friday) in summer (8:30am–1:30pm, 3:15–4:45pm in winter) and closed Saturday and Sunday. Some banks in the tourist resorts are open every afternoon, from 3–5pm. The bank desks in Larnaka and Pafos International Airports remain open until the last plane of the day lands.

Cash machines operate around the clock. They are typically installed outside banks and some hotels, as well as in larger towns and holiday resorts. You can withdraw cash using all major credit cards. Follow the instructions (given in English) on the individual machine.

Money Exchange

Bureaux de change are found in the centres of larger towns and at the airports. They are open 24 hours a day; currency exchange counters in the banks are open during normal banking hours. Money exchange transactions are always subject to a commission fee; look around to get the best deal – the rates are clearly posted for you to see.

Hotels also offer exchange facilities, but their rates of exchange tend to be less favourable than either banks or bureaux de change, and they usually charge a higher commission, too.

Both foreign currency and travellers' cheques are accepted, in exchange for euro or Turkish lira. Travellers' cheques are also honoured by many hotels, shops and restaurants.

Many shops in both the Republic of Cyprus and in North Cyprus accept common foreign currencies, including US dollars and British pound sterling.

ATM (cash machine) in one of Nicosia's streets

Banks and Currency Exchange in North Cyprus

In North Cyprus, the bank networks are less extensive than in the south. Banks are open from 8am until noon. Travellers' cheques are widely accepted in shops, hotels and restaurants. They can also be exchanged for Turkish lira in banks and bureaux de change. When exchanging money, use only reputable dealers. In light of the high rate of inflation, it is worth changing smaller amounts of money more frequently, rather than a large amount.

Entrance to a Turkish bank in North Cyprus

Travellers' Cheques and Credit Cards

Banks, bureaux de change and other exchange facilities will cash your travellers' cheques into either euro or Turkish lira.

Credit cards are accepted by most larger shops, restaurants and hotels, although in markets and small shops only cash is accepted. Many debit cards are accepted, but check with your bank that your card is valid internationally. It may be difficult to find a cash machine in provincial towns and villages, so it is advisable to bring enough cash with you.

Money can be obtained from 24-hour cash machines and banks that accept credit cards. The most widely accepted cards are VISA, MasterCard and American Express.

Currency

The Republic of Cyprus joined the Eurozone on 1 January 2008. Following a changeover period of one month, during which time both the Cyprus pound and the euro were in circulation, the Cyprus pound ceased to be legal tender.

The currency used in North Cyprus is the Turkish lira (TL or, more officially, TRY). This currency is not readily available abroad, so you need to change money on arrival in the island. North Cyprus also accepts payments in euro.

Republic of Cyprus

Banknotes

Euro banknotes have seven denominations. The 5 note (grey in colour) is the smallest, followed by the 10 note (pink), 20 note (blue), 50 note (orange), 100 note (green), 200 note (yellow) and 500 note (purple). All notes show the 12 stars of the European Union.

Coins

The euro has eight coin denominations: 2 and 1; 50 cents, 20 cents, 10 cents, 5 cents, 2 cents and 1 cent. The 1 and 2 coins are both silver and gold in colour. The 50-, 20- and 10-cent coins are gold. The 5-, 2- and 1-cent coins are bronze.

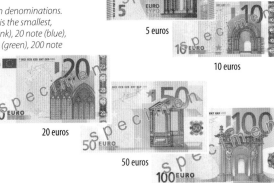

5 euros

10 euros

20 euros

50 euros

100 euros

200 euros

500 euros

North Cyprus

Banknotes

North Cyprus does not have its own currency; it uses the Turkish lira (abbreviated to TL). The banknotes, in six denominations from 5 to 200 TL, come in a range of colours, and bear Turkish national symbols and major historical figures. The euro is also accepted in the North.

Coins

There are six coins in circulation, ranging in value from 1 kuruş, 5 kuruş, 10 kuruş, 25 kuruş and 50 kuruş to 1 TL – Turkish Lira (100 kuruş).

5 lira

10 lira

20 lira

50 lira

100 lira

200 lira

TRAVEL INFORMATION

Most visitors travel to Cyprus on a package holiday which combines flights, accommodation, transport to and from the airport, and often car hire. This can be the most cost-effective option. International airports are located in Larnaka and Pafos; handling both scheduled flights and charters. Travel from mainland Europe to the island takes around 3–4 hours. Fares and schedules can be obtained from travel agents, airline offices and on the Internet. You can also reach Cyprus by boat, although this takes much longer. Boats sail from Greece to Limassol, and from Turkey to Kyrenia and Famagusta.

The road network is good, with clearly marked signs. Cars drive on the left side of the road. A decent bus service operates between main towns and big resorts.

Air Travel

The international airports in Pafos and Larnaka, both in the Republic of Cyprus, handle flights by the national carrier Cyprus Airways and other European airlines, serving many European capital cities and regional hubs. Budget airlines, such as easyJet and Ryanair, also fly to Cyprus. During summer, the airports become crowded due to the large number of charter flights. Scheduled flight tickets are generally more expensive than charters, but offer more flexibility and greater comfort.

Charter flights are at their busiest from April through October, with weekly departures. Most seats on charter flights are bought in blocks by tour operators, as part of their holiday packages, but "flight-only" charters are also available. These can be an affordable and convenient option for holidaymakers who prefer independent arrangements. Information concerning ticket availability

Pafos international airport

can be obtained from travel agents and from airline representatives. Airports have duty-free shops, cafés and restaurants, but the food and beverages on offer are over-priced.

Bus services from the airports to the main towns are frequent but it is worth checking the schedule to your destination in advance. The tourist information centres should be able to help you with this.

The best way of getting to town is by taxi or hired car. The taxi rank is situated immediately next to the exit from the arrivals hall. For short distances, taxis are a comfortable and affordable mode of transport. Many of the larger car hire companies have offices at the airports, as well as in major towns on the island.

Visitors travelling to Larnaka airport with a tour operator should turn left, towards the coach parking, after leaving the terminal building. Visitors hiring a car should take care to follow the signs after leaving the terminal building.

At Larnaka as well as at Pafos airport, services, amenities and transport links are clearly signposted at the terminal.

Ferries

Travel by ferry is often cheaper than flying, but currently there are few options to travel to Cyprus by sea. There are no passenger ferries to Cyprus at the present time.

Determined budget travellers can sail into Limassol from ports such as Piraeus (the port of Athens) and from some of the Greek islands, such as Patmos or Rhodes, but often this will be aboard a cargo ship. Journey times can be long: a direct sailing from Piraeus to Cyprus can take around 40 hours.

Cruise ships provide regular links between Cyprus and Haifa (Israel), Beirut (Lebanon) and Port Said (Egypt).

Regular service begins in spring, at the start of the tourist season. Between May and October, the ferries sailing

Larnaca international airport

to the Middle East are used mainly by people on holiday in Cyprus. From the south there are a number of popular trips, including the journeys to Israel, Egypt, Lebanon and the Greek islands. Regular services operate between North Cyprus and Turkey.

Some travel operators offer organized three-day trips to Egypt and the Holy Land, which include visits to Jerusalem and Bethlehem. These excursion vessels depart from Limassol Port.

There are a number of luxury cruiseliners that travel the Mediterranean and Middle East, with Cyprus being a popular stopping-off point.

North Cyprus

The quickest way to reach North Cyprus is by plane. All flights to Ercan airport originate in Turkey – from Alanya, Dalaman, Istanbul and Izmir. It is not possible to fly direct to Northern Cyprus from any other country. Flights are operated by Turkish Airlines. In order to reach Ercan airport you have to travel to Turkey from one of the European airports and then change for the flight to North Cyprus.

Convenient package holidays offer the same combination of flights, accommodation, airport transfers and, generally, car hire as those to the south, making this the easiest way to visit. You can also reach the North by ferry, which is a cheaper option, recommended for those who wish to bring their

Ferry harbour in Kyrenia, North Cyprus

own car to the island. The ferry companies serving these routes include Turkish Maritime Lines and Fergun Lines. Ferry journeys take much longer than flying: the journey from Taşucu to Kyrenia lasts six hours; from Mersin to Famagusta, 10 hours.

Travelling to North Cyprus can test your patience, as it usually involves long hours of waiting at Turkish airports for connecting flights – an important consideration when travelling with children or the elderly. These delays are due to the timetables not being very well coordinated.

Since the Republic of Cyprus joined the European Union in 2004, all citizens from the south are allowed to cross the border into North Cyprus without any hindrance, at least in theory, and stay as long as they wish. Visitors to the south who want to see North Cyprus can also cross the border to the North at the official checkpoints. Crossing anywhere other than an official checkpoint may result in arrest.

DIRECTORY

Cyprus Tourism Organization (Cto)

W visitcyprus.com
Larnaka
Tel 24 654 322.
Limassol
Tel 25 362 756.
Nicosia
Tel 22 674 264.
Pafos
Tel 26 932 841.
Troodos
Tel 25 421 316.

International Airports

Ercan
Tel 0392 600 5000.
Larnaka
Tel 24 816 400.
W hermesairports.com
Pafos
Tel 24 816 400.
W hermesairports.com

Cyprus Airways

W cyprusair.com

Ports

Cyprus Ports Authority (covers ports in Famagusta, Larnaka, Limassol and Pafos)
Tel 22 817 200.
W cpa.gov.cy

Airport terminal building at Ercan, North Cyprus

Travelling by Car

Most visitors to Cyprus explore the island by bus or hire car. Buses provide good links between the towns, while for shorter distances taxis are a good option – both comfortable and affordable. In Cyprus, vehicles are right-hand drive. The roads throughout the island are in good condition, and signposting is clear.

North Cyprus sign indicating cars should drive in the left lane

Car Hire

It is expensive to hire a car on the island, especially in the main tourist season from April through October. You may find more attractive prices during low season. The price usually includes full insurance, a certain mileage allowance and VAT (value-added tax). Drivers under the age of 25 require additional insurance. Cypriot authorities honour international diving licences, as well as foreign licences. Both manual and automatic cars are available for hire, as are motorcycles and scooters.

You really only need a four-wheel-drive vehicle if you are planning to tour the mountain regions in winter using some of the rough tracks, or go off-road in the Akamas peninsula. Major international car hire companies – Hertz, Avis and Europcar – have offices at the airports and in large cities, including Nicosia, Larnaka, Limassol and Pafos. Driving a hire car across the border to North Cyprus is not prohibited, but you will have to take out extra insurance on the Turkish side.

Rules of the Road

Driving is the easiest way to get around Cyprus. Roads are good, with motorways connecting Nicosia with Larnaka, Limassol, Pafos and Agia Napa. Distances are short – it is less than 160 km (100 miles) from Pafos to Nicosia.

Cypriots drive on the left side of the road, and drivers should give way to vehicles approaching from the right. Road signs are provided in both Greek and English in the south.

Distances and speed limits are in kilometres – 100 kmph (60 mph) on motorways, 80 kmph (50 mph) on most other roads, and 50 kmph (30 mph) in built-up areas. There are on-the-spot fines for speeding and for failing to wear a seat belt. Driving under the influence of alcohol is a criminal offence with serious consequences, as is using a mobile phone while driving.

Road sign in the south: sharp bend

Roads

The condition of the roads in Cyprus is very good. Since the 1980s many stretches of road have been built, and others modernized. Roundabouts (traffic islands) have also appeared at intersections; the right of way goes to drivers approaching from the right.

Finding your way to the major historic sites is not difficult, as brown road signs show the way. Difficulties may arise, however, in the narrow streets of small towns, where signs are usually absent.

Pedestrians, especially those who may not be used to left-hand traffic, should exercise caution when crossing the road, and warn children to be particularly careful when stepping into the road.

Maps

When hiring a car, you will usually be given a very basic road map of the island. It is certainly worth purchasing a more detailed map of Cyprus or the part of the island you'll be exploring; these are available in many book stores and petrol stations. It may be easier to purchase a map from home and bring it with you, so that you'll be prepared from the outset. Bear in mind that many mountain roads are accessible only by four-wheel drive vehicle or motorcycle (or scooter).

Remember, too, that place names in the North may be different from those on a map purchased in the South, so you may have to cross-reference maps.

Driving in Nicosia

The capital of Cyprus is the biggest and most congested city on the island. Traffic jams occur during rush hour and tourists may

A well-maintained road in the Troodos mountains

have difficulty negotiating the traffic here, and the narrow streets of parts of the city. The worst congestion can be expected on the trunk roads leading into and out of the city and – particularly in high season – on roads to the main historical sites. Outside the rush hour, driving in Nicosia is relatively easy and comfortable.

Street names throughout the city are clearly visible, and major tourist attractions are well signposted.

Buses

Bus service between the large towns is efficient and comfortable, and tickets are inexpensive. There are at least six services daily between the four main southern towns. Transport links to major seaside resorts are also good.

Local buses also connect outlying communities with the nearest main town, but they are geared to the needs of school children and villagers, so departures are only early morning and mid-afternoon. Travellers will find it harder to get to and from the smaller towns and villages.

Before travelling, check the timetable to see when the last return bus departs, to ensure that you will be able to get back. At weekends, there are reduced services.

Taxis

Metered taxis operate in all the main towns in Cyprus. Unmetered rural taxis serve most larger villages, charging

Traffic moving along one of Kyrenia's busy streets

31–49 cents per kilometre. There are also shared "service taxis" or minibuses, which take passengers door to door so you can choose the most convenient point for getting on or off. Service taxis operate between all the major towns half-hourly between 6am and 6pm (to 7pm in summer) Monday to Friday, and 7am to 5pm at weekends.

Taxi fares are reasonable – particularly when you take a larger car and share the cost between several people – and provide a very convenient way of getting around.

A taxi sign in North Cyprus

Hitchhiking

Hitchhiking is not illegal in Cyprus, nor is it recommended. It is better avoided altogether in the larger towns, where a decent public transport system and affordable taxis provide safer alternatives. In remote areas, the

locals readily give lifts to people standing by the road.

It can be difficult to hitch a lift during the peak holiday season, and temperatures soar, making the wait uncomfortable. Be sure to carry a bottle of water with you and wear a sunhat. Women who hitchhike should take special care.

DIRECTORY

Bus Timetables

Intercity
Intercity Buses
Tel 24 643 493.
🅦 intercity-buses.com

Larnaka
Zinonas Buses
Tel 24 665 531.
🅦 zinonasbuses.com

Nicosia
OSEL
Tel 22 468 088.
🅦 osel.com.cy

Pafos
Osypa Limited
Tel 26 934 252.
🅦 pafosbuses.com

Taxis

Acropolis Vassos Taxi
Akamia Centre, Larnaka.
Tel 24 622 000.

Euro Taxi
Ifigenias 24, Nicosia.
Tel 22 513 000.

Golden Taxi
Lysis Fasis 33, Limassol.
Tel 70 00 08 82.

Mayfair Taxi
Agapinoros 46, Pafos.
Tel 26 954 200.

Car Hire

Avis
Tel 22 713 333.
🅦 avis.com.cy

Europcar
Tel 25 880 222.
🅦 europcar.com.cy

Hertz
Tel 22 208 888.
🅦 hertz.com.cy

A local Cypriot MAN Evolution bus

General Index

Acknowledgments

Dorling Kindersley and Wiedza i Życie would like to thank the following people and institutions, whose contributions and assistance have made the preparation of this guide possible.

Publishing Manager
Kate Poole

Managing Editors
Vivien Antwi, Vicki Ingle

Publisher
Douglas Amrine

Senior Cartographic Editor
Casper Morris

Senior DTP Designer
Jason Little

Additional Picture Research
Rachel Barber, Rhiannon Furbear, Ellen Root

Revisions Editor
Anna Freiberger

Revisions Designer
Maite Lantaron

Revisions Team
Beverley Ager, Emma Anacoootee, Uma Bhattacharya, Emer FitzGerald, Carole French, Swati Handoo, Vinod Harish, Mohammad Hassan, Shobhna Iyer, Jasneet Kaur, Juliet Kenny, Sumita Khatwani, Vincent Kurien, Laura Jones, Jude Ledger, Deepak Mittal, Alison McGill, Sonal Modha, Catherine Palmi, Helen Peters, Andrea Pinnington, Rada Radojicic, Erin Richards, Lokamata Sahoo, Sands Publishing Solutions, Azeem, Siddiqui, Roseen Teare, Priyansha Tuli, Dora Whitaker, Sophie Wright

Production Co-ordinator
Wendy Penn

Jacket Design
Tessa Bindloss

Consultant
Robin Gauldie

Factchecker
John Vickers

Proofreader
Stewart Wild

Index
Hilary Bird

Additional Photography
Wojciech Franus, Carole French, Robin Gauldie, Konrad Kalbarczyk, Grzegorz Micuła, Bernard Musyck, Ian O'Leary, Ronald Sayegh, Jon Spaull, Andrzej Zygmuntowicz

Special Assistance
Dr. Fotos Fotiou, Aleksander Nikolaou, Irfan Kiliç, Suleyman Yalin, Latif Ince, Artur Mościcki, Joanna Egert-Romanowska, Maria Betlejewska, Małgorzata Merkel-Massé.

The publishers would also like to thank all the people and institutions who allowed us to use photographs from their archives:

Bernard Musyck, Ronald Sayegh (www.CyprusDestinations.com, skiing and agrotourism site)

Picture Credits
a = above; b = below/bottom; c = centre; f = far; l = left; r = right; t = top.

Alamy Images: Jon Arnold Images Ltd 64; Ros Drinkwater 158-9; Greg Balfour Evans 45b, 116, 128; Peter Horree 169tl; Hemis 11tc; Doug Houghton40 203bl; Iconotec 17b; imagebroker/ Maria Breuer 190cra; imagebroker/Siepmann 169c; iWebbtravel 106; Andrey Kekyalyaynen 200bl; LOOK Die Bildagentur der Fotografen GmbH 13tr; Victor Lucas 186-7; nagelstock.com 2-3; David Newham 10tr; Piamen Peev 55bl; Stuwdamdorp 197cr; Peter Titmuss 200c; Rawdon Wyatt 173br, 203tc; Zoonar GmbH 1c. **Brasserie Au Bon Plaisir:** 175t; **The Trustees of the British Museum** 97bc. **Cleopatra Lebanese Restaurant:** 172t; **Corbis** Bettmann 30, 38clb, 75br; Jonathan Blair 28c, 29cra, 38tr; Tom Brakefield 155cr; James Davis/Eye Ubiquitous 20clb, 95crb, 152cla; John Heseltine 168cl; Jo Lillini 26bc, 185bl; Chris Lisle 28bl; Hans Georg Roth 6–7. **Cyprus Police** 194bl. **Cyprus Tourism Organisation:** 13bc, 56tr; Y.Vroullou 10bl; **Domus Lounge Bar & Restaurant:** 167tr, 176bl; **Dreamstime.com:** Rostislav Ageev 12tr; Senai Aksoy 12br; Debu55y 9tr, 9cr; Gillian Hardy 8br; Bensliman Hassan 100-1; Kirill Makarov 40-1; Nushahru 8cl;Michalakis Ppalis 11b, 185tr; Tetiana Zbrodko 16; **Four Seasons, Cyprus:** 160br, 163tr; Carole French 196bl; **Getty Images:** Esen Tunar Photography 44; Nejdetduzan 146-7; **Hilton Cyprus:** 161bc, 164tl; **Jashan's:** 177tr; **Loel Winery** 181tl. **Grzegorz Micuła** 21ca/bl, 22t, 23br, 56cb, 53c, 71cr, 96tr, 186br, 187tl, 196cla. **Bernard Musyck:** 29bl; **Oleastro Restaurant:** 172bc; **Oliveto Stonegrill Dining:** 167bl, 170br, 182br; **Onar Holiday Village:** 161tl, 165bl; **TAGO** Konrad Kalbarczyk 17b, 182t; Wojciech Franus 19br; **Superstock:** imagebroker.net 88; **Thanos Hotels - Anassa:** 162bl; **Vouni Panayia Winery:** 174bl

Front Endpaper

Alamy Images: Jon Arnold Images Ltd Rbl; Greg Balfour Evans Rcra; Rbr; iWebbtravel Lbl; **Getty Images:** Esen Tunar Photography Ltl; **Superstock:** imagebroker.net Ltr.

Jacket
Front and Spine - **Alamy Images:** Eyebyte.

All other images © Dorling Kindersley

For further information see www.dkimages.com

English–Greek Phrase Book

There are no clear-cut rules for transliterating modern Greek into the Latin alphabet.
The system employed in this guide follows the rules generally applied in Greece, adjusted to fit in with English pronunciation. On the following pages, the English is given in the left-hand column, the right-hand column provides a literal system of pronunciation and indicates the stressed syllable in bold.
It is also worth remembering that both the Cypriot Greek and Cypriot Turkish alphabets differ slightly from those used on the mainland, and their accents are distinctive, too.

In Emergency

Help!	**Voítheia**	vo-ee-theea
Stop!	**Stamatíste**	sta-ma-tee-steh
Call a doctor!	**Fonáxte éna yatro**	fo-nak-steh e-na ya-tro
Call an ambulance!	**Kaléste to asthenofóro**	ka-le-steh to as-the-no-fo-ro
Call the police!	**Kaléste tin astynomía**	ka-le-steh teen a-sti-no mia
Call the fire brigade!	**Kaléste tin pyrosvestikí**	ka-le-steh teen pee-ro-zve-stee-kee
Where is the nearest telephone?	**Poú eínai to plisiéstero tiléfono?**	poo ee-ne to plee-see-e-ste-ro tee-le-pho-no?
Where is the nearest hospital?	**Poú eínai to plisiéstero nosokomeío?**	poo ee-ne to plee-see-e-ste-ro no-so-ko-mee-o?
Where is the nearest pharmacy?	**Poú eínai to plisiéstero farmakeío?**	poo ee-ne to plee-see-e-ste-ro far-ma-kee-o?

Communication Essentials

Yes	**Nai**	neh
No	**Ochi**	o-chee
Please	**Parakaló**	pa-ra-ka-lo
Thank you	**Efcharistó**	ef-cha-ree-sto
Excuse me	**Me synchoreíte**	me seen cho-ree-teh
Goodbye	**Antío**	an-dee-o
Good morning	**Kaliméra**	ka-lee-me-ra
Good evening	**Kalinychta**	ka-lee-neech-ta
Morning	**Proí**	pro-ee
Afternoon	**Apógevma**	a-po-yev-ma
Evening	**Vrádi**	vrath-i
Yesterday	**Chthés**	chthes
Today	**Símera**	see-me-ra
Tomorrow	**Avrio**	av-ree-o
Here	**Edó**	ed-o
There	**Ekeí**	e-kee
What?	**Tí?**	tee?
Why?	**Giatí?**	ya-tee?
Where?	**Poú?**	poo?
How?	**Pós?**	pos?

Useful Phrases

How are you?	**Tí káneis?**	tee ka-nees
Very well, thank you	**Poly kalá, efcharistó**	po-lee ka-la, ef-cha-ree-sto
Pleased to meet you	**Chaíro polę**	che-ro po-lee
What is your name?	**Pós légeste?**	pos le-ye-ste?
Where is/where are…?	**Poú eínai?**	poo ee-ne?
How far is it to…?	**Póso apéchei…?**	po-so a-pe-chee?
I understand	**Katalavaíno**	ka-ta-la-ve-no
I don't understand	**Den katalavaíno**	then ka-ta-la-ve-no
Can you speak more slowly?	**Miláte lígo pio argá parakaló?**	mee-la-te lee-go pyo ar-ga pa-ra-ka-lo?
I'm sorry	**Me synchoreíte**	me-seen-cho-ree teh

Useful Words

big	**Megálo**	me-ga-lo
small	**Mikró**	mi-kro
hot	**Zestó**	zes-to
cold	**Kreyo**	kree-o
good	**Kaló**	ka-lo
bad	**Kakó**	ka-ko
open	**Anoichtá**	a-neech-ta
closed	**Kleistá**	klee-sta
left	**Aristerá**	a-ree-ste-ra

right	**Dexiá**	dek-see-a
straight	**Eftheía**	ef-thee-a
between	**Anámesa/ Metaxey**	a-na-me-sa/ Metaxÿ
on the corner….	**Sti gonía tou…**	stee go-nee-a too
near	**Kontá**	kon-da
far	**Makriá**	ma-kree-a
up	**Epáno**	e-pa-no
down	**Káto**	ka-to
early	**Norís**	no-rees
late	**Argá**	ar-ga
entrance	**I eísodos**	ee ee-so-thos
exit	**I éxodos**	eee-kso-dos
toilets	**Oi toualétes**	eee-kso-dos

Shopping

How much is it?	**Póso kánei?**	po-so ka-nee?
Do you have…?	**Echete…?**	e-che-teh
Do you accept credit cards?	**Décheste pistotikés kártes**	the-ches-teh pee-sto-tee-kes kar-tes
Do you accept travellers cheques?	**Décheste pistotikés travellers' cheques?**	the-ches-teh pee-sto-tee-kes … travellers cheques
What time do you open?	**Póte anoígete?**	po-teh a-nee-ye-teh?
What time do you close?	**Póte kleínete?**	po-teh klee-ne-teh?
this one	**Aftó edó**	af-to e-do
that	**Ekeíno**	e-kee-no
expensive	**Akrivó**	e-kree-vo
cheap	**Fthinó**	fthee-no
size	**To mégethos**	to me-ge-thos
white	**Lefkó**	lef-ko
black	**Mávro**	mav-ro
red	**Kókkino**	ko-kee-no
yellow	**Kítrino**	kee-tree-no
green	**Prásino**	pra-see-no
blue	**Mple**	bleh
antique shop	**Magazí me antíkes**	ma-ga-zee me an-dee-kes
bakery	**O foúrnos**	o foor-nos
bank	**I trápeza**	I trápeza
bazaar	**To pazári**	to pa-za-ree
bookshop	**To vivliopoleío**	o vee-vlee-o-po-lee-o
pharmacy	**To farmakeío**	to far-ma-kee-o
post office	**To tachy- dromeío**	to ta-chee -thro-mee-o
supermarket	**Supermarket**	"Supermarket"

Sightseeing

tourist information	**CTO**	CTO
beach	**I paralía**	ee pa-ra-lee-a
Byzantine	**vyzantinós**	vee-zan-dee-nos
castle	**To kástro**	to ka-stro
church	**I ekklisía**	ee e-klee-see-a
monastery	**moní**	mo-ni
museum	**To mouseío**	to moo-see-o
national	**ethnikós**	eth-nee-kos
river	**To potámi**	to po-ta-mee
road	**O drómos**	o thro-mos
saint	**ágios**	a-yee-os
theatre	**To théatro**	to the-a-tro

Travelling

When does the … leave?	**Póte févgei to…?**	po-teh fev-yee to..
Where is the bus stop?	**Poú eínai i stási tou leoforeíou?**	poo ee-neh ee sta-see too le-o-fo-ree-oo?
Is this bus going to…?	**Ypárche I leoforeío gia…?**	ee-par-chee le-o-fo-ree-o yia…?
bus ticket	**Eisitírio leoforeíou**	ee-see-tee-ree-o le-o-fo-ree-oo?
harbour	**To limáni**	to lee-ma-nee
bicycle	**To podílato**	to po-thee-la-to
taxi	**To taxí**	to tak-see
airport	**To aero- drómio**	to a-e-ro-thro- mee-o
ferry	**To „ferry-boat"**	to fe-ree-bot

alternatives for a female speaker are shown in brackets

In a Hotel

Do you have a vacant room?	**Echete domátia?**	e-che-teh tho-ma-tee-a?
double room	**Díklino me dipló kreváti**	thee-klee-no meh thee-plo kre-va-tee
single room	**Monóklino**	mo-no-klee-no
room with bathroom	**Domátio me mpánio**	tho-ma-tee-o meh ban-yo
shower	**To douz**	To dooz
key	**To kleidí**	to klee-dee
I have a reservation	**Echo kánei krátisi**	e-cho ka-nee kra-tee-see
room with sea view	**Domátio me théasti thálassa**	tho-ma-tee-o meh the-a stee tha-la-sa
room with a balcony	**Domátio me théasti mpalkóni**	tho-ma-tee-o meh the-a stee bal- ko-nee
Does the price include breakfast	**To proïnó symperi-lamvánetai stin timí?**	to pro-ee-no seem-be-ree-lam-va-ne-tehsteen tee-mee?

eating out

Have you got a free table?	**Echete trapézi?**	e-che-te tra-pe-zee?
I'd like to reserve a table	**Thélo na kratíso éna trapézi**	the-lo na kra-tee-so e-na tra-pe-zee
The bill, please	**Ton logariazmó parakaló**	tonlo-gar-yas-mo pa-ra-ka-lo
I'm a vegetarian	**Eímai chortofágos**	ee-meh chor-to-fa-gos
menu	**O katálogos**	o ka-ta-lo-gos
wine list	**O katálogos me ta oin-opnevmatódi**	o ka-ta-lo-gos meh ta ee-no-pnev-ma-to-thee
glass	**To potíri**	to po-tee-ree
bottle	**To mpoukáli**	to bou-ka-lee
knife	**To machaíri**	to ma-che-ree
fork	**To piroúni**	to pee-roo-nee
spoon	**To koutáli**	to koo-ta-lee
breakfast	**To proïnó**	to pro-ee-no
lunch	**To mesimerianó**	to me-see-mer-ya-no
dinner	**To deípno**	to theep-no
main course	**To kyríos gévma**	to kee-ree-os yev-ma
starter	**Ta orektiká**	ta o-rek-tee-ka
dessert	**To glykó**	to ylee-ko
dish of the day	**To piáto tis iméras**	to pya-to tees ee-me-ras
bar	**To „bar"**	To bar
tavern	**I tavérna**	ee ta-ver-na
café	**To kafeneío**	to ka-fe-nee-o
wine shop	**To oinopoleío**	to ee-no-po-lee-o
restaurant	**To estiatório**	o e-stee-a-to-ree-o
ouzeria	**To ouzerí**	To ouzerí
kebab take-away	**To souvlatzídiko**	To soo-vlat-zee dee-ko

Menu Decoder

coffee	**O Kafés**	o ka-fes
with milk	**me gála**	me ga-la
black coffee	**skétos**	ske-tos
without sugar	**chorís záchari**	cho-rees za-cha-ree
tea	**tsái**	tsa-ee
wine	**krasí**	kra-see
red	**kókkino**	ko-kee-no
white	**lefkó**	lef-ko
rosé	**rozé**	ro-ze
raki	**To rakí**	to ra-kee
ouzo	**To oúzo**	to oo-zo
retsina	**I retsína**	ee ret-see-na
water	**To neró**	to ne-ro
fish	**To psári**	to psa-ree

cheese	**To tyrí**	to tee-ree
halloumi cheese	**To chaloúmi**	
feta	**I féta**	ee fe-ta
bread	**To psomí**	to pso-mee
hummus	**To houmous**	to choo-moos
halva	**O chalvás**	o chal-vas
Turkish Delight	**To loukoúmi**	to loo-koo-mee loo-koo-mee
baklava	**O mpaklavás**	o bak-la-vas
kléftiko (lamb dish)	**To kléftiko**	to klef-tee-ko

Numbers

1	**éna**	e-na
2	**dyo**	thee-o
3	**tría**	tree-a
4	**téssera**	te-se-ra
5	**pénte**	pen-deh
6	**éxi**	ek-si
7	**eptá**	ep-ta
8	**ochtó**	och-to
9	**ennéa**	e-ne-a
10	**déka**	the-ka
100	**ekató**	e-ka-to
200	**diakósia**	thya-kos-ya
1,000	**chília**	cheel-ya
2,000	**dychiliádes**	thee-o cheel-ya-thes
1,000,000	**éna ekat--ommyrio**	e-na e-ka-to-mee-ree-o

Days of the Week, Months, Time

one minute	**éna leptó**	e-na lep-to
one hour	**mía óra**	mee-a o-ra
half an hour	**misí óra**	mee-see o-ra
a day	**mía méra**	mee-a me-ra
week	**mía evdomáda**	mee-a ev-tho-ma-tha
month	**énas mínas**	e-nas mee-nas
year	**énas chrónos**	e-nas chro-nos
Monday	**Deftéra**	thef-te-ra
Tuesday	**Tríti**	tree-tee
Wednesday	**Tetárti**	te-tar-tee
Thursday	**Pémpti**	pemp-tee
Friday	**Paraskeví**	pa-ras-ke-vee
Saturday	**Sávvato**	sa-va-to
Sunday	**Kyriakí**	keer-ee-a-kee
January	**Ianouários**	ee-a-noo-a-ree-os
February	**Fevrouários**	fev-roo-a-ree-os
March	**Mártios**	mar-tee-os
April	**Aprílios**	a-pree-lee-os
May	**Máios**	ma-ee-os
June	**Ioúnios**	ee-oo-nee-os
July	**Ioúlios**	ee-oo-lee-os
August	**Avgoustos**	av-goo-stos
September	**Septémvrios**	sep-tem-vree-os
October	**Októvrios**	ok-to-vree-os
November	**Noémvrios**	no-em-vree-os
December	**Dekémvrios**	the-kem-vree-os

alternatives for a female speaker are shown in brackets

English-Turkish Phrase Book

Pronunciation

Turkish uses a Roman alphabet. It has 29 letters: 8 vowels and 21 consonants. Letters that differ from the English alphabet are: **c**, pronounced "j" as in "jolly; **ç**, pronounced "ch" as in "church"; **ğ**, which lengthens the preceding vowel and is not pronounced; **ı**, pronounced "uh"; **ö**, pronounced "ur" (like the sound in "further"); **ş**, pronounced "sh" as in "ship"; **ü**, pronounced "ew" as in "few".

In an Emergency

Help!	**İmdat!**	eem-**dat**
Stop!	**Dur!**	door
Call a doctor!	**Bir doktor çağrın!**	beer dok-**tor chah-**ruhn
Call an ambulance!	**Bir ambulans çağrın!**	beer am-boo-**lans** chah-ruhn
Call the police!	**Polis çağrın!**	po-lees chah-ruhn
Fire!	**Yangın!**	yan-**guhn**
Where is the nearest telephone?	**En yakın telefon nerede?**	en ya-**kuhn** teh-leh-**fon** neh-reh-deh
Where is the nearest hospital?	**En yakın hastane nerede?**	en ya-**kuhn** has-ta-**neh** neh-reh-deh

Communication Essentials

Yes	**Evet**	eh-**vet**
No	**Hayır**	h-**eye'**-uhr
Thank you	**Teşekkür ederim**	teh-shek-**kewr eh**-deh-reem
Please	**Lütfen**	**lewt**-fen
Excuse me	**Affedersiniz**	af-feh-der-see-neez
Hello	**Merhaba**	**mer**-ha-ba
Goodbye	**Hoşça kalın**	hosh-**cha ka-**luhn
Good morning	**Günaydın**	gewn-**eye'-duhn**
Good evening	**İyi akşamlar**	ee-**yee** ak-sham-**lar**
Morning	**Sabah**	sa-**bah**
Afternoon	**Öğleden sonra**	ur-leh-**den son-**ra
Evening	**Akşam**	ak-**sham**
Yesterday	**Dün**	dewn
Today	**Bugün**	**boo**-gewn
Tomorrow	**Yarın**	**ya**-ruhn
Here	**Burada**	**boo**-ra-da
There	**Şurada**	**shoo**-ra-da
Over there	**Orada**	**o**-ra-da
What?	**Ne?**	neh
When?	**Ne zaman?**	neh **za**-man
Why?	**Neden**	neh-**den**
Where?	**Nerede**	**neh**-reh-deh

Useful Phrases

How are you?	**Nasılsınız?**	na-suhl-suh-nuhz
I'm fine	**İyiyim**	ee-**yee**-yeem
Pleased to meet you	**Memnun oldum**	mem-**noon ol-**doom
That's fine	**Tamam**	ta-**mam**
Where is/are …?	**… nerede?**	…**neh**-reh-deh
How far is it to …?	**… ne kadar uzakta?**	…**neh ka-**dar oo-zak-ta
I want to go to …	**… a/e gitmek istiyorum**	… a/eh geet-**mek** ees-**tee**-yo-room
Do you speak English?	**İngilizce biliyor musunuz?**	een-**geel-eez**-jeh bee-**lee**-yor moo-soo-nooz?
I don't understand	**Anlamıyorum**	an-**la**-muh-yo-room
Can you help me?	**Bana yardım edebilir misiniz?**	ba-**na** yar-**duhm** eh-deh-bee-**leer** mee-see-neez?

Useful Words

big	**büyük**	bew-**yewk**
small	**küçük**	kew-**chewk**
hot	**sıcak**	suh-**jak**
cold	**soğuk**	soh-**ook**
good/well	**iyi**	ee-**yee**
bad	**kötü**	kur-**tew**
open	**acık**	a-**chuhk**
closed	**kapalı**	ka-pa-**luh**
left	**sol**	sol
right	**sağ**	saa
straight on	**doğru**	doh-**roo**
near	**yakın**	ya-**kuhn**
far	**uzak**	oo-**zak**
early	**erken**	er-**ken**
late	**geç**	gech
entrance	**giriş**	gee-**reesh**

exit	**çıkış**	chuh-**kuhsh**
toilets	**tuvaletler**	too-va-let-**ler**

Shopping

How much is this?	**Bu kaç lira?**	boo **kach** lee-ra
I would like …	**… istiyorum**	… ees-**tee**-yo-room
Do you have …?	**… var mı?**	… **var** muh?
Do you take credit cards?	**Kredi kartı kabul ediyor musunuz?**	**kreh**-dee **kar**-tuh ka-**bool** eh-**dee**-yor moo-soo-nooz?
What time do you open/close?	**Saat kaçta açılıyor/ kapanıyor?**	Sa-**at** kach-ta a-chuh-**luh**-yor/ ka-pa-**nuh**-yor
this one	**bunu**	boo-**noo**
that one	**şunu**	shoo-**noo**
expensive	**pahalı**	pa-ha-**luh**
cheap	**ucuz**	oo-**jooz**
size (clothes)	**beden**	beh-**den**
size (shoes)	**numara**	noo-ma-**ra**
white	**beyaz**	bay-**yaz**
black	**siyah**	see-**yah**
red	**kırmızı**	kuhr-muh-**zuh**
yellow	**sarı**	sa-**ruh**
green	**yeşil**	yeh-**sheel**
blue	**mavi**	ma-**vee**
bakery	**fırın**	fuh-**ruhn**
bank	**banka**	**ban**-ka
cake shop	**pastane**	pas-ta-**neh**
chemist's/pharmacy	**eczane**	ej-za-**neh**
hairdresser	**kuaför**	kwaf-**fur**
barber	**berber**	ber-**ber**
market/bazaar	**çarşı/pazar**	char-**shuh**/pa-**zar**
post office	**postane**	pos-ta-**neh**
travel agency	**seyahat acentesi**	say-ya-**hat** a-jen-teh-**see**

Sightseeing

castle	**hisar**	hee-**sar**
church	**kilise**	kee-**lee**-seh
mosque	**cami**	**ja**-mee
museum	**müze**	**mew**-zeh
square	**meydan**	may-**dan**
theological college	**medrese**	med-**reh**-seh
tomb	**türbe**	tewr-**beh**
tourist information office	**turizm danışma bürosu**	too-**reezm** da-nuhsh-**mah bew**-ro-soo
town hall	**belediye sarayı**	beh-leh-dee-**yeh** sar-**eye'**-uh
Turkish bath	**hamam**	ha-**mam**

Travelling

airport	**havalimanı**	ha-**va**-lee-ma-nuh
bus/coach	**otobüs**	o-to-**bewss**
bus stop	**otobüs durağı**	o-to-**bewss** doo-**ra**-uh
ferry	**vapur**	va-**poor**
taxi	**taksi**	tak-**see**
ticket	**bilet**	bee-**let**
ticket office	**bilet gişesi**	bee-**let** gee-sheh-**see**
timetable	**tarife**	ta-ree-**feh**

Staying in a Hotel

Do you have a vacant room?	**Boş odanız var mı?**	bosh o-da-**nuhz var** muh?
double room	**iki kişilik bir oda**	ee-**kee** kee-shee-**leek** beer o-**da**
twin room	**çift yataklı bir oda**	**cheeft** ya-**tak**-luh beer o-**da**
single room	**tek kişilik**	**tek** kee-shee-**leek**
a bathroom	**banyolu bir oda**	**ban**-yo-loo beer o-**da**
key	**anahtar**	a-nah-**tar**
room service	**oda servisi**	o-**da** ser-vee-**see**
I have a reservation	**Rezervasyonum var**	reh-zer-vas-yo-**noom** var
Does the price include breakfast?	**Fiyata kahvaltı dahil mi?**	fee-ya-**ta** kah-val-tuh da-**heel** mee?

Eating Out

Do you have a table	**… kişilik bir masa**	… kee-shee-**leek** for …people
The bill please	**Hesap lütfen**	heh-**sap** lewt-fen
I am a vegetarian	**Et yemiyorum**	et yeh-**mee**-yo-room
restaurant	**lokanta**	lo-**kan**-ta
waiter	**garson**	gar-**son**

menu	**yemek listesi**	ye-**mek lees**-teh-see
wine list	**şarap listesi**	sha-**rap lees**-teh-see
breakfast	**kahvaltı**	kah-val-**tuh**
lunch	**öğle yemeği**	ur-**leh** yeh-meh-ee
dinner	**akşam yemeği**	ak-**sham** yeh-meh-ee
starter	**meze**	**meh**-zeh
main course	**ana yemek**	a-**na** yeh-**mek**
dish of the day	**günün yemeği**	gewn-**ewn** yeh-meh-ee
dessert	**tatlı**	tat-**luh**
glass	**bardak**	bar-**dak**
bottle	**şişe**	shee-**sheh**
knife	**bıçak**	buh-**chak**
fork	**çatal**	cha-**tal**
spoon	**kaşık**	ka-**shuhk**

Menu Decoder

bal	bal	honey
balık	ba-**luhk**	fish
bira	**bee**-ra	beer
bonfile	**bon**-fee-leh	fillet steak
buz	booz	ice
çay	ch-'eye'	tea
çilek	chee-**lek**	strawberry
çorba	chor-**ba**	soup
dondurma	don-door-**ma**	ice cream
ekmek	ek-**mek**	bread
elma	el-**ma**	apple
et	et	meat
fasulye	fa-**sool**-yeh	beans
fırında	fuh-ruhn-**da**	roast
gazoz	ga-**zoz**	fizzy drink
kkahve	kah-**veh**	coffee
karpuz	kar-**pooz**	water melon
kavun	ka-**voon**	melon
kayısı	k-'eye'-uh-**suh**	apricots
kıyma	kuhy-**ma**	minced meat
kızartma	kuh-zart-**ma**	fried
köfte	kurf-**teh**	meatballs
kuzu eti	koo-**zoo** eh-**tee**	lamb
lokum	lo-**koom**	Turkish delight
maden suyu	ma-**den** soo-**yoo**	mineral water
meyve suyu	may-**veh** soo-**yoo**	fruit juice
muz	mooz	banana
patlıcan	pat-luh-**jan**	aubergine (eggplant)
peynir	pay-**neer**	cheese
pilav	pee-**lav**	rice
piliç	pee-**leech**	roast chicken
şarap	sha-**rap**	wine

sebze	seb-**zeh**	vegetables
şeftali	shef-ta-**lee**	peach
şeker	sheh-**ker**	sugar
su	soo	water
süt	sewt	milk
sütlü	sewt-**lew**	with milk
tavuk	ta-**vook**	chicken
tereyağı	teh-**reh**-yah-uh	butter
tuz	tooz	salt
üzüm	ew-**zewm**	grapes
yoğurt	yoh-**urt**	yoghurt
yumurta	yoo-moor-**ta**	egg
zeytin	zay-**teen**	olives
zeytinyağı	zay-**teen**-yah-uh	olive oil

Numbers

0	**sıfır**	**suh**-fuhr
1	**bir**	beer
2	**iki**	ee-**kee**
3	**üç**	ewch
4	**dört**	durt
5	**beş**	besh
6	**altı**	al-**tuh**
7	**yedi**	yeh-**dee**
8	**sekiz**	seh-**keez**
9	**dokuz**	doh-**kooz**
10	**on**	on
100	**yüz**	yewz
200	**iki yüz**	ee-**kee** yewz
1,000	**bin**	been
100,000	**yüz bin**	yewz been
1,000,000	**bir milyon**	beer meel-**yon**

Time

one minute	**bir dakika**	beer da-kee-ka
one hour	**bir saat**	beer sa-at
half an hour	**yarım saat**	ya-ruhm sa-at
day	**gün**	gewn
week	**hafta**	haf-ta
month	**ay**	'eye'
year	**yıl**	yuhl
Sunday	**pazar**	pa-zar
Monday	**pazartesi**	pa-zar-teh-see
Tuesday	**salı**	sa-luh
Wednesday	**çarşamba**	char-sham-ba
Thursday	**perşembe**	per-shem-beh
Friday	**cuma**	joo-ma
Saturday	**cumartesi**	joo-mar-teh-see